Contents

Author's Note

The laws relating to taxation in virtually every country are constantly changing and are subject continuously to the discretionary interpretation of commissioners of taxation, inland revenue or the equivalent in all or most countries. References to taxation in this book should be placed in that context. While every care has been taken, neither the author nor the publisher accepts any responsibility or liability for any action taken by any person(s) or organisation(s) on the purported basis of anything contained in this book.

This applies equally to references to any other matters in the book, including pension, superannuation, insurance and social services matters, investment in its various forms and the management of money in all its forms. While again every care has been taken, no person(s) or organisation(s) should act in any way whether in investment or any other matters in reliance on anything contained in this book but should satisfy themselves independently and by consulting other sources of their choice before embarking on any proposed course of action.

TO

GUS SHARKEY

who, long ago, needed to read this book and

to my wife,

HEIDE SCHULTE VON BÄUMINGHAUS CUMES

who, more recently, caused it to be written

Prologue

$1,000,000.

One million lovely dollars.

That used to represent vast wealth.

The riches of a Monte Cristo.

Today it's a lot, or not very much, depending on your financial standards. Many years ago, an American banker confided to me, 'A million's nothing any more. You need *ten* million dollars now before you even *begin* to count.' I thought he must be joking. Even half a million was a fortune to me then.

The Working Poor

A million still is to most of us. A middle-income earner in the rich countries will take twenty years to earn it. An average earner will take forty years — the whole of your working lifetime — and you'll spend it as fast as you earn it. At the end you won't have much left. Perhaps a house, a car and some pension entitlements. That's about all. To *accumulate* a million dollars — to have assets worth a million at any one time — is an achievement of quite another dimension. The vast majority of people will never have enough, in whatever assets, to declare themselves 'millionaires'.

The 'Can't Count' Rich

Of course, as the real value of money has fallen, it *has* been getting easier to join the millionaires' club. So I'd better define a 'millionaire' more precisely. Strictly, a millionaire is

1

anyone whose net worth equals a million dollars (or, for example, a million pounds sterling, but *not* a million Italian lire or a million Japanese yen). One writer has established four categories for the wealthy:

'Rich: £1 million to £5 million.
Very rich: over £5 million to £20 million.
Super-rich: over £20 million to £35 million.
Can't count (the Getty definition): Any family worth more than £35 million.'[1]

For my present purposes, I take the strict dollar definition: a millionaire must have a net worth of at least a million American dollars. As the dollar continues to lose real value, your basic millionaire will progressively have command over less real wealth than the fabled million dollars on the face of a pile of greenbacks used to represent. So we might need a looser, more flexible definition: a millionaire is he who knows himself to be comfortably rich and is overtly or tacitly acknowledged by his community to be one of its best-heeled citizens — to be included, let us say, among the wealthiest 1 per cent of the community.

Taking that as our yardstick, let's get a few things clear.

Millionaires are You and Me

The first, and in many ways the most important, point is that anybody can become a millionaire. If not quite as easy as falling off a bike, it's an achievement open to everyone, without discrimination as to age, sex, class or most other *imposed* characteristics. The *voluntary* acceptance of, for example, a religion that looks unkindly on riches, can be a bar. Some societies also respect ancestrally acquired wealth but look down their noses at those who grub for money: 'the top ranks of British society had money and spent it cheerfully, but they were brought up in their "public" schools and universities to think that making it was not the done thing'.[2] However, leaving such attitudes as these aside,

---

1 Davis, *The Rich, A Study of the Species,* p.15.

2 The *Economist,* London, 24 December 1988/6 January 1989, pp.44–5, which added that 'this aversion to making money had spread wide'. But that was some twenty years ago, 'when the British élite found the idea of making money more distasteful than it does now'.

you don't need any qualifications. It's better if you're literate and reasonably numerate; but you don't need to be capable of graduating through medical or law school. Nor do you need to be an economist, an accountant or a mathematician. In fact, being a clever chap might make it harder for you to make heaps of money: it could give you pretensions or build in inhibitions.

What you *do* need is a common-sense grasp of what makes the business world go round. But that's about all. For proof that money-makers are not members of some exclusive club, just look around you. The great majority of millionaires are ordinary people — like yourself. If they didn't happen to be rich, you probably wouldn't notice them. Indeed, you probably never give a second glance to most of the millionaires who *do* cross your path. Conversely, the clever chaps — the university dons, the brilliant mathematicians, the economists — are often dog poor. If you notice them at all, it's because they've got the seat out of their pants.

Historically, most of the richest men in their communities have started modestly: Ford and Rockefeller in the United States; Morris (Lord Nuffield) and, among our contemporaries, Robert Maxwell in Britain. 'From a wretched village in Czechoslovakia', Maxwell came 'through a wartime Military Cross and some unmemorable years as a Labour member of Parliament,...to head a huge publishing empire.'[3]

In the newer countries, Samuel Terry was transported to New South Wales as a convict in the early nineteenth century. Some thirty years later, he died as Australia's first millionaire, reputedly worth £1 million, an enormous fortune for those days. He had had little education, boasted no special talents and had come, if anyone had, from the ultimate social underclass. A century later, Edwin (Ted) Street and his wife Daisy arrived in Australia as poor immigrants at about as unpropitious a time as ever was. It was 1931, the worst year of the worst depression of modern times. But Daisy could make ice-cream. Ted hawked it round the streets in a small horse-drawn cart. Some thirty years later, they sold their ice-cream company to Unilever,

---

3 Ibid.

one of the world's great multinationals, for $4 million.

There have been many others. Immigrating to Australia after the Second World War, Arvi Parbo became head of Western Mining Corporation, one of Australia's largest mining houses, and chairman of Broken Hill Proprietary Limited, Australia's largest company. Alan Bond, having immigrated as a teenager with his parents, started with the legendary nothing and now runs a multi-billion-dollar corporate empire. None of these 'stars' in the capitalist structures of the large or smaller Western countries had unusual resources, remarkable talents or special advantages. They had a not-easily-identifiable mix of energy, vigour, enterprise and ambition; but, otherwise, they were as ordinary as anyone in their origins and as modest in their prospects.

The Brash Face of 'New' Money

The popular image of the millionaire is more spectacular:

> Adnan Kashoggi — A.K. to his associates — is a flamboyant character, a wheeler-dealer who was the model for the principal character in the best-selling Harold Robbins' novel, *The Pirate*. His father was personal physician to King Ibn Saud; it established a royal connection which has been useful ever since. Adnan was sent to a British-style boarding school in Alexandria, where he scored his first entrepreneurial success: he introduced the father of one classmate who wanted to import towels to the father of another who owned a textile factory, and received a present of £200. He later took a course in business studies at California's Stanford University and, when he returned to Saudi Arabia, became an agent. He soon had the Saudi agencies for Marconi, Fiat, Chrysler and Rolls-Royce aero-engines. His royal links got him involved in lucrative arms deals. He was paid a commission of $45 million from the sale of French tanks to the Saudi army and, in the years that followed, earned more than $100 million from Lockheed and another $54 million from its rivals, Northrop. The Lockheed and Northrop deals first brought him to the attention of the American public: it was alleged that the fees paid to him had been bribes. Kashoggi denied it; he insisted that the proper term was 'commissions'. He issued a press statement which argued that:

This is what the free economy is all about. The more you produce, the more you are rewarded. This is how companies sell their products and it was on this basis that the American economy was founded and still thrives today. We have offices in six cities and five countries and seventy or eighty persons who work on the business we are trying to develop for our clients. If we don't produce for them we get no return for our work. Is 50 million dollars for all that work by all those people in the company working for five years wrong? I don't believe that anyone who believes in the free enterprise system would think it's wrong, or anyone who wants to see more prosperity and more jobs in the U.S. thinks that a sale which produces 4 billion dollars is wrong.

John D. Rockefeller and his fellow 'Robber Barons' would have accepted his case; his American critics, still shaken by Watergate, didn't. Nor, it seems, did the Saudi Government: the Ministry of Defence no longer buys weapons through Kashoggi or any other Saudi middlemen. But Kashoggi does not have to rely on agents' fees, these days, to finance his extravagant lifestyle. He has built up a formidable business empire outside Saudi Arabia. His Triad group, based in Liechtenstein, is a conglomerate with operations in thirty-eight countries: banking, property development, hotels, ship chartering, meat packing, insurance, fashion, hospital management and so on. It owns property in Florida, Texas and Arizona; steak houses in San Francisco; an industrial trade zone in Salt Lake City; and two Californian banks. (There was strong resistance when he tried to buy a third, the First National Bank of San Jose.) Kashoggi — a small, portly man blessed with great energy — flits from one country to the next in his private jet. He has eight homes waiting for him, in London, Rome, Paris, Cannes, New York, Beirut, Riyadh and Jeddah. He also has a luxurious yacht, which is reckoned to have cost him $25 million, and a fleet of expensive cars. He likes to give lavish parties and is invariably surrounded by beautiful women. Islamic puritans may disapprove, but he is unrepentant: he says he enjoys living pleasantly and can afford it.[4]

---

4 Davis, op. cit., pp.86–7. Kashoggi has now fallen on tough times. The yacht has been sold to American billionaire Trump, and allegations have been made of improper associations with ex-President of the Philippines Marcos.

The Discreet Face of 'Old'

Other millionaires are less flamboyant. I once attended, in Hong Kong, a session of the Williamsburg Conference, an institution financed by the Rockefeller Foundation. John D. Rockefeller III chaired the meeting. He was brought up in a spartan tradition, described by his brother David: 'From our earliest days we are told not to leave food on our plates, not to allow electric lights to remain burning when we are not using them, and not to squander our money thoughtlessly, because these things are wasteful...of all forms of waste, however, that which is most abhorrent is idleness.'[5]

John D. III was true to this tradition. He was not 'idle'; nor did he waste money on food or clothes, at home or abroad. I ran into him later in Beekman Towers in New York. He was dressed in the rather scruffy, unfashionable mode of a gentleman belonging securely within the old-money establishment. In the late eighteenth and early nineteenth century, Jane Austen presented, in her novels, the newly rich as having fine houses and clothes and doing those things thought to be smart and fashionable. They were perhaps the Adnan Kashoggis of their day. But those who had had money for a couple of generations had libraries within their fine houses; they read books but didn't bother quite so much to dress in the latest styles. They were the John D. Rockefellers III. He had not only 'libraries' but also a Foundation respected world-wide and such intellectual diversions as the Williamsburg Conference and the Asia Society.

Exploiters, Caste — and Social Mobility

However, whether Kashoggis or Rockefellers, successful 'capitalists' have not always been held up as our finest models. On the contrary, they have often been regarded as 'exploiters' whom a militant socialism would justifiably eliminate. But the incontrovertible evidence of recent years has been that, in destroying the essential spirit of capitalism, socialism produced less, less efficiently, so that less was

---

5 Ibid., p.20.

available to distribute whether to the rich or to the poor, who are ever with us. We have come to acknowledge a need to allow the spirit and practice of capitalism to evolve so as to enable more people to participate directly in the capitalist process. John Maynard Keynes wrote that, 'Capitalism, wisely managed, can probably be made more efficient for attaining economic ends than any alternative system yet in sight, but..in itself it is in many ways extremely objectionable'.[6]

One of the objectionable features of the past has been the tendency to think of the 'capitalists' as belonging to an exclusive caste: they are the rich, the leisured and the pleasured. The rest contribute to their wealth and power but have little of their own. That was never a valid picture of capitalism, which created a mobile society in which the poor — or a few of them — could become rich and powerful. What we now need is to ensure that, in the modern renaissance of the capitalist spirit, more should have a chance, indeed be inspired to become practising capitalists. A first step is for all of us to be aware that we can be successful investors and entrepreneurs, that nothing of the 'great' capitalists' achievement is beyond us.

That's the first thing to learn. Just how easy it is. Getting to be a millionaire is not beyond the capacities of everyday, commonsensical people. Fix that firmly in your mind. If you're willing to sacrifice some hang-ups and throw away any residues of unwarranted modesty, you can comfortably crouch yourself into the starting-blocks for the race to riches. You'll need to follow a few simple rules which I'll outline for you. Apart from that, just being yourself will be enough, provided only that you start with some basic, quite simple attitudes.

For example, it's better if you don't mind making money — and better still if you find it positively enjoyable. That doesn't mean you have to be obsessed, so that you spend every waking moment — and some sleeping ones — dreaming of being a millionaire. That's not necessary. If you allow yourself to become obsessed, you'll miss the delights that flow from being rich. In what we're going to say, we're going to assume that, for you, making money is a

---

6 Keynes, *The End of Laisser-Faire*.

means to an end, not an end in itself. It's an old but still valid cliché that you can't take it with you. So we'll assume you don't lust to pile up money to count it, Scrooge-like, day and night; but that you yearn only to assemble enough to give you the good things of life, as *you* define them.

Some will want to jet-set around the world — buy jewels and furs and ocean-going yachts and out-Kashoggi Adnan himself. Others will be content with a less conspicuous lifestyle — a small part of an island in the sun, rest and repose with congenial and appreciative friends, leisure to perfect some personal talents. You don't have to be selfish with your money. You can squander a little on your family, your loved ones and friends. It's pleasing to give nice surprises — a diamond necklace, a Pacific cruise, an apartment in Surfers' Paradise or even in Cannes or Hawaii — to someone you love. You'll like it — and so will they. They'll be glad you learned how to make money. At worst, they won't hold it against you. If they didn't appreciate you before, they might well do so now — and show their appreciation in warm and friendly ways. That's nice too.

Money-making is Only Part of Life

So you shouldn't mind making money but you shouldn't make it an obsession nor should you stop doing other things that constitute a full life. Of course, if you want to spend all your time piling up wealth — twenty-four hours a day, seven days a week — that's for you to decide. But then you'll be a professional. What I'm going to say might still have value for you; even the best professional can benefit from it. But, in what follows, I'll really be addressing the 'amateurs': those who just want to occupy themselves part-time in making enough money to do what they like in financial comfort.

As a part-time money-maker, you can be a full-time whatever-you-want: an artist, a Shakespearean actor, a plumber, a clerk or a taxi-driver. You can, if you like, be a marbles player; or sit in the sun doing nothing. You can be any of these and many other things and still make plenty of money on the side. (But religiously avoid being such a compulsive workaholic at *anything* that you can't idle part of your time away at money-making.) When you've made all the money you thought you wanted, then you can forget about it. Or, if you've come to enjoy it as a relaxation, you can keep on making money — perhaps for your kids or your local church or whatever. The economist John Maynard Keynes was an accomplished money-maker who didn't need it all for himself; so he spent much of his time enlarging the endowments of his college in Cambridge through sound investments. You could do something the same. But, whatever the other interests, this book is directed to the part-timer — the person who doesn't want to devote a whole life to Mammon — although even the devotee might well keep it in his library for careful reference, especially if things start to go awry.

The Morality of Making Money

What about the morality of money-making? When we speak of serving Mammon, we speak pejoratively: to be or seek to be rich is evil; to suffer in poverty, and be content, smacks of saintliness. If that's the way you feel, that's fine. I'm not trying to talk you into doing anything you find morally offensive; it's up to you. I'm not seeking to set moral standards, to be moral or immoral. If this book is anything, it's amoral, although both author and readers will be normally responsive to moral considerations. If you reject wealth as morally wrong, then you've got no business reading this book — unless you're prepared to discover what an agreeably innocent pastime it can be. If you can bear to make money — and you've got no moral reservations about it — then this book won't make you any less moral than you were before: it won't encourage you to rob banks or snatch money from widows and orphans or do any of those things that the society regards as immoral — or downright illegal. All it will do is enable you to become richer in those ways that your society, in its wisdom, regards as acceptable.

No Genetic Hurdle

A couple of other things need to be cleared away. First, your family background doesn't matter all that much. It does matter a little. It will certainly help if you're descended from John D. Rockefeller or J. Paul Getty and some of the great man's pile came down to you. But, if you start with quite a large amount of money in the kitty, bear in mind that it won't necessarily take care of itself, so you'll need to ensure it's not fecklessly lost. The advantage will be that you won't have to take many initiatives. Indeed, if your inheritance is already well invested, you might do best only to supervise it. Most large fortunes carry their benefits forward to younger generations. However, some evidence exists of a cycle in which a family rises from rags to riches in one generation, holds its riches in the second and completes the cycle back to rags in the third. It's the completion of any such cycle that the rich must avoid.

But the point especially to underline is that it doesn't matter if your family has always been poor. You can still become a millionaire. Being rich or being poor is something you inherit. But *becoming* rich — or, for that matter, becoming or staying poor — is really up to you. You don't inherit an incapacity to make money as you inherit blue eyes, knock-knees or baldness. All the capacity you need to become rich is there at birth. All you have to do is utilise it — learn the simple rules, as you learn to play tennis or write a letter or drive a car. Most families have had their poor and their rich members. Some have had family lines which have been rich for a couple of generations and then slipped back again into poverty. But poverty hasn't been a scourge afflicting families like an hereditary disease, generation after generation. Some members have lifted themselves out of poverty with comparative ease. So it doesn't matter what your family has been. Don't be dissuaded if all your known ancestors have been poor. You can become rich nevertheless. If you had to change the colour of the blue eyes you've inherited, that really would be tough. But to get rich, the worst you have to do is change your family ways and be confident — confident that, however many family members have failed, you have the capacity to be rich. It's that self-confidence, or the putting aside of any attitudes of inferiority, that is crucial to success.

No Sweat about the Midas Touch

All right, you say, 'If I don't need qualifications and my

genes don't count, then what I must have is luck: I have to be the sort of person on whom money showers down from the skies every time I walk down the street'. No, not a bit of it. This book isn't concerned with luck. It's all about making money by those who have good luck and equally by those cursed with bad luck all their lives. This book is the cautious person's guide. It's for the person who never likes to take a risk. It's not the gambler's guide — not even the cautious gambler's. Indeed, to the full extent practicable, it takes the gambling out of money-making. For us, nothing depends on good luck — on a simple throw of the dice. Everything depends on applying rules that eliminate the sinister influence of ill fortune. Of course, if good fortune *does* smile, so much the better: you'll get to be a millionaire so much the quicker. But that's a bonus. Essentially, this book says that, in the pursuit of the comfortable life, luck doesn't matter. You don't need good luck and you can quiet your fears of bad luck by following rules which reduce or eliminate it.

1
What You Need

Work's a Poor Way to Get Rich

To make money, the one thing you need above all is money. Most people work for it. That's not the best way of making it — if only for the reason that, unless you're already President of General Motors or, these days, Disney Productions or Reebok Shoes, you can't make enough of it. Most people — the 'average wage-earners' — earn up to $500 a week. That's $25,000 a year. Over a working life of forty years, that amounts to just $1,000,000. So you would have to save, tax-free, every cent you ever earned to get to be a millionaire from wages alone; and you wouldn't do that until the end of your working life. After you'd eaten, and clothed yourself, found some shelter, bought some transport, raised a family, paid your taxes and all the rest, you'd be likely to end your career pretty well where you started it. You'd have damned near nothing. Even the self-employed often do little better: the writers, the solicitors, the doctors, the accountants, the sportsmen, unless they reach the upper echelons of their occupations. Even my GP, whom I'd thought 'comfortably off', confided to me that he was lucky to clear $15,000 a year. He might have been looking for sympathy; but many self-employed professional men and women earn far below the alleged 'stars' of their profession. Certainly, some people do earn a pile of money. The captains of industry, the admirals of commerce, the world champion boxers, the Wimbledon champions, the best-seller novelists and a few others earn much more than a million dollars through what might be called 'personal exertion'.

But, for most of us, working steadily at a job, thirty-five to forty hours a week, for forty years of our life, is a poor way of getting rich. In fact, without a lot of help from someone or something else, we're not going to make it. It won't be possible, unless inflation sweeps us into millionaire status and that's not going to be worth much in real terms: we won't be any richer and might well be poorer than we were as a struggling wage-earner on $500 a week.

So we've got to think of something other than work, preferably something that isn't immoral — certainly not illegal. Of course, there will be some 'work' in making any sort of money. There has to be a little effort in everything we do. But becoming a millionaire doesn't necessarily call for 'work' in the accepted sense. You don't have to swing a pick or thump a word-processor for thousands of hours every year. The crucial thing is so to arrange your life that you take advantage of everyday opportunities. Life is mostly a question of organisation — good or bad. If your life is well organised, most things become easy. If not, even trivial day-to-day chores become a trial.

Do Things that Matter

Part of good organisation is that you need to know where you're going. Some people, with a lot of ability and an abundance of energy, get side-tracked into inconsequential activities - things that don't count in any context. So you need to choose an activity of significance and then organise your life to participate in it. That doesn't mean you have to give up all your other interests and objectives. On the contrary, all your objectives will be easier to realise if you're well organised. Most people's lives contain a huge amount of wasted time — just drifting about doing nothing or nothing that gives them any joy or satisfaction.

The child is asked, 'Where have you been?'

'Out,' he replies.

'What have you been doing?'

'Nothing.'

That carries over into adult life. Most of us get no enjoyment from doing nothing: it bores the hell out of us. The main element in a *satisfying*, as well as successful, life is that time is put to good purpose; effort is well directed;

talents — though limited — are given a chance to express themselves. So we're not talking about hard labour or even extra effort so much as organising and directing much the same volume of time and effort in ways to get us what we want — in this case, making enough money to keep us in comfort.

Banks: Familiarity and Contempt

To do this, we need first to know some very simple things. We need some exercises in elementary living — things that sadly are not so very elementary in most people's lives. We need to know about simple methods of handling our money in a bank. Surprisingly, even today, many people don't have a bank account and many more have never had a cheque account. So you need to know about dealing with banks, not just having an account but also utilising the full range of their services that might be of value to you. You should understand the virtues and vices of savings accounts, cheque accounts, time deposits, CDs (certificates of deposit), bank bills and so on. There's nothing in the least difficult about this.

The Canadian writer Stephen Leacock said banks terrified him.

> 'When I go into a bank I get rattled. The clerks rattle me;...the sight of the money rattles me; everything rattles me...I become an irresponsible idiot...
>
> 'The accountant was a tall, cool devil...The manager was a grave calm man. I held my fifty-six dollars clutched in a crumpled ball in my pocket...
>
> '"I have come to open an account. I intend to keep all my money in this bank."...
>
> '"A large account, I suppose," he said.
>
> '"Fairly large," I whispered. "I propose to deposit fifty-six dollars now and fifty dollars a month regularly."
>
> 'The manager got up and opened the door. He called to the accountant.
>
> '"Mr Montgomery," he said unkindly loud, "this gentleman is opening an account, he will deposit fifty-six dollars. Good morning."
>
> 'My face was ghastly pale...The bank swam before my eyes...

'"Is it deposited?" I asked in a hollow, vibrating voice.

'"It is," said the accountant.

'"Then I want to draw a cheque".

'My idea was to draw out six dollars of it for present use...Then I realized that I had written fifty-six instead of six. I was too far gone to reason now...

'"You withdraw your money from the bank?"

'"Every cent of it."...

'He gave it me and I rushed out.

'As the big door swung behind me I caught the echo of a roar of laughter... Since then I bank no more. I keep my money in cash in my trousers pocket and my savings in silver dollars in a sock.'[1]

Bank buildings themselves are often intimidating. They're meant to proclaim just what formidable financial institutions dwell within. They're meant to impress as places for people to entrust their money to. But they can frighten the wits out of the small saver and, even more, the small borrower. The piles of cash at the teller's command make the customer's assets — the pathetic few notes you've brought along to add to your little 'money box' — seem trifling.

Even the clerks can be supercilious, their status inflated by the enormous amounts of cash they handle. To someone seeking finance, the bank manager might seem a man of enormous authority to be approached with a respect bordering on reverence. That is of course a nonsense; so, if you know yourself to be infected with this nonsense, you must rid yourself quickly of the virus. The easiest way to do that is to have frequent dealings with banks and bankers. Convince yourself that, however vast the resources of the bank, the financial status of bankers — bank staff — is often as modest as your own. Make yourself immune from feelings of inferiority. Destroy any allergies that banks bring on. Then keep practising until familiarity breeds contempt. You don't need actually to end up with *contempt* of banks and bankers. Early in 1989, the French Bankers' Association launched a therapeutic 'be rude to your bank' campaign,

---

1 Leacock, 'My financial Career', in 'Literary Lapses', *The Penguin Stephen Leacock*, pp.1-3.

urging customers to make offensive gestures and name an animal they associate with their bank manager, such as a shark, a rat, a vulture or a hyena. You don't really need to go as far as that; but see enough of them to be on easy terms with them. You'll soon realise that bankers are no more formidable than your grocer or butcher — and often not half as smart.

Banks and bankers do indeed deal in a commodity no more exotic than meat and bread. Their commodity happens to be money. They'll pay a price to use yours. You must pay them a price to use theirs. Give or take a few frills, that is, in essence all they do. They pay as little for your money as they can and charge you as much for their money as the market or the usury laws allow. The difference is their profit to put in their coffers or distribute to shareholders. In the process, they create credit by betting that depositors will not demand all their money back at any one time and that therefore they can safely lend far more than they borrow. There's nothing 'evil' in this. Butchers buy their meat as cheaply as they can and sell it for as much as they can.

The difference is the profit. So with bankers. Bankers use more esoteric jargon than butchers or grocers. Jargon that sounds impressive. But any person of average intelligence can get hold of what they're on about as easily as you can understand racing or cricket terms, transient teenage jargon or any other 'club' communication.

Bankers are ordinary traders. In the old days, if you had a bit of cash and wanted to trade in it, you could set up a bank yourself. You could even issue your own banknotes. At one time, the United States had a different bank in every small town — almost on every street corner. Many were unstable and subject to sudden demise. Their numbers have been eroded by time and crashes; but there are still many more banks in the United States than in most other developed Western countries. However, most banks, whether in the United States or elsewhere, have now become so huge that average citizens no longer imagine they can set up a bank of their own. The biggest banks in Japan and the United States have assets worth billions — even hundreds of billions — of dollars and single transactions can run into billions of dollars too.

But, however big they may be, they still deal in money in much the same way as the small-town bank on a main-street corner. So you shouldn't be overawed. There's nothing hard to understand about banks' operations. They buy in cash — or hire it — from depositors and sell it out — or rent it — to borrowers at a higher price. They do this in varied ways: in domestic and foreign currencies, in commercial, investment and retail transactions. They provide certain services — money for travellers, consumer credit, safe-custody facilities. But essentially they deal in money — as others deal in bread or meat — in order to make a profit from the trade.

Banks now include many financial institutions which, in the past, operated under distinct charters: such institutions as building societies, hire purchase companies or 'thrifts' have taken on more and more the character of banks. They accept deposits, issue passbooks and sometimes cheque books and credit cards, and lend on a wide range of securities. Building societies tend to approximate most closely to banks: they attract deposits and lend at rates competitive with traditional banks. Finance companies, still operating heavily in the consumer credit market, offer higher rates for deposits and charge higher rates of interest on loans. A 5 per cent margin will not be unusual. They operate at the higher-risk end of the credit market, being willing, for example, to accept second or even third mortgages on property. You should borrow from them only if you can't get the money you want more cheaply from banks or building societies. (Some building societies and even banks in Britain during the 1985–88 real estate boom were willing to extend 100 per cent mortgages on property, thus eliminating second mortgages.) While there are these distinctions, financial institutions are fundamentally the same: they trade in money, borrowing low and lending high to make their profit.

That's the nub of the issue as far as you're concerned. Knowing what the banks do and have to offer, you should use them for *your* benefit and not let them take advantage of you. That doesn't mean you should try to take them down. That would be foolish. Banks are crucial to your money-making. You need them. So you must win and keep their trust. But you must make sure that, when you open a savings account or a cheque account or whatever you do with a bank, you gain a real benefit for yourself, as part of a mutual benefit, because the bank will gain from having you as a customer just as you should expect to gain from having a bank on whose resources you can draw. Bank transactions can and should form part of the process of creating a more egalitarian society:

> The function of credit in a simple society is...remarkably egalitarian. It allows the man with energy and no money to participate in the economy more or less on a par with the man who has capital of his own. And the more casual the conditions under which credit is granted and hence the more impecunious those accommodated, the more egalitarian credit is. It is also that agreeable equalisation which levels up, not down, or seems to do so. Thus the phenomenal urge in the United States, one that lasted through all of the last century and well into the present one, to create banks. And thus, also, the marked if unadmitted liking for bad banks. Bad banks, unlike good, loaned to the poor risk, which is another name for the poor man.[2]

The 'bad banks' moved the balance of mutual benefit between borrower and lender too far to the customer's side and so sideswiped themselves. You must be sure that, in dealing with banks and other financial institutions, you balance mutual benefit nicely or tilt it in your favour — whether dealing with 'good' banks or 'bad' ones. What does this mean for the practical conduct of your banking business?

First, if you open a savings account, bear in mind that you will be selling the bank the use of your savings at a price — usually well below that at which the bank will resell the use of your savings to others. If that turns out to be the sum-total of your dealings with the bank, then you're likely to come out pretty poorly. You'll never become a millionaire. If — through inflation — money is losing value faster than the price the bank is paying you to use your savings — and the tax the government charges you on it — then you'll be worse off when you get your money back than when you

---

2 Galbraith, *Money: Whence It Came, Where it Went*, pp.70–71.

lent it to the bank. The bank won't lose, because they're dealing in money — yours and other people's. But you will, because in the end you're dealing in real goods and services — bread and bus fares and cinema tickets and, if your savings buy fewer of these things than before, then some of your hard-earned wealth has gone down the drain. Of course, it didn't really go down the drain — someone else got a benefit, at your expense. Just who got it and what you need to do to ensure you don't lose again, we'll come to later. But the point here is to be sure that you get *your* benefit out of dealing with a bank. You're entitled to it and should see you get it. Of course, even if you lose some real value of your savings by depositing them in a bank, you'll still be better off than if you'd put your savings in a sock. Stephen Leacock's sock paid him no fee at all for the joy of keeping his silver dollars warm. A sock never inflation-proofed anything. So you're better off getting *some* interest than none. And another thing puts the bank ahead of the sock.

Depositing your money with a bank helps build goodwill with that bank. Goodwill means getting something out of the bank — something now or, perhaps on several occasions, in the future. One of your objectives should be to have your bank manager regard you as a sound, reliable, respectable feller — someone he's pleased to be seen with, whom he and his superiors see as a 'good risk'. That 'good risk' status is something to be cherished and nurtured as your money-making career proceeds. I remember long ago asking my bank manager for what, in retrospect, was a trivial loan. He agreed unhesitatingly, adding, in the oleaginous way some bankers have, that I was 'a man of substance'. That meant that, although I was still poor, I had, in one sense, already made it: through the bank, I could count on drawing on other people's financial resources. So a bank's goodwill is not merely prestigious; it adds crucially to your financial resources. Consequently, a savings account can do for you what a sock never can: it can help you establish goodwill, give you a respectable credit rating and add to the financial resources on which you can call.

As the term 'credit rating' implies, you need to look to something more substantial than goodwill. A savings account doesn't take you into the world of 'business'. You need a cheque or current account — an account that enables you to instruct your bank to pay amounts of money to certain people and debit your account accordingly. It implies two things. The first is that you're involved in fairly numerous financial transactions that require movement of money in a way and with a frequency that a savings account can't accommodate. A savings account means, in effect, that you normally deal in cash — in notes and coin of the realm. A cheque account means that you've gone beyond that and that you now deal in credit: you offer a cheque and the cheque is accepted as a token that you stand in good 'credit'. Equally, if you accept another's cheque, you imply that his 'credit' is good with you. If his or your cheque bounces, his or your credit takes a dive; so it's vital to ensure your cheques are honoured. Much of your success in making money, especially in the early years, depends on your good repute with those whose credit is important to you. That doesn't mean you should be frightened of banks or nervous in your dealings with bankers. On the contrary, you must be confident and show it. But keep on their right side. Don't do anything that might cause your banker — or your Tax Commissioner — to have any doubts about you.

But remember you're being careful for a purpose. You're keen to preserve your reputation with your banker, not just please him but get something out of him. Banks don't deal in charity. They 'don't really want customers who are social security beneficiaries', Labor Parliamentarian Roger Price said. He went on to ask, 'Should everybody have equality of access to banking facilities or are they only for those with a lot of money?' [3] We might be unhappy about it but we all know the answer. Banks are less fidgety when they're dealing with the securely rich and the big-transaction customer. So, in the absence of charity from their side, we have no obligation to be charitable to them.

Get Your Hands on Others' Money

That brings us back to the difference between a savings account and a cheque account. With the savings account, you're lending your money to the bank. You're the creditor

3   The *Bulletin*, Sydney, 2 May 1989, p.45.

and the bank is in your debt. The bank is using your money to make money; to make millionaires out of its shareholders and those of its customers who borrow your money. It might make you feel good to be a creditor but, if you're to make a fortune, you have to stop letting others use your money and become a sort of banker yourself. Like the bankers, you must get your hands on someone else's money at a price low enough to ensure you will be able to use it to produce more than you've had to pay for it.

Remember how we started this chapter. You stand no real chance of becoming a millionaire by working a forty-hour week for a forty-year working life. To become a millionaire, you must, without committing highway robbery or pinching the boss's petty cash, get your hands on some money, legally. That's crucial. Money-making depends on using someone else's money. You can use some of your own — if you've got any — but, whoever you are, however rich you are, you'll probably need, at some time, to use some of someone else's or, at least, you'll be better off if you do.

> Few [millionaires] have actually had a million in the bank. The self-made rich believe in putting their cash to good use, which means investing it. Many are heavy borrowers: one of Britain's most successful entrepreneurs once told me that he had *always* had an overdraft. When I asked the late Lord Thomson, on his eightieth birthday, how much cash he had on him he turned out his pockets and produced a single five pound note. 'But,' he said, 'I have a credit card.'...[4]

With the likes of Lord Thomson, the bigger the borrower gets, the easier it often becomes to borrow huge sums. Borrow a hundred dollars, the cliché runs, and it's your worry; borrow a hundred million and it's the bank's worry. To be realistic, you're never likely to borrow enough to worry a modern bank; if you do, you've lost your amateur status. But you might have noticed 'how much easier it is to borrow ten thousand dollars than ten, how much easier still to borrow a hundred thousand, and that when you come at last to raising an international loan of a hundred million the thing loses all difficulty'.[5]

---

4   Davis, op. cit., p.10.
5   Leacock, op. cit., p.286.

Love Your Debt — But Use it Well

So let's underline this fundamental point: the formula for getting rich is to get hold of someone else's money and use it in a way that gives you a higher return than the price you've had to pay for it. In the end, that's all there is to it. In effect, that's what banks do; so, when you do it, you become a bit of a banker too. You can't readily set yourself up as 'The William and Mary Jones Bank'; but you can act in a way that will win you the same sort of benefits a bank gets from dealing in money.

Let's assume you've got yourself on to a basis of familiarity with banks and bankers and you've begun to accumulate experience in dealing with savings and cheque accounts. Now you've reached the stage where you might go along to your bank and ask for some money. Don't be afraid to do this. If no one ever went along to a bank to ask for a loan, the bank would go bust — it would simply have no business to do. Banks have to 'sell' the use of money just as a greengrocer has to sell carrots. If you're in a position to pay the greengrocer, he will happily sell you his carrots; that's what he's there for. If you're in a position to pay the banker, he'll be equally delighted to sell you the use of his money. He'll be eager to do business with you, provided he can be reasonably sure he can make a profit out of it. He won't do business with you if he thinks he's likely to lose his money. So don't be afraid to ask a banker for money. Like the greengrocer, that's what he's there for. But make sure you put a proposition to him that is good both for you *and the bank*.

There's nothing difficult or astonishing about this. It's all part of ordinary everyday living. We've already noted that many people still don't have any bank account and many others have only a savings account. There are also many inhibitions about borrowing, whether from banks or anyone else. The puritan ethic of some protestant churches condemns borrowing. The word 'debt' has a pejorative ring. Savings are good; debt is bad. You should pay your way — in cash; not rely on credit. History and literature support the case against lending. Shakespeare says,

'Neither a borrower, nor a lender be;

For loan oft loses both itself and friend,
And borrowing dulls the edge of husbandry...'

Some people, when forced to seek credit, for example, to buy their own house, pay off their mortgage as quickly as they can, whether or not it is in their interests to do so. They feel ashamed of a mortgage, as they might of a skeleton in the family cupboard. They feel relieved and proud when they haven't got one any more. They're 'free of debt'. They stand tall — and perhaps look down on others who still have some dread 'mortgage' hanging around their necks.

Of course, we must distinguish between debt incurred for consumption and debt incurred for the acquisition of real assets and especially debt incurred for the acquisition of income-earning assets. Runaway consumer credit can be disastrous: the recent massive expansion of plastic card credit — deriving from its too-easy availability — is a destabilising factor for personal, private sector and public sector well-being. The claim is made that consumer debt in Australia has risen from 9 to 12 per cent of disposable household income in the past decade. In other countries, the same trend has been apparent. This debt is frightening. But investment credit wisely directed to accumulating income-earning assets paves the way to riches.

In any event, despite a good deal of traditional resistance to credit, more people than ever before now deal with banks and other financial institutions, and their financial transactions have become more and more varied. Consumer credit is used to buy a multitude of goods and services. Hire purchase or personal loans are used to buy cars and other consumer durables.

Acquiring Assets: The Family Home

Raising finance is even more obviously essential to buy an individual or family house. Most young, newly-married couples, when they find their dream house, must approach a bank for a loan. They go through much the same procedures as investors in real estate — indeed, they *are* investing in real estate. They stand to gain or lose according to whether the price of houses goes up or down, although their capacity to exploit movements in the real estate market is limited.

If the market goes up, they might be able to borrow more against their asset. But they themselves are the consumers of the services their investment provides. They don't rent the house to a tenant; in effect, they rent it to themselves. If they calculate that the cost of using their own money, plus the interest on the money they've borrowed from the bank, is *more* than they would have to pay in rent for the same house, then in terms of immediate cash flow, they would be better off to rent rather than buy. If they do buy, then they are the landlords to themselves as tenants. They might gain or lose as compared with renting from someone else; and they might make a capital gain or loss as the value of the property rises or falls. There might be only a limited opportunity to realise on these capital gains so long as they occupy their own house. But, as we shall see later, they can realise these gains in some measure, so that, although they are consumers of their own investment, that investment can still be part of the process of accumulating wealth and contribute over time to income earning and capital accumulation.

In the past, a home-buyer tended to take out a mortgage on a house and repay the mortgage regularly over a period of twenty or more years. It was a single, long-term transaction. In recent years, especially when real estate values have been highly volatile, a practice has emerged for home-owners to realise early on capital appreciation of their house or flat. This has been true, for example, in Britain — more particularly in London and south-east England. A house bought for, let us say, £100,000 in 1984 was worth, say, £250,000 in 1988. The owner could then realise the capital gain and buy a more expensive house. (Of course, the new house was bought at 1988 prices so the real gain was not as great as the paper gain by the time the upward conversion was finished.) Another possibility was to use the house, with its enhanced value, as security to raise a loan, additional to the original mortgage. The loan might then be used for commercial/investment purposes or consumer spending. These arrangements underline the point that an owner/occupier's house is an investment which, as a real-estate asset like any other, can be used to raise funds for a variety of purposes.

There is no reason why the process of real estate acquisition should stop. If most people can manage the purchase of their own family house, they can equally well accomplish the acquisition of other property. It is just a matter of repeating the process and perfecting it with each new transaction. Perhaps for many the trauma of such a large single purchase is too much; but there's no reason it should be.

Getting a Stake and Finding Funds

The vital key to acquiring property is to find a first small stake. With that, you go to the bank with a proposition. The bank provides some money at the going price and you provide the bank with a sufficient security. The acquired property, if you do not use its 'services' yourself, is rented so as to provide an income sufficient to pay the bank the price it charges for the use of its money. From then on, a self-sustaining process can be established. The element crucial to this process is that you continue to have access, usually through the intermediary of a bank, to someone else's money that you can then use to earn more than you have to pay for it. In brief, you've set yourself up nicely to make a profit — and add to your net assets — that is, to your wealth. That is what getting rich is all about.

A couple of things should be said about this. The first concerns the stake you need before you can really get going, whether with credit from a bank or anyone else. If your dad left you a goldmine, you've got your stake ready-made. But if, like most of us, your dad left you little more than his good wishes, you'll have to put your stake together yourself. For the most part, there's no way of overcoming this problem except by work. Work won't make you a millionaire but it can get you started down the road. The same Stephen Leacock mentioned earlier used to tell how fascinated he was by stories of people who, having walked into a city with only sixpence in their pocket, became millionaires overnight. So he decided to try the trick himself. He walked out of town, then walked back in again with only sixpence in his pocket. He waited for something to happen. Nothing did.

The only way to make your sixpence grow is to make it work — or go to work yourself. The latter nearly always provides the initial stake. It doesn't have to be great. A hundred or a few hundred dollars could be enough to get you on your way. If the stake is small, the gains will initially be small in absolute terms, though perhaps great in percentage terms. If you double $100, you still have only $200 — hardly enough to live it up — but if you keep on making useful percentage gains, the absolute profits quickly become pretty large too. Double $50,000 to $100,000 for a $50,000 gain and you've made at a blow as much as the average wage/salary-slave on $500 a week earns in two full working years. As we shall see in a moment, what you need initially is patience and modesty in your early expectations.

As an alternative to working for your stake, a 'patron' might provide it for you. Theoretically, that is always possible — a rich uncle might be eager to be charitable; or a stranger might be impressed with your investment proposals or your potential as a money-maker. But remember what Dr Samuel Johnson said about the patron:

> Is not a Patron, my Lord, one who looks with unconcern on a man struggling for life in the water, and, when he has reached ground, encumbers him with help? The notice which you have been pleased to take of my labours, had it been early, had been kind; but it has been delayed till I am indifferent, and cannot enjoy it; till I am solitary, and cannot impart it; till I am known and do not want it.

So a patron might be hard to find when you're starting and too many might want to sponsor you — *for their benefit, not yours* — after you've reached the high road to great fortune.

But the idea of the patron does illuminate the point that banks aren't the only source of funds. Though sometimes devious and always ready to top up their charges, banks are often the cheapest and most reliable source, but you should get to know other places where you might pick up some money. Never forget that your capacity to get the use of other people's money will determine how successful you will be and how quickly. The great economic empire-builders have been those who've been able to assemble financial packages. Alan Bond has demonstrated a formidable capacity to borrow billions of dollars. 'Get me inside any boardroom', he is reported to have said, 'and I'll get the decision I want'. Though his touch hasn't always been sure, his success provides a lesson for all of us to learn: research on sources of finance will pay off handsomely, not only when you're starting but also when you're rich. Research isn't something arcane; mostly it means keeping your eyes and ears open for opportunities to pick up more funds at reasonable cost.

Some sources are obvious. Finance companies and building societies are in the business of selling the use of money — of hiring it out, if you like, usually at rates higher than the banks although competitive conditions often bring rates, especially of the building societies, very close together. Non-bank financial institutions usually demand less security. But, to offset this, their interest rates are higher, sometimes steeply, so you must shop around for the best bargain. Never pay a higher rate of interest than you have to — but, of course, a higher rate might be justifiable if you get some other benefit for it such as a higher percentage loan on the security you offer. Don't go to a finance company if you can get the loan you want, at a lower rate, from a bank. But, if you can't get the money you want from a bank, then consider whether the project would still be viable even at the higher price you must pay the finance company for your funds. If the higher price would make your project unprofitable, then forget it — without regret. If it would still be profitable, then a case exists for going ahead, even if the profit margin is small. Any profit means progress on the road to riches.

Remember, however, that a profit is seldom guaranteed. So you need to balance a prospective small profit against whatever might be the risk. If you think the chances are good of coming out on the right side of the ledger even after paying a high price for your funds, then you could be justified in going ahead, provided other elements in the equation are favourable. But don't forget that the smaller the potential profit margin the more easily it can be eroded by fluctuations in other cost and market elements. Not only should you balance potential profit against risk but you should also balance one project against another. If one is a high risk/small profit prospect and the other is a low risk/high profit prospect, then the latter is obviously to be preferred.

Funds can often be obtained from less well-known institutions and sources. Trustee companies lend money at prices somewhere between those of the banks and the finance companies. Solicitors have clients' funds which they are keen to place on good terms to reliable borrowers. (Unfortunately, funds in the hands of solicitors have declined in recent years, especially as outlets for surplus funds have become better known and more accessible. Investment advisers, whether directly or through the media, have become more common so that the financial function of the family solicitor, especially in country areas, has been eroded.)

You need to become familiar with the sources of funds and their usefulness to you for particular purposes and for specific projects as they come up. You might need long-term money — from banks, finance or trustee companies, building societies or solicitors' clients. Or you might want short-term money for a building project. That could come from banks or finance companies. Apart from the institution, what sort of finance should you look for? Bank bills with terms 30, 90 or 180 days might be cheaper and more appropriate than a long-term mortgage for what is called bridging finance for a building project. Bridging finance 'bridges' the ravine between outlays during building and receipts when the project is completed.

Be cautious — and sceptical. Some people offer foreign money, say, American dollars, at rates of interest much lower than domestic rates. But you'll have to repay in American dollars and the Australian dollar — 'the little Aussie battler' — might fall in value. If your cash flow is entirely in 'the little Aussie battler', you could get into trouble. The very act of borrowing foreign money — by you and many others — for projects that don't help the Australian foreign payments position can itself contribute to weakness in the Australian dollar, thereby compounding your interest and repayment burdens. So be prudent when you're offered cheap money. Look a little down the road and consider the problems that might arise.

Familiarity with these matters is crucial. Never forget: you must get access to other people's money, at the best price. It's not your lending power that counts but your borrowing power. That will make you rich. Do careful research in advance so that, when a chance to make a smart investment comes up, perhaps unexpectedly and requiring funds at short notice, you will know what the financing options are. You might need to act quickly, so keep your standing in apple-pie order with those sources of finance which offer the best options. Research can consist largely of following the relevant newspapers and magazines: the *Wall Street Journal*, the *Financial Times, Investors Chronicle*, the *Australian Financial Review, Business International*. Turn the pages, run your eye over the financial advertisements, respond occasionally if only to extend your awareness of what finance is on offer and on what terms. Build up your understanding of what might be suited to your purposes. Tuck the information away in your memory or your diary for when you might need it. When you acquire a computer, store it on the inexhaustible memory of that invaluable appliance.

Don't be too wildly optimistic, of course, about the latest 'smart' investment and remember that even the most sober institutions can mislead. Don't let bankers or stockbrokers encourage unhealthy enthusiasms. They can make huge misjudgements themselves about investing billions of dollars internationally or a fistful of dollars on small local projects. Of the booms and busts in the United States up to the Great Depression of the 1930s, one analyst has written that:

> The banks...provided the money that financed the speculation that in each case preceded the crash. Those buying land, commodities or railroad stocks and bonds came to the banks for loans. As the resulting notes and deposits went into circulation, they paid for the speculative purchases of yet others. It helped that the banks were small and local and thus could believe what the speculators believed, be caught up in the same euphoric conviction that values would go up forever. The banking system, as it operated in the last century and after, was well designed to expand the supply of money as

speculation required. Banks and money also contributed to the ensuing crash. A further constant of all the panics was that banks failed...A bank failure is not an ordinary business misadventure...it has not one but two adverse effects on economic activity: Owners lose their capital and depositors their deposits, and both therewith lose their ability to purchase things...[6]

The penchant of even the most sober banks to make misjudgements has not declined in what we imagine now to be more sophisticated times. Many of the world's most splendid financial institutions continued lending billions of dollars to African and Latin American countries long after they should have quit their addiction to what was clearly a high-risk fashion. Many also continued to lend to companies whose financing exposed them to high risks in the stock exchange crash which eventually hit in October 1987; and many have continued to lend to individuals with doubtful capacity to service either consumer or investment loans. Banks' unsecured credit card lending has often been reckless and irresponsible.

So don't imagine that, because a bank is prepared to lend you money, yours is a sound investment. It might or might not be. You must form your own judgement. Don't let yourself be carried away by topical enthusiasms or fashions. Use other people's money — as you would use your own — only when you've made a serious and rational assessment of the project on which you propose to spend it. You're unlikely to get rich except by getting your hands on other people's money, but you're almost certain to go bankrupt unless you use wisely all the money — yours and other people's — that you do get your hands on.

The Tax System

At some stage in your career, you'll need an accountant to keep your business affairs in order and handle your tax work. Don't spend money on him too soon. As a wage or salary earner, you'll have Pay-As-You-Earn tax deducted in each pay period. Your tax return will be pretty simple, with

---

6 Galbraith, *Money: Whence It Came, Where It Went*, pp.110–11.

standard deductions and family rebates. You can easily handle that yourself; and the exercise will do you good. Only as you get richer in income and assets — as your affairs get more complicated — will you need an accountant. Get a good one who's sober in his wider judgements as well as expert in his technical skills.

Remember your aim should be to minimise tax, that is, to pay no more but no less than you're legally required to. You must be sure you don't avoid or evade tax — and that the Taxation Office won't be led to suspect you've been trying to. So, as you travel along your Millionaire's Freeway, you'll need an accountant at some point if only to ensure that you don't unwittingly stray across the line from minimisation to avoidance or evasion. You'll need to keep good books too, for tax and general business purposes. The 'good books' needn't be elaborate; rather they need to be clear and simple. Your accountant can help in keeping your books in order.

The tax system in Australia and most other Western developed countries purports to be progressive, that is, the higher your income, the higher the proportion of it you pay in income tax. The progressive concept is not always implemented in practice. Sales and other so-called indirect taxes — which, in fact, hit the consumer directly and immediately — are regressive, that is, they hit the average and lower income groups proportionately more heavily than the higher income groups. Even the income-tax system has a regressive quality in that taxpayers at the higher levels, deriving income from varied sources, have much more scope than simple wage and salary earners legitimately to cut their tax. We'll come up against this phenomenon time and time again: despite our much-vaunted social and economic policies purporting to help the less advantaged, the little bloke is constantly required to bear more of the pain, to the benefit of the rich and powerful. It's an incentive for us all to join the club of the rich and powerful, although we might hope that, when we do, we'll turn out to be more caring of the poor we've left behind.

Progressive income tax means that the *average rate of tax* on, say, $20,000 is less than that on $25,000. But the *average* rate will be lower than the *marginal* rate which, in Australia in 1989, rises to 49 per cent on incomes over $35,000 a year.

The marginal rate applies to your earnings only above a certain level, not to all your earnings. If you can get your taxable income down below the level at which the maximum marginal rate applies, you'll make substantial savings.

One way to do that might be to convert current income into capital gains. In other words, your investments might cause your income to fall, thus reducing your income tax, while your real assets — shares, property and the rest — grow. A recent well-publicised method of achieving this is through negative gearing, that is, investing borrowed funds in such a way that current returns from the investments are lower especially than interest charges on borrowings. The object is not, of course, to lose money but to make capital gains. If and when those gains are realised, they'll incur capital gains tax which, however, is subject to fairly complex formulae one of whose most significant features is that taxpayers can sift inflationary elements out from their nominal capital gains. That's something that income tax, with its fiscal drag, does not allow taxpayers to do. (Fiscal drag means that inflation lifts you into a higher tax bracket, with a higher marginal rate of tax, even though your real income hasn't risen.)

When you buy shares, you should find out how much of your dividend income is franked, that is, tax-paid before distribution and therefore offering you an imputation credit in your own income tax return. Again, when you choose a superannuation scheme, you should be clear about the tax regime applying to it both during the contributory period and when, on maturity, you'll get a regular income from it and/or a lump-sum payout. Often tax treatment will significantly affect the value and so your choice of the most appropriate investment.

Therefore, you should keep abreast of the taxation system and the almost constant changes to it. Don't become obsessed with saving tax. Remember you have to get it before they tax it. So your objective should be to increase your tax base for the tax man — to gather more income and wealth — rather than save a few tax dollars on persistently low income and few assets. Try for a bigger cake rather than a bigger slice of the same small cake to share with the tax man.

Patience and Realism

That's the broad position on getting money and the taxing of it. But a couple of other points can be made at this early stage. The first is to be patient. You're not aiming to become a millionaire overnight. If your sights are so short-term, you're likely to shoot yourself in the foot — or inflict an even more serious wound. Some people are lucky. Some *do* win million-dollar lotteries. But not many; and this book isn't for them. It's for those who are never going to win a five-cent raffle. (Those who, like me, were born in the Year of the Dog, should quickly abandon all hope of making a fortune through unqualified good luck.) So don't go round looking for the biggest coup of all time. It might turn up; but the odds are against it. Don't expect to get rich in a few months. If you're careful and stick to some simple rules, you could be rich in a few years — and that's not long to wait. It doesn't call for much patience; but it does call for some. Especially, don't be so impatient that you rush in to buy when you don't really know whether you should or shouldn't. Don't buy just because you've got some spare cash and you're anxious to put it somewhere — *anywhere!* Wait for the right moment.

A corollary is to be optimistic but sober in your expectations. Don't count on the next investment producing an instant jackpot. It might; but that will be a bonus. The important thing is to ensure you make a profit — that you're richer when its returns have been realised than you were before. The profit might be modest but no one — so the cliché runs — ever went broke taking a profit, however small. If you keep on making modest profits, they'll add up to a handsome total over time. You mightn't have any one mighty coup to boast to your friends about but you'll be quietly getting rich day by day.

The best approach is to take the world as it is. Don't expect too much of it. 'No one ever went broke,' Henry Mencken also said, 'underestimating the intelligence and taste of the American people.' That goes too for the Australians, the British, the Europeans and even the seemingly can't-make-a-mistake Japanese. The world and its inhabitants are pretty pedestrian and will allow you to make small, pedestrian advances most days. That's all you need.

After a few years, you should be able to look back on an accumulation of profits that will have moved you to a higher level of wealth and affluence. That should be your target.

Tools of Trade and Information

What apparatus do you need? Not very much that you don't have already. You don't need a big office or much office impedimenta. You can 'work' from home. Use the family telephone and the family library, reinforced with a few books like this one. Take in a couple of financial newspapers and magazines. And, as soon as you can afford it, invest in — that's right, invest in — a personal computer. They're getting cheaper and more user-friendly all the time. You can store data, write letters, plot charts and graphs if you want to — you don't *have* to — and, as time goes by, even run expert-analysis systems on your computer. When you're not using it to become a millionaire, the kids can play games on it — or educate themselves in its more serious use. You can link it with other people's systems — legally, of course. Through it, you can be more efficient and have more data available to you in your own home than most banks, stockbroking firms and other large institutions a decade ago.

Whether by computer or otherwise, keep yourself informed. One of the most significant human talents is the capacity to communicate. You'll make money by knowing something others don't — or knowing it sooner. The 'king of the junk-bond traders', Michael Milken, was reported to arrive for a talk

> ...carrying under his arms two enormous files, each weighing about thirty pounds. He said, 'Every bond you want to talk about is here' (pointing to the files) 'or in here' (pointing to his head). There were about 150–175 issues — however many, he could tell you the name of the chairman's cat. He cut the wheat from the chaff — 'This is what's good about these guys, this is what's bad.' [7]

You don't have to know 'the name of the chairman's cat',

---

7 Bruck, *The Predators' Ball*, pp.55–6.

aspire to be an obsessed workaholic or get yourself into trouble as eventually Milken did; but you do need to do your homework, assemble the facts and, as an investor, act on the best information you can get.

Read a bit more widely, too. Milken read a book by W. Braddock Hickman, called *Corporate Bond Quality and Investor Experience.*

> Hickman, after studying data on corporate bond performance from 1900 to 1943, had found that a low-grade bond portfolio, if very large, well diversified and held over a long period of time, was a higher-yielding investment than a high-grade portfolio. Although the low-grade portfolio suffered more defaults than the high-grade, the high yields that were realised overall more than compensated for the losses. Hickman's findings were updated by T.R. Atkinson in a study covering 1944–65. It was empirical fact: the reward outweighed the risk.[8]

Milken read Hickman, applied his findings and so made billions of dollars. It's an example that, adjusting for scale, all of us might follow.

---

8 Ibid., p.28.

2
Killing the Stock Market

All right, you say, we've got the preliminaries out of the way. Now, where do we start?

Join the Yuppies

The most painless and effortless way of making a fortune is on the stock market. It can be the lazy person's race-track to wealth. 'Ah, yes,' you retort, 'that's all very well; but how do I get to play the stock market? I'm not rich — and the stockmarket is for well-heeled, clever people — stockbrokers, financial wizards, entrepreneurs, yuppies, all that lot.'

Fair enough. You're nervous. Mark Twain said October was 'a peculiarly dangerous month to speculate in stocks'. He said all the other months were, too. So a healthy caution is wise. But any feelings of inadequacy are not.

You can be assured, first, that you do NOT need *already* to be a millionaire before you start trading on the stock exchange. You can be as poor as a church mouse — or almost. To get started, all you need are a few dollars to buy a minimum parcel of shares, from 'blue chips' — the eminently respectable shares — to 'penny dreadfuls' — those held in contempt by conservative investment advisers. Quite a few blue chips started their stock exchange lives as penny dreadfuls; so the dreadfuls shouldn't be disregarded. Nor should the many shares in between: some will be good — that is, offer you prospects for worthwhile profits. David Jones, the retailer, paid an interim dividend, fully franked, of 200 per cent for only six months trading in May 1989. Others were not so good. Mount Isa Mines, the big miner, paid only 12 per cent for the last full year. But MIM is a strong company and most of the 'in-between' shares will justify careful assessment. Whatever the parcel, the amount needed for your initial investment can be quite small.

The second point on which you can be reassured is that, just as with banks, there is nothing difficult or mysterious about dealing on the stock exchange. Stock exchanges are not exclusively 'yuppie country'. Of course, you'll find yuppies there; but you should see that as an invitation to join in the action, not be frightened away. It should make you say to yourself, 'If they're using the stock market to buy themselves fancy houses, cabin-cruisers and fast cars, the pickings must be good. I'm going to find out all about it and share in the pickings!'

Of course, the stock market has its own jargon and rules of the road. But neither jargon nor rules are beyond anyone of modest understanding. Indeed, the jargon is just part of everyday language — a means of enabling people associated with stock trading to communicate with one another quickly in familiar ways. This means that *anyone* can easily become expert in the jargon. If this were not the case, the stock market 'language' would fail in its essential purpose of facilitating communication among large numbers of people, varying greatly in their intellectual and other capacities. So far as the 'rules of the road' are concerned, once again these rules are to facilitate trading in stocks: they are as simple and easily understood as 'keep to the left' and 'no overtaking' when you're on the highway. They make life as easy for traders in stocks as diplomatic protocol makes life easy for those who practise diplomacy. Leaving aside the jargon and the stock exchange rules, there are no special rites, no initiation ceremonies, no occult procedures, nothing to upset even the most anxious before setting out to trade on the stock exchange. It's all perfectly straightforward. Let's take a closer look at these two initial points.

What's a Stock Market?

The stock exchange or stockmarket is simply a place that deals in shares of, or loans to, or other interests in public companies. (You can also buy and sell government and municipal bonds, that is, loan paper of those authorities; but we'll leave that aside for the moment.) It's a place where you buy and sell shares in a *public* company. When you buy those shares, you become one of the owners of that company — you 'share' in its ownership. It's as simple as that. If you keep on buying shares until you have, say, more than 50 per cent of the company's shares on issue, then you own enough to have a 'controlling interest'. You can outvote all the other shareholders combined at company meetings and appoint directors and company managers of your choice. In certain circumstances, you can acquire a controlling interest with fewer than 50 per cent of the company's shares. If you buy all its shares, then it's your wholly owned company or, if you buy it through another company that you own, it becomes a wholly owned subsidiary of your company. You might have enough subsidiaries or enough controlling or other interests to form a holding company to manage or control and bring together the profits (or losses) of the companies under its umbrella. You can 'take over' another company by acquiring a majority or all of its shares. But the essential point to note is that a share represents a share in the actual ownership and therefore in the control of that company. The more shares you own, the greater your proportionate ownership and (perhaps) control of that particular company.

So far, I've been talking about ordinary shares in a company. Some shares have 'preference' over ordinary shares in payment of dividends. This preference may be cumulative, that is, if a dividend is passed in one year, it must be paid later when profits allow. Other shares are classified as non-voting shares, normally in order to ensure that the original owners of the company maintain their controlling interest. However, ordinary shares are those most commonly traded on the stock exchange and allow full participation in ownership, but not necessarily in control or management, commensurate with the size of the holding.

Generally speaking, when you own other 'paper' of a public company, you do not thereby acquire any rights to ownership or control of that company. If you hold such paper as fixed-interest-bearing notes or debentures, you have a right only to receive interest on whatever money you have lent the company by acquiring that paper. You do not have any right to determine policy, to vote at annual meetings, to appoint directors and so on. Sometimes fixed-interest paper does confer some shareholders' rights — perhaps in the future when certain requirements have been met. An example is the convertible note. A note is convertible when the fixed-interest rights may be converted into ordinary shares, usually at the option of the holder and during or at the end of a specified period. When you convert the notes you hold into shares, you acquire all the rights of a shareholder. Convertible noteholders often have equal rights with shareholders to new issues — that is, they can take up a proportion of a new issue of company shares made from time to time by the directors with the approval of the shareholders. If a note-holder has 1000 notes and a share issue is made of one new share for every five shares or notes held, then the note-holder is entitled to buy 200 shares. You are *entitled* to buy, *if you want to*. You don't have to buy. It's up to you. If you don't exercise your rights — that is, your rights to buy or 'take up' new shares — you can sell those rights, through the stock exchange, to others. Those rights might be worth just a few cents or a dollar or even many dollars for each share. So, if you have rights to 200 shares, you can sell those rights for $200 if they are worth $1 each or for $4,000 if they are worth $20 each. Sometimes the convertible notes are or may be converted into shares at the time of a new issue; at other times, you can continue to hold your original notes until, at some later time, you sell or convert into shares. But the point here is that when you convert notes into shares, at the time of a new issue or otherwise, you then acquire the rights of an ordinary shareholder in respect of ownership and control of the company.

That gives something of a quick glimpse at the sort of interests that can be bought and sold on the stock exchange. The stock exchange is a market for various pieces of paper representing those interests. Just as a greengrocer sells carrots, a butcher sells meat and a bank sells the use of money, so the stock exchange, through its brokers, enables people to buy and sell shares and other interests in public companies. It's as simple as that; but, without adding any great complexity, I need to make a couple of elaborations.

The greengrocer owns the carrots he sells; but the stock exchange and its brokers do not own the shares or other paper in which they deal. Those shares and other paper are owned by you and your next-door neighbours and your colleagues in the office and anyone else who has bought shares or other interests in public companies. Large public institutions, including insurance companies, pension and superannuation funds, trade unions, unit and investment trusts and many others also invest in shares and other stock exchange paper. Without itself owning any such paper, the stock exchange brings the various buyers and sellers together to effect sales, rather in the way that an auctioneer brings buyer and seller together to strike a bargain on the price at which a painting or a house or a Chippendale chair or a Spanish doubloon will change hands.

The people who assist such exchanges are called stockbrokers. They are the intermediaries between buyers and sellers of interests in public companies. They facilitate stockmarket trading, just as real estate agents facilitate trading in property. In theory, there is no need for stockbrokers. If you want to buy BHP or BP or General Motors shares you can search around until you find someone who wants to sell those shares; that person can then make you an offer; and, after some haggling, you can settle on a price at which to buy. That's possible; but it would be a clumsy way to conduct business, especially on the present scale of share-trading around the world.

Bulls and Bears

So a centre is needed where buyers and sellers can come or be brought together to buy and sell. The centre is the stock exchange and the brokers are the salesmen who, along with clerks, 'operators', 'chalkies' and others, 'staff' those centres, enabling bargains to be struck among hundreds, thousands or — world-wide — many millions of buyers and sellers.

The price at which a share changes hands is a reflection of the demand for and supply of that stock. In some stock markets, such as those in Britain, 'market-makers', usually specialising in particular market sectors, set the price of a share; but, since they do this through demand for and supply of the share at a given time, they rather reflect than 'make' the market.

If there are many buyers and few sellers, the price will rise sharply, so creating a 'bull' market. A bull market tends to attract more and more investors buying for a further rise in price. Sellers will tend to hold their shares back from the market until they think the bull market has peaked or they're satisfied to take their profits.

Contrarily, if there are many sellers and few buyers, the price will fall sharply. A 'bear' market will emerge, which will tend to attract more and more sellers fearful of further price falls. Buyers will tend to hold off until they think the bear market has bottomed — or until the market decline encourages them to go bargain-hunting.

A bull market will be influenced by the number of shares coming on to the market. If a large proportion of the shares of a company is held by one person or family determined to maintain their shareholding, then relatively few shares will be available for trading. An explosion in demand for the small volume of shares might then drive the price up dramatically. A big foreign order directed to a limited number of Australian shares might do the same thing.

Equally, a bear market might develop in the shares of another company if a huge new share issue floods the market or a large institutional investor decides to unload its shares on the open market. In fact, the holder of a large block of shares will usually try to sell gradually or off-market under some special arrangement rather than depress the market, to its own disadvantage, with a sudden large volume of sales.

But the important thing to note is that the price of a share will reflect demand and supply. That price will bring supply and demand into an equilibrium which might last only an instant before a new bargain creates a new equilibrium. The price at which you happen to buy or sell that share will be determined by the equilibrium between supply and demand for the share at the moment when your broker places your buy or sell order through his operator in the stockmarket.

The Screen of Noise

I must here enter an early note of warning: the stock market is not a 'perfect' market, in which all sellers and all buyers are fully informed and in which they act rationally in full conformity with their perfect knowledge.

> It used to be assumed that...stockmarkets were 'informationally efficient'. This means that, at any given moment, share prices take account of all the information there is to be known about the underlying shares. This does not imply that everyone knows everything. There will be informed traders and uninformed ones. Informed traders will bid prices up or down to accord with the value of the shares; uninformed traders can ask for no better information than the current price...[However] there can be no such thing as an 'informationally efficient' market...Prices are influenced not just by the actions of informed traders, but also by economic shocks coming from beyond the market, and by the willingness of traders to accept the financial risk that the possibility of such shocks creates. This uncertainty means that trading takes place behind a 'screen of noise' ...[1]

The 'shocks' and the 'noise' might emanate from wars or threats of war; from new governmental economic policies; from sudden strength or weakness of the economy in which the company whose shares are being traded is located; or from some charismatic value attaching to the shares themselves. The charisma may come from the industry — gold, uranium, high technology — or from the specific share, for example, its launching by a well-known entrepreneur or because a new discovery, such as cold fusion, has caught the imagination of the stock market or the public at large. The public mood of the moment can be a contributing factor, even though that mood might have little or nothing to do with the potential profitability of the enterprise whose shares are being traded.

The stock market can therefore be rational; or it can be highly emotional. When an idea or a spirit or a fever takes hold, the market can be caught up and driven helplessly by

---

1 The *Economist*, London, 24 December 1988/6 January 1989, p.90.

it. The market — or the masses of professional and ordinary people operating within it — can be lifted by an elation akin to irresistible gold-rush fever, or they can dump a share in a panic akin to a mob of depositors confronted with a bank collapse. In these situations, the market is not rational, operating in accordance with fundamental strengths and weaknesses, but wildly irrational, driven up or down by crowd impulse.

The stock market might also react unpredictably to particular phenomena. For example, in January 1989, the United States reported a blowout in its current account deficit. That might have been expected to depress the value of the dollar. It didn't; the dollar went up. It did so — perhaps — because the currency markets expected the Federal Reserve to hike up interest rates, thus attracting a greater inflow of international money. But, if interest rates were to go up, that expectation should have depressed the stock market. It didn't; the stock market raced away to new post-October-1987-crash highs. So, in most situations, you need to qualify rational assessments with what you assess to be the mood and fashions likely to affect the market at the moment.

In other words, what is important is to assess not only the economic fundamentals but also how the market will react to those fundamentals and, more than that, to 'shocks coming from beyond the market' and the 'screen of noise'. If you have ordinarily sensitive antennae, you can do this quite as well as, perhaps better than, your stockbroker; but the combined responses of your stockbroker and his colleagues, together with your fellow investors, will determine how the market will react to particular stimuli and with what force. If you can feel their heartbeat when a war is about to break out or when a company strikes oil or when a new product comes on the market or when a new company raider rides over the horizon, you could have riches within your grasp.

New Issues and Stags

Sometimes, a stockbroker isn't needed at all. When a company makes a new share issue, that issue may be taken up by existing shareholders direct with the company, without the intervention of the stockbroker. (Of course, if you want to sell your rights as a shareholder to the new issue, in whole or in part, then you will need a stockbroker to trade your rights for you.) Again, as an existing shareholder you might invest all or part of your dividends, as they accrue, in more shares of that company, bought direct from the company at a discounted price. Many companies now make such arrangements for their shareholders, under which no stockbroker is needed for the regular acquisition of shares. Some allow shareholders to purchase shares at the same small discount through 'cash contributions', thus saving stockbrokers' commissions.

Nor is a stockbroker needed in many of the 'privatisations' made by governments. For the most part, these issues of shares to the public are well advertised and application can be made direct to the privatised company. When those privatised shares are sold — perhaps immediately after they have been bought by the 'stags' — a stockbroker will, of course, be needed.

That term 'stag' is a good example of the jargon used in share trading. The term may be unknown to the newcomer; but the concept is simple. A stag is simply a person — or an institution — who buys shares in a new flotation with the intention of selling them as soon as they begin to be traded on the stock exchange. You buy in the belief that the offer price will prove to be below that which the market will put on them as soon as trading starts. Sometimes stags are right — and make a profit. Sometimes they are wrong — and get out of the market with fingers burnt. (The stag who bought BP shares just before the stock market crash of October 1987 would have had the unpleasant experience of holding shares acquired at well above market valuation. But those who bought British Telecom made money; and those who waited until the more impatient stags had sold out made more.)

So stags are just ordinary people trying to take advantage of a market situation that recurs from time to time. Some stags are so eager that they break the rules, for example, by using several false names, in making applications for shares in privatised companies and so get themselves into serious trouble. In this, as in other respects, stags, like stockbrokers, bulls and bears, are part of and share the virtues and vices of the everyday share-trading world. So, if you see a stag situation coming up, make a careful assessment and, if you're convinced, put in your application to the issuing house together with your cheque and then line up to take your profits — remembering that, even if you've judged correctly, it might be best not to rush in with the thundering herd on the first day but wait until the stag stampede has played itself out.

In broad compass, that's all there is to it. Stockbrokers have no more mystique than butchers or greengrocers. They have certain professional skills, acquired as a result of day-to-day experience of the routines of the stock exchange, just as butchers or greengrocers have skills acquired from day-to-day dealings in wholesale and retail meat and fruit markets.

A broker normally buys his seat on the stock exchange. Sometimes, depending on the economic circumstances of the time and the stock exchange involved, he has had to pay only a small price for his seat — perhaps less than for a taxi-driver's licence. More recently, as world-wide trading has boomed, stock exchange seats have come to cost a great deal of money, running into hundreds of thousands or millions of dollars, depending on the exchange. He does not need any outstanding qualifications. He does not need any university training. He is not necessarily an economist or a lawyer; nor is he necessarily someone with any exceptional economic and financial expertise. He might happen to be; but that would be a bonus. Essentially he is a trade-facilitator — someone who helps in the buying and selling of public company paper.

I shall take this further later on, particularly in the degree to which reliance should be placed on a stockbroker's advice, but for the moment, the point to be noted is that the stock exchange and its denizens are not fiendishly complicated, mysterious and terrifying. The exchange is an ordinary marketplace and its operators ordinary marketeers or salesmen. You should approach them with as much self-assurance as you approach anyone else with whom you want to transact everyday business. You should be critical of their service — or applaud it — as you do the services provided by other tradesmen. Don't hang back from dealings on the stock market because you feel the market itself or the people who operate within it are too clever or too rich or too sophisticated or, generally, beyond your financial, intellectual or social league. They aren't. If you deal with them on a basis of equality, you'll find that, after a while, you're twice as clever — and know twice as much — as most of the 'wizards' who hang up their shingle around the stock market's precincts.

Playing the Market: Flexible Outlays, Limited Liability

I talked a moment ago about how much — or how little — money you need to launch yourself into the business of trading on the stock exchange. You really need very little. The regulations vary from one exchange to another, so generalisations might not apply exactly in every case; but they won't be too far out. Most stock exchanges set a number for the minimum parcel of shares that can be traded. This number varies with the value of the share. If the share changes hands at, say, 10 cents then the minimum parcel might be 1000 shares. That means that you must be prepared to spend at least $100 on the minimum parcel of those shares. For more highly priced shares, costing, say $10 each, the minimum parcel might be 50, so that you would have to be prepared to spend at least $500 on a minimum parcel. Stockbrokers' commissions, generally about 2.5 per cent of the value of the shares bought or sold, can be lower for large transactions and proportionately higher, through minimum charges, for small parcels.

But the amounts of money are not large. Minimum parcels cost perhaps as little as a day's pay or as much as a week's earnings of the average wage-earner in the more affluent countries. Anyone who can afford to buy a car or a television set or take the family for a summer holiday at a nearby beach can afford to trade on the stock exchange. You don't need to be rich — nor do you need to be a reckless gambler. Buying shares could well be less expensive than a day at the races; the returns much more certain; and the excitement, from time to time, quite as exhilarating.

Stock market trading has tended to be associated with men of great wealth around whom myths have been woven in the popular memory — men like John Pierpont Morgan and John Paul Getty. Joseph Kennedy, the father of President John Kennedy, was reputed to have made his fortune — or one of them — out of the stock market and particularly through his timely exit from the market just before the Great Crash of 1929. There are names today well planted in the public mind and in the popular press that dramatise activity on the stock exchanges. Such men as James Goldsmith in Britain, who made his own timely exit from the stock market before the crash of October 1987. Rupert Murdoch, Robert Holmes a'Court, Larry Adler and John Elliott have caught the public imagination in Australia. Larry Adler, like so many others, was a migrant who had built up a fortune from nothing before his death in December 1988.

Alongside the heroes are the anti-heroes, such as Ivan Boesky, found guilty of insider trading in the United States. But these men are only the stars and villains. There are millions of others — small, walk-on actors who do the crowd scenes in the stock exchange 'theatre'. For every big trader, there are millions of small players around the world. They come from all walks of life — professional men and women, farmers, widows, bankers, aircraft captains, cricketers, soldiers and many others. Some have invested millions of dollars in shares; most just a few hundred or a few thousand.

As that illustrates, stock exchange trading is one of the most flexible forms of trading in the world. Indeed, that was intended from the start. It was an essential accompaniment to the limited liability company, the foundation on which modern capitalism was built. The limited liability company made the Industrial Revolution possible and is vital to the post-industrial economies in which we live. The limited liability company means that your liability — to creditors of the company or whatever — is limited to the extent of your shareholding in that company. If you have invested $1,000 in a company, you cannot lose more than that shareholding if the company goes bust. Your liability is limited to $1,000. If you have bought shares to a face value of $1,000 for $200, then you stand to lose only your $200 if the company goes bust. Again, your liability is limited to the market value of your shareholding. *You are not liable to lose any other of your assets to meet the liabilities of the company in which you have bought shares.*

The creation of the *public* limited liability company also meant that shareholders could sell their shares on the open market or investors could buy shares on that market. So now you can move into or out of a company as freely as you wish, provided only that you can pay the price of the share you want or can get the price you are asking for your share in the ownership of the company. You can choose almost exactly how much of your resources you want to commit. If you have the money, you can dive in for a big killing. Or you can cautiously outlay a few dollars. You can put everything into the shares of one single company that appeals to you; or you can spread your money around a dozen or a hundred companies, so that, if your judgement turns out to be poor for one company, it might turn out to be brilliant for another or others.

If you buy an apartment or a house, you must spend, say, $50,000 or up to $1,000,000 (perhaps much more) on one single investment. If you invest in Rembrandt paintings or rare stamps or champion racehorses, you can't slice your investment up into very little pieces (unless you form a syndicate, which introduces difficulties of its own). But you *can* do that when you trade on the stock exchange. It's for you to say how much you want to spend and how you want to spread it round. You won't find any greater flexibility anywhere in the investment world. And the storage costs for share certificates and other public company paper are nil. You don't have to worry about finding tenants; you don't have to take out insurance; and you don't have to feed share certificates like racehorses. The market is always open for you to buy more or sell out. Delay in realising on your holdings — a very important consideration if you need money quickly for personal or investment purposes — is reduced to a minimum. It's the lazy person's racetrack to wealth. It can be the cautious person's track too — the way of the man who wants to look twice over his shoulder and never chance his future on a single roll of the dice. When you trade on the stock exchange, there's not much you need for success. But you do need judgement and the discipline to follow a few simple rules.

Let's have a look at what those simple rules are.

Learn on the Job: Charlie's Coup

Many years ago, I'd just met a good mate I'll call Charlie. Charlie'd had what most people would say was an excellent education — a brace of universities, a higher degree, that sort of thing, all on scholarships, of course. He'd taken a public service job that conferred some status; occasionally talked to the political mighty, wrote paragraphs for their more intelligible speeches and slaved over Cabinet submissions on problems the pollies saw as 'intractable'. But he had little money and little prospect of acquiring much from the worthy but poorly paid career on which he'd embarked. He began to feel cheated.

'I work like a navvy,' he told me, 'and what do I get for it? Just about enough to give me the strength to go on workin' me poor bloody backside raw on their rotten hard bureaucratic seats. Bugger-all else, I tell you that.'

Why should he be constrained in so many ways by lack of money, he asked himself, while others, not obviously more deserving, had masses of the stuff to throw around in all directions? Then, out of the blue, Charlie got some 'inside information' — which really came from somewhere about as close to the legendary nag's hay-cruncher as Sydney Cove is to Gunn's Gully. Never mind. Here was someone who knew all about everything and this someone had whispered in his ear that he should put his money — what little there was of it — into a company I'll call Happy Bounty. Charlie tingled with excitement. Here was his big chance. The market was rising, especially in mineral stocks. Happy Bounty was a mining company. Charlie heeded the urgings of greed and sank most of his few dollars into his hot tip, at a cost of 1.5 cents for each share. Happy Bounty promptly collapsed to half a cent. He felt a stab of pain but then thought of his 'inside information' and elation engulfed him. He knew something few others did. His chances of gain hadn't died; they were now even greater. He bought some more. The shares didn't move. Paralysis persisted week after week. They couldn't go any lower than half a cent or they'd have disappeared off the board altogether. That was probably all that saved them.

Then the company announced they were prospecting for uranium — the glamour metal of the day. Their shares lifted off the ground and started to walk — slowly at first and then more rapidly. Charlie invested some of his paper profits in a bottle of champagne and started to celebrate. The shares reached 8 cents — sixteen times what he'd paid at their low. He bought some more. They rose to 20 cents, because someone or other had found some uranium — or at least had got some tremors on his geiger counter — some fifty kilometres from a spot at which Happy Bounty had been 'prospecting' — which meant no more than they had bought their own geiger counter and aimed it vaguely in the direction of some virgin rock.

At 20 cents, Charlie sold enough to get his money back. The shares rose to 50 cents. He invested in another bottle of champagne and hung on. The shares hit $1. It was unbelievable — but a bonanza. They reached $1.50 — 300 times the price at their low. Making money, Charlie thought, was just too easy. Why hadn't he been in on this racket before? Then the market began to totter. Not just Happy Bounty, but the whole market began to sway dizzily, especially for companies associated with mining. But by now Charlie'd come to believe in miracles. The stock market was a blessing especially created to make him rich. He believed in it, as though in some amiable deity. He hung on.

It did him no good. Happy Bounty plummetted — like the heavy metal it was supposed to be seeking — at great speed from an unnatural height. Just in time, his good sense returned. He sold all he still had at 50. A nice profit. He'd got all his money back with what he'd sold at 20 cents, and now at 50 he'd sold his remaining shares for none of which he'd paid more than 8 cents. He'd have been even better off if he'd sold at $1.50. But he couldn't complain. He'd done splendidly. He laughed all the way to the bank.

But what about all those other people out there in the market? *Some* had done as well as or better than Charlie. But the odds were they were a small minority. Who were the unlucky ones who'd bought Happy Bounty between $1 and $1.50? Who were the unlucky ones still holding Happy Bounty when, just a couple of weeks after they'd hit their peak, they were back to half a cent again? Someone must have lost quite a bit of money during that fortnight; and not many people know what's happened to Happy Bounty since. I certainly don't. Even Charlie remembers it only during those few glorious weeks so many years ago. Somewhere along the line, the company disappeared from the stock exchange lists — and someone's money along with it.

That episode taught Charlie — and me — quite a few lessons — lessons that can be useful to all of us.

If you're dirt poor, you're tempted to try for big, spectacular gains. Gains of huge magnitude come mostly from speculative shares, many of them low-priced penny-dreadfuls, at the sucker's end of the market. Dirt-poor investors go for them, first, because they can afford them — they're the *only* ones they can afford in quantity. Second, the percentage gains can be enormous. If you buy at half a cent and sell at 10 cents, the increase in price has been only 9.5 cents, but you've made twenty times your original investment. Not bad. So, if you want to build your capital quickly, that could be the way to do it.

What you must bear in mind, however, is that the stock exchange should not be regarded as a place for gamblers: as a casino or totalisator, another way to play roulette or punt on the ponies. Trading in speculatives should be a strictly limited exercise. One widely known investment adviser wrote that 'there is not a single member of the public in North America today who has made a sizable sum of money by investing in the penny mining market'.[2] That's nonsense; certainly many 'members of the public' in Australia have made 'a sizable sum of money' out of penny dreadfuls. Charlie was one.

But a warning note is still in order. You should never speculate more than your desperate circumstances compel you to; you should never outlay more than you can afford to lose; and you should make sure you're taking no more than a calculated and well-controlled risk. Little as Charlie had, he didn't put *all* his money into Happy Bounty, but only as much as he knew he could risk losing. He also knew he had to risk something if he were to lift himself out of his dirt-poor rut.

As a safeguard against risks, he'd had 'inside

---

2 Shulman, *Anyone Can Make a Million*, p.16.

information'. That's another lesson to be learned. If you've got a million people, you'll have at least a million pieces of 'inside information' on something. Charlie'd never heard of Happy Bounty before, so his 'inside information' at least told him the company existed and what it did or was allegedly trying to do. But then he had to assess how reliable his informant was and whether, on what he could find out, he should risk his money. *He* had to make the judgement. No one else could. It was *his* money that he'd miraculously snowball or, as Charlie worried, 'do like a dinner'.

He could have talked to his stockbroker; but, in the days before Happy Bounty, Charlie hadn't the faintest idea what a stockbroker looked like. Anyway, if he'd asked the typically conservative broker, he'd have told Charlie, in severe tones, not to touch Happy Bounty with a barge-pole. If, on the other hand, the broker'd had an active interest in the stock, he might well have advised Charlie to put his shirt on it. That could have misled more dangerously than conservative advice.

As it was, Charlie never got to know what a stockbroker's advice might be. As a newcomer to stock trading, he didn't have the good sense to check his 'inside information' with his new-found stockbroker even at the point at which he asked him to buy some Happy Bounty for him. He made his own decision which was to buy modestly at 1.5 cents. That wasn't as bad a decision as might appear. His 'inside' informant was a decent man, whose judgement and honesty he respected. The 'insider' was risking some of his own money. So, in making a modest investment, Charlie wasn't necessarily making a gross blunder.

Then Happy Bounty slumped to half a cent, at which point Charlie bought more. That's a tactic of which you must beware. It's known as following a stock down. You average the cost of your holding downwards. On the surface, that seems to have something to commend it: you bought at a bargain price and now you're compounding your bargain by getting more even more cheaply. That looks good, and for some shares, soundly based on fundamentals, it might be; but, in most circumstances, it's a blunder — a really first-class, classic, sucker's blunder.

Your general rule should be to get out if your stock

slumps substantially, especially if it's a speculative. 'Stop-loss' orders have long been a feature of stock market trading: the broker is instructed to sell if the stock falls by a certain margin, for example, if it falls from its current $5 to, say, $4.50, he is instructed to sell immediately. That protects the individual investor against more than a pre-calculated loss. But it can also mean that, if a crowd of investors use stop-loss techniques — and especially with computer-assisted trading — a modest downturn in a stock can suddenly become a collapse under an avalanche of sell orders. That was one of the contributing factors to the crash of October 1987, a traumatic event we'll discuss shortly.

But in the Happy Bounty days, computer-assisted trading was many years away and greenhorn Charlie was yet to hear of stop-loss. He knew of no rule that, if your stock slumps to a third of the price you paid and looks like going right off the bottom end of the board, you'd better save what you can before the *Titanic* goes under. He believed, almost religiously, in his 'inside information' or perhaps he had a hunch that Happy Bounty, like Lazarus, would rise again. Was it really a hunch — or was it no more than a hope? There might have been a little conceit too — an unwillingess to admit he'd been a sucker to fall for that 'insider' stuff and buy at all. Even if it were a genuine hunch and even though hunches sometimes pay off, you should be very careful about relying on them; certainly you should attempt some more rational assessment either of the fundamentals of the stock or — what can often be much more important — the mood of the market, created by the 'screen of noise'.

Remember that trading in stocks should not be regarded as another form of gambling. It's not a question of it being your day for cracking jackpots. Stock market trading shouldn't be a matter of feeling lucky, but a matter of exercising careful judgement and acting in the light of hard facts and — especially — what the market's judgement is of those hard facts or the blue sky above them.

When Happy Bounty slumped to half a cent, the market was saying that it regarded the stock as almost worthless and, in the end, it's what the market thinks — however irrationally — that determines a stock's value. If, at any moment, the market thinks Happy Bounty is worth only half a cent, then that's what it's worth. You can argue about the 'fundamentals', scream about how irrational the market is; but, at least in the short term, the fundamentals and rational assessments of intrinsic values mean little. It's the mood of the market that counts. But, despite all the portents — and indeed the fundamentals — Charlie bought more. He was brave — or reckless — enough to believe that the market and its mood would change.

As it turned out, he was right. Happy Bounty suddenly shot up. Why? The only reason was that the market suddenly reversed its assessment of the stock. Or not so much its assessment as its mood about the stock.

The company had announced that it was looking for uranium. To this day, I don't know whether it ever looked or not; certainly it never found any. But, in the short term, that didn't matter. The market believed the company was looking for uranium and considered — or hoped or wagered — that it might find some. Value depends on the market's view of a stock — however superficial or ill-informed or just plain wrong that might be. That is especially so with speculatives. Therefore, you must assess not what the company might really be doing — or what its real worth might be in some objective terms — what its fundamentals are — but what the market, in its wisdom or unwisdom, thinks of it. In this case, the market reacted positively and very favourably to the news that Happy Bounty had its geiger counter out and was looking for uranium. The price of Happy Bounty shot up.

Now another element entered. Because the price shot up, whole regiments of new investors, who'd never heard of Happy Bounty before, thought someone must be on to something. They hadn't been privy to any 'inside information'; but they thought they now had plenty of public evidence that Happy Bounty was going places. That being so, they weren't going to miss out on a great opportunity. They wanted to be in on the ground floor — or the mezzanine at least. Perceiving a bull market for the stock, they bought so as to benefit from what they were convinced would be a further rise in the price of the stock. In doing so, they fulfilled their own expectations. Their buying pushed the price up even more, confirming and reinforcing the existence of an eager bull market. That in turn drew in new regiments of eager investors. These investors, acting together, were again the architects of their own expectations. They themselves built up the market to accord with their own assessments and, looking at their creation and seeing it was good, they proceeded to pour in ever more reinforcement to what they had created. In short, having observed a bull market and confirmed it by their own efforts, they rushed to cash in on their own illusions and so ensured that the process would continue. It was what might be called the South Sea Bubble effect, a phenomenon observed early in the history of the modern enterprise economy and recurring frequently, if not regularly, since. The snag is that the bubble will only 'last until the supply of new buyers that affirmed the expectations ran out or something happened to reverse the expectations'.[3]

The first big surge took the price from half a cent to 8 cents — a gain of 7.5 cents on each share. That doesn't seem to be much. But, if you'd invested $100 at half a cent, your $100 had now become $1,600. That was an enormous gain. Whether built on faith or hope or sound assessment of fundamentals or the mood of the market, the profit was splendid. At that point, Charlie's faith had held and he'd bought more. That wasn't necessarily a blunder. The market had got the stock moving up. His guess was that a good head of steam was still behind the movement. He was a persistent bull — continuing to buy for a rise. And again it happened he was right.

What was his reason for buying? Did he really believe that Happy Bounty would find uranium and make enormous profits for its shareholders? I don't know. I never formed any very clear judgement. Nor, I think, did he. Like many others, he probably did have in the back of his mind that the company might find something. But he did little to assess the probabilities — or the size of any find or the cost of extraction in relation to the going market price for the commodity. A vague feeling was abroad in those days that mining uranium promised more of a bonanza than mining solid hunks of pure gold. But few investors in Happy Bounty did any sums. Charlie certainly didn't. Did he then carefully

---

3 Galbraith, *Money: Whence It Came, Where It Went*, p.173.

assess the mood of the market? Again, like many others, he didn't in any sober, well-organised way. Rather he got caught up in the fever of the market — a fever that applied to the market as a whole, to a range of minerals stocks and particularly to stocks directly or indirectly believed or claiming to be associated with uranium. Gripped by this fever — as millions had been gripped by a fever that sent them rushing to California, the Klondike or the Australian goldfields — investors forgot about rational assessments and fought with one another to get some part of the action.

Happy Bounty then hit 20 cents. By any standards, that was a huge paper gain on shares Charlie'd bought at 1.5 cents, at half a cent and at 8 cents. Just $100 invested at half a cent had now become $4,000. Charlie decided to sell enough to get his stake back and hold the rest for a free ride. That was good, sober, cautious trading. 'I'm beginning to get the hang of this, mate,' he told me. And he was. At the same time, there was no way he could have known whether the steam had gone out of the Happy Bounty market. If you think you can you are nourishing a conceit that can lead you to disaster. The best you can hope for is to guess when the steam will run out or to hedge your bets as Charlie had done.

Charlie was not experienced enough in those days to appreciate just how quickly a turnaround from a bull to a bear market can be. If you take your eye off the market for a day — sometimes even for an hour — a frenzied upward market can topple into a precipitous slide. But he didn't know that then. All he had was a gut feeling — the coward's salvation — that it was best to play it safe. He had the added satisfaction that he was in a position to play it both ways. At twenty cents, he was already — on paper — well ahead. He had to sell only a small part of his holdings to get back all the money he'd invested and then enjoy his free ride. As it turned out, at 20 cents, the stock still had a lot of lift in it. It briefly touched $1.50 before it began to stagger.

Charlie did *not* sell his Happy Bounty at the ceiling price. There's a lesson in that too. You're going to be dead lucky to sell any shares — and especially speculatives — right at the top of the market. With very volatile stocks in a frenzied market, you might sell at the top once in a lifetime — if you're lucky. But you'd be wise not to count even on that.

And when the market begins to slide, don't dig your toes in and beg the market to lift the price of your stock up to the top again. You can't rule out a recovery; but the odds are against it. You'd be much wiser to get out before the slide becomes an avalanche. In the case of Happy Bounty, the price had plunged to 50 cents by the time Charlie's broker acted on his sell order. (In a frantic or even an unusually volatile market, brokers can suddenly become less accessible and process orders less promptly than normal.) In a short time, Charlie's Great White Hope had tumbled two-thirds of the way down the mountainside from its peak. That's disappointing. You can't help calculating how much better off you'd have been if you'd decided to sell earlier and/or your order had been processed more quickly. It's like winning second prize instead of first. But what you've won might be a splendid prize nevertheless. Fifty cents was one hundred times the half cent Charlie'd paid for Happy Bounty at the bottom of the market. Every $100 invested at half a cent had become $10,000 at 50 cents. Again, not bad. So you should count your blessings and not lose too much sleep about the even grander blessings that have passed you by.

Certainly you shouldn't think you've 'failed' because you didn't sell at the peak, that your genius for investment has turned out to be an illusion. No matter how great your 'genius', your chances of selling right at the top in a volatile market are small; and whether you succeed or not will depend not so much on genius — whose achievement will be only to get you close — as on almost unadulterated luck. No one can really tell precisely when a market is going to turn and, if he claims he can, look closely at him: the chances are he's a liar or a swindler. So, don't waste tears on missing the top, but gratefully accept the profits you *have* made and settle down to consider how to apply your profits to generate more.

That might mean you will have to be patient. A wildly speculative market, with prospects for large gains, occurs only periodically, usually with some years of relative tranquillity between. If you get a wildly speculative market once in five or ten years, that's about as much as you can hope for. And then you have to see it coming. You have to know it or sense it far enough ahead to be able to buy low, before the market catches fire and then sell high, before the fire goes out. It's no good buying when the market is already headed for the peaks. If you buy then — when all the taxi-drivers and their gullible passengers are stoking up the market — you're likely to lose your shirt. You could be like those who bought Happy Bounty at a dollar plus and still be looking twenty years later for someone to give you half a cent for them. A wise bull is one who's waved goodbye to the market just before the bears arrive. He'll be a very sad bull if he's still buying with a pack of bears stampeding up behind him.

So when a dynamic market collapses, the wise investor, having got out in good time, waits patiently on the sidelines until an opportunity returns to make profitable investments. Just as it's very difficult to pick the top of a market, so it's hard to pick the bottom. There are often several stages in the decline from the top. You might think the bottom has been reached and a recovery has begun, only to find that the decline has resumed. If you buy too early, you'll see your investment decline in value and perhaps have to wait months or years before any full-bodied recovery gets under way. So be careful. But bear in mind that you'd be very lucky to pick the absolute bottom of the market. Try to get somewhere near it and you'll be safe to buy.

Although the market is often irrational, you'd be wise to keep your eyes on fundamentals. In Australia, for example, boom markets often form around the miners — or one group of them. So you should keep an eye on the commodity markets as reported, say, in the *Wall Street Journal,* the *Financial Times,* the *Economist* and the *Australian Financial Review.* Is the price of, let us say, copper moving upwards? Are metal stocks falling, as reported, for example, on the London Metal Exchange, or are reserves piling up to depress the market? Are uses for copper being enlarged? Are old copper mines going out of production and no new finds being made? Is production and investment falling in Zambia? Is there a prospect of political instability in Chile? What are the broad growth prospects in the world's major economies? This information should enable you to make a pretty informed guess about the trend in the price of copper shares in the coming months. Some regard copper as a bell-wether for other metals, so you might look for like trends in aluminium, lead, zinc and other mining shares. But each will call for an individual assessment of much the same kind as for copper.

In this way, you should get a good idea of when the time will be ripe to enter the market again. But, above all, don't rush in and buy just because some cash is burning a hole in your pocket. And don't pit hope against reason. If your best judgement is that the stockmarket has nothing to offer, forget it and look elsewhere for investment opportunities. Wait patiently until you see a genuine opening to buy the right stock at the right time — and don't be afraid to sell.

That's another good rule: don't fall in love with your holdings. Don't be a collector. If you want to collect something, collect stamps or (less profitably) match-boxes or paper dolls; but don't collect stocks and shares. They're for trading or holding for income and/or long-term capital gain. Buying them must imply a willingness to sell to realise the gains you bought them for or, sadly, to dump when the prospect of gain has dimmed. It's no good buying at the right time — that is, at or near the bottom of the market — if you can't bring yourself to *sell* at the right time — that is, as close as you can manage to the top of the market. It's that difference — and, in stock trading as in love, *vive la différence* — the difference between the price you paid and the price you get that puts you in the fast lane on the racetrack to becoming a millionaire.

You must strive to maximise the difference. That doesn't mean you get into the business of buying and selling every day. You're not a professional. (Bear in mind that, if you trade like a professional, the taxation office will treat you as one.) You're an enthusiastic and gifted amateur, making short-term gains from time to time but also making long-term investments which will give you security and provide security backing for other investment enterprises. But don't hold on to shares too long — especially shares with highly volatile markets. If you do, the cycle will complete itself and you'll find that the share you bought for a song and that swelled to a grand chorus is back where it came from and selling for a song again.

Penny Dreadfuls and Blue Chips

That leads to the distinction to be drawn between speculative investment and investment in blue chips or, at least, in solid, reliable stocks with good management and earnings records. Especially at the beginning of your career, you'll welcome a few coups on speculatives. A small absolute gain on a penny dreadful — say, a gain of one cent on a one cent share — makes a huge percentage profit. Happy Bounty showed how the profits can shower down. Because of this potential, some markets offer a special analysis of low-priced stocks. The London market, for example, has advisers who monitor and recommend low-priced shares for investment. These shares need not be priced as low as Charlie's Happy Bounty but might, for example, be selling for less than 50 pence (about one Australian dollar). Some advisers who specialise in these shares contend that the market has written at least some of them down to low levels because of their *past* vicissitudes but that their future looks more rosy and they can be bought for good, solid growth. If so, they can be among the best performing investments on the stockmarket, with enticing prospects for capital gains. But they need to be watched and assessed carefully. The mere fact that their prices are low — that they are in a slump — does not mean that they are now necessarily about to experience a boom and that their prices will inevitably rise. And even if they do rise, perhaps dramatically, don't take your eye off them. Too often we think that what goes up, goes up forever. It doesn't! And some penny-dreadfuls will have slumped for good; so you need to make balanced judgements about each share and decide, for yourself, whether a particular penny-hopeful is due for a comeback — if only because of the 'screen of noise' — or will be carried out of the ring, on a stretcher, forever. Practise assessments, without necessarily buying. Look at fundamentals; and the blue sky above them. Don't over-rate but don't under-rate them either.

So low-priced speculatives should have a place in your portfolio and in your trading. But don't have too many, don't chase them too hard, keep them under constant review and get rid of them right smart when the time comes. Let them reveal themselves to you, from your reading and your friends and, for example, from watching the daily stock exchange reports. Get the sniff of them. Learn to identify those that offer a good chance to increase your investment stake. That stake, snowballed as time goes by, is destined for salting away in things you can rely on to finance the good life and provide security in your old—even your middle—age. If you've just increased your stake, you might start looking for an increase in your current income. You will then fall into that category of investor who understandably wants to benefit now from his assets, rather than eternally recycle them to build more and more assets for the future.

That income-seeking investor should look for well-priced stocks offering a good dividend return. Remember that, in the income context, *yield* will be important, rather than the dividend paid on the face value of the shares. If the dividend is 15 per cent and you pay twice the face value to acquire the shares, then your yield will be half the dividend, that is, 7.5 per cent. So if you are looking for income your needs will probably be met best by buying stocks which are paying a good dividend but which the market has not yet valued much beyond their issue price, that is, the face value of the share as shown on the share certificate. On the other hand, I mentioned earlier the 200 per cent *interim* dividend of David Jones. The stock was then selling at about $9.50 — nineteen times its face value. So the yield came down to about 10.5 per cent for six months or 21 per cent at an annual rate. Of course, this dividend — and yield — might not be maintained. But, as a well-managed, long-established company, David Jones can be worth buying, even at a price way above par value, both for income and long-term growth.

Assessing Stocks

How good can a high-dividend, well-priced stock be? What qualifications should the wise investor look for? Let's take a specific example, CSR — the Colonial Sugar Refining Company. A few years ago, CSR had fallen on difficult times. It had expanded, too far and too late, into areas of oil, coal and metals untraditional to it. It had paid too much for its acquisitions, when the market for their products was already beginning to soften. In the process, the company had become too highly geared or leveraged, that is, the ratio of its interest-paying debt to its shareholder equity had risen steeply. Its earnings rate fell, its dividend was cut, the market value of its shares dipped. It looked like a company to get out of. What does it look like now — in 1989?

During 1988, the company divested itself of $842 million of oil, gas, coal, minerals and steel interests. Capital investment for the year exceeded $1 billion. Long-term debt was cut by $124 million and gearing (leverage) from 30 per cent to 21 per cent. Half-yearly operating profit to September 1988 rose 85 per cent to $147.2 million, enabling an interim dividend of 14 cents on 50-cent ordinary shares. The company had concentrated its activities on sugar — its traditional sphere — building materials and aluminium.

CSR therefore looked like a company that had survived a bad patch and envisaged a high-growth, high-profit future. Was that a fair précis? Generally, yes. But some less flattering points need to be made. First, sugar is a volatile industry. During the 1980s, the world sugar price varied from below three to about twelve US cents a pound in 1989. How will it move in the next few years? How will CSR's profits be affected by those fluctuations? The answer could be, 'Not disastrously if prices collapse, but still substantially.' Profits from sugar were about 29 per cent of total operating profit in 1988.

Second, however, building and construction materials and timber products contributed $85.8 million to operating profit — more than 52 per cent of the total. The CSR management claimed to have achieved 'significant cost savings and operational efficiencies...through the integration and rationalisation' of various building products divisions so that 'margins improved for most products'. However, the building and construction industry is volatile too, with boom and bust years sometimes following one another in quick succession. High and climbing interest rates through much of 1989 hit residential building. In addition, surpluses in office accommodation in the central business districts of most capital cities seemed likely to emerge by 1992, if not much earlier. Would high interest rates, too long maintained, provoke a deep and bitter recession in the economy as a whole? How would these developments affect the profitability of CSR's building products division? If the short-term impact was adverse, would the building products market nevertheless bounce back strongly as soon as interest rates came down, in response to the fundamentals of an acute housing crisis in most Australian cities? CSR's short-term profitability could be closely related to the answers to these questions.

Third, bauxite, alumina and aluminium, which contributed $23.7 million to the half-yearly operating profit — 16 per cent of the total — also have volatile world markets. CSR claimed to have cut costs and improved efficiency. It had some medium-term contracts which would iron out fluctuations and it had engaged in 'some forward pricing and currency hedging...to secure revenue in Australian dollars for part of future aluminium production'. These wise precautions reflected well on the company's management; but they again underlined that CSR was operating in challenging industries, with a large international exposure.

Fourth, the question must be asked whether CSR got out of its resource, mostly energy investments too precipitately. It bought high and has now sold low, with the real prospect that world markets for oil, gas, coal and minerals might grow strongly during the 1990s. Will demand for energy resources lift dramatically at a time when major new discoveries, especially of oil and gas, have been lacking? Has CSR too hastily surrendered the prospect of strong markets for these resources when they might have usefully offset future declines in revenues from sugar, building materials and aluminium? The question is difficult to answer but should be put.

These are the sorts of considerations you should examine before giving your buy order to your stockbroker. He should also look at the current yield and the way the CSR share price has recently moved. The half-yearly dividend was 14 cents — an annual rate of 28 per cent. The company's shares were selling at the relevant time at more than $4, so the yield came down to about 1.75 cents or about 3.5 per cent for the half-year. Not bad for a first-class stock, especially since the immediate outlook for the company's products was good. Nevertheless, the share price had gone up in the last couple of years and, even allowing for the turbulence caused by the October 1987 crash, the price of more than $4 might have nearly exhausted its upward potential. (CSR would have been a better buy a few years ago in the midst of its troubles when the price was nearer $2. Buy as close as possible to the bottom is the general rule to follow.)

So the investor in CSR in the earlier part of 1989 could not expect a high rate of income return nor probably much capital appreciation in the near future. Rather were its shares a first-rate stock to be held over a long period for modest income yield and useful capital growth. The investor looking for higher immediate income with potential for capital gain might well turn away from ordinary shares, whether in CSR or some other company, and consider the advantages of taking up some convertible notes. Such notes usually give a fairly high and immediate fixed-interest return, with the prospect of profitable conversion into shares later on. Dividend hikes might encourage, and increase income on, conversion. New and bonus issues, in which convertible notes often participate, can be held to add to income or sold to boost cash flow. Any advantages which flow from takeover proposals will usually extend to holders of convertible notes. Thus they can add to immediate income without surrendering most of the blessings accruing to the ordinary shareholder.

The real blue chips, such as Broken Hill Proprietary Limited, will be worth holding through a modest stock market cycle, but don't be too proud to move into and out even of BHP from time to time. Though not a volatile stock in the sense of the speculatives, BHP has, over the past twenty years or so, doubled in value and then halved, in reaction to broadly based movements in the economy or the stock market or to more narrowly based movements in the markets for steel, oil and other natural resources. They have sold as low as $2 and as high as $20. They have been affected by changes in fundamentals — the markets for oil and steel — and by such things as takeover proposals which, during the 1980s, introduced dramatic changes in dividend and other management policies affecting shareholders. The Holmes a'Court takeover attempts in the years preceding the stockmarket crash of October 1987 had a particularly dynamic impact on the BHP share price and management's dividend, bonus and new-issue policies.

So if you can see an upturn coming in the BHP share price, then buy; if you can see the market turning down — either generally or in the areas in which BHP is most active — then consider reducing or eliminating your holdings. But remember that BHP is a valuable long-term holding and you should not too precipitately get in and out of the company. You're unlikely to make the same *percentage* gains as with more speculative stocks, although *absolute* gains can be large in special circumstances. But, short of those special circumstances or widespread disaster, shares in BHP and other blue-chip stocks can be held through modest cyclical down-turns, to come good again — or even better — when the slump gives way to recovery. Remember though that this assumes you bought low, as you always should with any stock.

At the time you buy, the income return on blue chips might be low — much lower than, for example, interest on gilt-edged government bonds or middle-ranking company debentures or convertible notes — but they constitute a solid security with good prospects for capital gains. Always try to buy when the price, even of blue chips, is near the bottom. Don't buy if you think the market is likely to drift lower. As we said before, the absolute bottom of the market is hard to pick but get as close to it as you can. Then you can hold on to some blue chips through the ensuing boom and, if need be, back to the slump. If you've bought well you'll get your rewards in reliable and increasing dividends and in new issues at prices near par value — or at any rate at a pretty good discount on what the market will charge you even in a slump. The record of BHP for new and bonus issues has been impressive over the years; so has the record of Western Mining Corporation and several other blue-chip stocks. The consequent accretion of wealth — in the form of readily marketable shares — has to be balanced against the relatively low dividend yield of blue chips. (Although dividend rates are almost always high in relation to the $1 par value of BHP shares, the dividend *yield* is almost always modest in relation to the shares' market price, recently between about $5 and $10. The dividend on the $1 share rose from 10 cents in 1984 to 32 cents in 1988 and, for the first six months of 1989, 34 cents on an annualised basis. But the yield was several times less and it's that yield you must consider: what you get for the money you had to pay for the shares, rather than the dividend as expressed as a percentage of the face value of the shares.)

So with a few, carefully selected blue-chip stocks, you can afford to be patient, without neglecting opportunities for profitable trading. Provided there's no hard evidence to make you lose confidence in a blue chip and the market continues in a secular mood of support, you can stay with it for long-term benefits, buying from time to time 'on weakness', taking up your entitlements to new issues and holding on to bonus issues, and, if the company offers such blessings, accepting payment of dividends in the form of shares. In brief, increase your blue-chip holdings when you can get them cheaply. Sell if you see a significant longer-term decline in market value ahead.

Whatever the composition of your portfolio, you should keep all your stocks under review: speculatives, blue chips and those fair to good stocks in the middle. All will be subject to change. Demand fluctuates; fashions change; managements come and go; the supply situation might move into surplus through higher domestic production or imports. All of these things — and others — will affect your assessment of the future of the stocks you're holding. For example, use of optic fibres might mean a long-term drop in the world demand for copper, so you might want to get rid of your shares in Mount Isa Mines. If many people think that way, the price will fall, so try to get out before the slide becomes a slump. On the other hand, you might believe that demand for copper, in 1989, will remain high, some of the high-cost mines having been forced out of production because of the sharp drop in price between 1982 and 1987, sliding production in Zambia, enhanced demand from manufacturing industry in the newly industrialising countries and record low world stocks. You might also think that Mount Isa Mines has done a good job cutting production costs, identifying new deposits and investing in new technology. So you might congratulate yourself that you held on to your MIM shares during the dark days and that you 'bought on weakness'. If the price hasn't already risen too high, you might consider adding more MIM shares to your portfolio. In any event, you might eagerly take up any rights to new issues at discount prices and take your dividends in more shares (issued at a small discount on the ruling market price, without any stockbroker's commission).

Income and Growth: Stocks as Security

Now let's assume you're at a different stage of life and your capital/income needs have changed. You've converted your speculative gains into substantial holdings of sound stocks in well-managed companies. You're getting to the point at which you don't need so much immediate income, especially since it will attract a high rate of tax. Rather you're now looking for capital gain from your investments. If that's the case, you'll need to look for growth stocks — including companies in fairly new sectors or comparative newcomers in older sectors. Companies producing or distributing new technology, for example, in the computer and communications field, might be interesting. A new company with lively management that is taking over old companies whose dynamism has faded might be another. Older companies, provided they're still vigorous or have been reinvigorated, will also qualify. Good management is always a vital ingredient to look for. A touch of genius also helps. Some years ago, a company founded by the brilliant Ralph Symonds made timber products of outstanding quality; when he died, the company faded.

It won't be so important to you now if the growth companies pay no or very low dividends. What is vital is that they're well-managed companies in lively sectors poised for growth and offering good returns some distance down the track. You'll have to make a judgement about how long you're prepared to hold them — perhaps a few months, perhaps two or three years, before they begin to pay off in capital gain, income or both. With a capital-gains tax, don't forget that you'll need to hold stocks for a longer term to minimise tax, so it'll pay you to identify them ahead of the market and hold on to them. The Tax Office will probably charge you less on capital gains than on income, your nominal gains will be discounted with an allowance for inflation and, in any event, you won't have to pay capital gains tax until you realise your capital gains, that is, until you actually sell your shares at a profit in excess of the rate of inflation during the period you've held them.

Bear in mind that capital gains can be of great value even *before* you realise them — *and even if you never realise them.* That is because your shares are not only an investment but can also serve as security for further investments. Exactly how much use you can make of them depends on your banker; but, if you've got a good portfolio of shares, held in safe custody by him, it certainly won't hurt his opinion of you. Most bankers are extremely conservative. They might make mistakes; but they don't like risks. They like plumb 100 per cent dead certainties. Therefore, don't highlight to your banker the speculative stocks you hold or have held; and be coy about any penny dreadfuls on which you're currently taking a punt. You might make good money on them but your bank manager will rarely have much faith in them and he could form an impression that you're reckless — and that's a reputation you must never have with your banker. (We've got plenty of evidence that bankers themselves can be incredibly reckless but that's different; *you* mustn't appear to be.) So emphasise your portfolio of blue and near-blue chips and let him hold them for you. He'll be impressed with this incontrovertible evidence that you're a person of substance. That reputation and the value of the shares will be a well for you to draw on. If its waters aren't so deep that they're worth a million dollars, they could nevertheless be deep enough to persuade your bank manager to provide funds for your next project. So hold good stocks over time and store them with your bank. Though they'll be only part of the close association you should build up with your banker over the years, they'll pay off handsomely. You might note too that, if you deposit them with him as security, you probably won't have to pay anything to have your share certificates sitting in his vaults. (If you ask him to hold them in safe custody, he'll charge you for the service!)

However the bank holds them, don't forget that those share certificates can be a valuable security. You don't want to tie them down too tightly. You'll want to recycle them from time to time, to take advantage of market opportunities. You'll want to sell those that have lost or are losing form and buy others with more life in them. You'll add to your total stock from time to time through new or bonus issues or new acquisitions. So you'll have a revolving fund of shares of fairly stable or increasing value, lodged with your bank over a long term. If he's got confidence in your ability to handle this portfolio, he'll probably be ready to regard it as a direct and adequate security for loans he'll extend to you. He might want you to assign specific shares to him as security or he might be content with a gentleman's agreement that, although the components of the portfolio will vary over time, you'll maintain the portfolio with him at a certain agreed value.

In either case, the portfolio strengthens your position when you need funds. You can sell part of the portfolio or you can borrow against it. If you borrow money against the portfolio as security, you don't need to sell shares. As share values rise, so does the value of the security. Usually, your banker won't be willing to accept a peak price, at the top of a runaway boom, to calculate the value of the security, especially if the individual stocks as well as the market are volatile. (Even blue chips can be volatile in a runaway bull or severe bear market and in some takeover situations.) He'll write values down to cover some pretty grim contingencies; but, if the stocks in your portfolio are sound, there should be an accretion of value from which you can benefit without having to realise on your shares by sale on the stock market; and you won't have to worry the Taxation Office with any admission that you've made capital gains by selling them.

More and more, the way to wealth has consisted in the effective use — perhaps even the manipulation — of pieces of valuable paper and the gradual accumulation of entries to your 'credit' in registry and accounting ledgers. You should use all the pieces of paper you can acquire to add to your 'credit' in these ledgers. The person with a flair for acquiring and moving these pieces of paper around — for ensuring that they're in the right place at the right time — will prosper. Those pieces of paper might seem insubstantial but they represent command over real wealth — over farms and factories, houses and offices, mines and transport. The more of them you have, the more wealthy you will be.

Is that all there is to becoming rich? You scratch together a stake of a few dollars, buy a few shares with it and hit a jackpot by buying the right speculatives in a bull market. Then you invest the takings in blue chips and lodge your sound stock with your banker to use as security for further bank loans. That's not a bad scenario but there are a few other things you will need to know.

Advisers: Grand Masters or Blind Monkeys?

One thing is guidance on the professional advice you should take. After you've made some progress and accumulated some worthwhile assets, you might think that the challenges of further progress have become too great for the amateur. Perhaps you've been lucky and, you think, your luck mightn't hold. You'd like a little more assurance by talking to some people — some 'experts' — who know all the right moves for investing, minimising taxation and the rest. As with playing chess, you think you could learn something from the Grand Masters.

Let's look at the Grand Masters to whom you might go for advice and see how competent they're likely to be. Especially these days, there are a lot of advisers about, ready to serve you, sometimes at quite a high price. Some governments require or propose to have these advisers registered, after undertaking some qualifying examination. But, in many contexts, anyone can offer himself or herself as an 'investment adviser', perhaps without any identifiable qualifications or any relevant or creditable track record. Without calling themselves advisers, journalists on television and radio, or in the printed press, will give reports and commentary which constitute 'advice' or which will tend to guide viewers or listeners or readers towards or away from certain investments. Often these journalists will have little relevant background in business affairs.

Some advisers will have ability and integrity. But you must regard them all with a certain scepticism. Keep your feet planted firmly on the ground. Their interest will not necessarily coincide with yours. They might want to make money out of you rather than for you. Their judgement will sometimes be good but it will also often be faulty — inexcusably faulty. The time they can or will want to give you will often be limited and their attention span for your concerns will be much narrower than their attention span for·their own. Their advertisements in the daily and financial press will be beguiling and their 'investment' and 'financial' newsletters will claim an authority they seldom deserve. They will highlight the few past occasions on which they have been right and be silent about the many occasions on which they have been wrong. Their promises will be spectacular; their performance pedestrian. So be careful. Practise being a sceptic. It will keep you financially fit.

There are some recognised, orthodox sources of advice.

One is your stockbroker. Especially these days, he can be someone with considerable training and experience in economic and financial affairs, sometimes a university graduate in economics or commerce. He deals in shares all the time, so he should know something about them. He should be able to give 'good', 'sound', 'reliable' advice. Sometimes he does. Dig out of him all the information you can. Some stockbrokers issue periodical, usually monthly, appraisals of the investment climate and of specific companies. Read them. Sometimes they contain useful data and analyses.

But your stockbroker is not always the whizz-kid you imagine. Test whatever information he gives you. Does it stand up to what you've heard elsewhere? If he tells you that the management of, say, the Colonial Sugar Refining Company is going to change for the better, does that accord with assessments others are making of the respective merits of CSR's outgoing and incoming management teams? You ask him, as I asked my broker on one occasion, whether a takeover offer by Spargos Gold is reasonable at rather less than one Spargos for one share of Queen Margaret Mines. 'Yes', he advised me. And what was the market some two years later, in the latter half of 1988? Spargos was selling at 23 cents and Queen Margaret Mines at $1.30. Not exactly a brilliant piece of advice. So sometimes your stockbroker's advice might be good; sometimes it will be terribly wrong.

That means that, although there's never any perfect hedge against poor advice, you must carefully analyse your stockbroker's recommendations to see whether they stand up both to the facts and to the criteria that are important to you. He tells you to buy gold shares. Do you think that the price of gold will continue to fall or do you agree with him that, in the short term at least, it has bottomed and is more likely to rise? Will the gold price leap upwards in terms of a rapidly depreciating dollar? Or will 'the little Aussie battler' come good again and cut the gold price in local dollar terms?

Then again, your stockbroker might be recommending 'safe' stocks that he's kept on his list for his well-heeled, ultra-cautious 'granny' clients for the last twenty years. He retains them on his list partly so that his old clients will continue to rate him 'sound': it's his means of reassuring them. Fair enough. But do *you* want granny stocks? Has all the dynamism gone out of them long ago? Are the jowls of their chairmen and managing directors sagging with age and exhaustion? Have they lost drive and imagination, do they ignore new technology and flounder about new, real investment? If the answers are 'Yes', they won't provide you with growth investments or give you extra income. About your only interest might be in taking them over, if they're asset rich; but then you'd lose your amateur status.

So look closely at your stockbroker's advice. Get all the data you can from company reports, watch the media financial news and commentaries and weigh the data against what your stockbroker says. Don't gather so much data that you're overwhelmed. Practise sifting the wheat from the chaff. Much reporting in the daily press and business periodicals is pretty thin and often little better than gossip. Reporters often have little expertise or experience. Last week, their job might have been to compose the daily horoscope. With a little persistence, you'll quickly become expert at throwing out the dross and polishing the gems. Don't gather too much data but always be prepared to accept 'the slaying of a beautiful hypothesis by an ugly fact'. Everything might be fine — the management good, the capital equipment excellent, the mine next door to Sydney Harbour, the gold price reaching to the sky — everything splendid — but if the gold lodes just aren't there, that 'ugly fact' will kill the 'beautiful hypothesis' stone dead — unless you're buying for blue sky alone.

As with your stockbroker, so with your banker — listen to him but don't be dominated by him. The odds are he's no wizard either. Nor will his interest necessarily be the same as yours. He'll be conscious of his bank's concerns and want to protect his own steady income rather than promote your rapid rise to riches. So the banker's advice, like your stockbroker's, will often be precautionary and, to that extent, a valuable deterrent against recklessness. Listen to it. Apply the brakes on your rush into wilder schemes if, after analysing his advice, that seems prudent. But don't let banker or stockbroker dominate you. Don't regard their advice as Holy Writ. If, after due reflection, you're convinced you should act contrary to it, then do so. In the end, if you're to come out on top — and rich — you're going to have to make your own judgements and occasionally make your own mistakes, so the sooner you start practising self-reliance the better.

Apart from stockbrokers and bankers, there is that battery of investment advisers we spoke of before, who have so proliferated in recent years. The daily newspapers now devote much more of their space to financial and business affairs. 'Business' magazines of various kinds and of greatly varying quality have blossomed everywhere. The daily newspapers and, even more so, the business magazines often purport to tell you how to get rich; but their performance is almost invariably disappointing. Much of their coverage is of the activities of the more dramatic of the entrepreneurs and their treatment of matters of substance concerned with the stock market and individual stocks is slight and jejune. They carry advertisements for or commentaries on various share purchase propositions. Organisers of share trusts — North American trusts, property trusts, Asian trusts — explain the virtues of what they have to offer; but they are promoters, interested in making a profit out of you. There are weekly and monthly investment letters, 'hot-lines' to give you the latest tips, seminars at which you are invited to hear the 'masters' of investment magic. Some of these enterprises have merit. But many do not. Many are simply out to get *your* money so that they can make a fortune out of it. That's not what you want: you want to get the use of *other people's* money so that you can make your own fortune.

So select carefully. Apart from those who are self-interested, many so-called advisers and experts have little ability and few insights, their advice consisting of little more than a collection of clichés that appeal to the fashions and preoccupations of the moment. Many offer little clear-cut advice, for example, about the wisdom of investing in the stock market, as distinct from property or precious metals or whatever and, within these broad categories, offer little coherent advice on the virtues of particular companies. They indulge in generalities that get you nowhere. You will also find little agreement on or rational debate about what the prospects are for the stock market as a whole or for particular companies. Some newspapers and television stations will do a round-up of the opinions of half a dozen 'experts'. Two will say the market will go up, two that it will go down and two that it will stay where it is. Some will say, 'Buy A'. Others will say, 'Sell A'. The rest will ignore A and tell you to buy or sell B. Any rational analysis in support of one course or the other is usually entirely lacking.

The better advisers are more specific and give well-considered reasons for recommending a particular share or other investment in a specific sector of the economy. They attend to the fundamentals. For example, they give their assessment of the future of the commercial property market in the central business district in, say, Perth. If the fundamentals are right, then you can consider whether shares in a company operating in that market in Perth are likely to be a sound buy or not. You've got some depth to your approach to your investment. So those in-depth advisers dealing in specifics are the ones you'll find most helpful. But they're going to make mistakes too, no matter how able they might be, on fundamentals as well as peripheral elements. Very few people can accurately and consistently pick trends in the future price of wool or computers or air-fares. We'll deal with some of these things later when we deal, for example, with the people who saw too soon that the price of sugar *had to* rise — and it didn't or not until some years later.

So even the good advisers will make mistakes and their

interests won't necessarily be yours. They'll direct their recommendations to those things of most interest to a majority of their readers or viewers or subscribers. They'll rarely give advice in the light of their own personal experience: most of them are *observers* rather than *doers*. Especially as you become more experienced, you'll find that your judgement is often better than theirs. So exercise your own judgement as early as possible and see how it stands up to the advice you get from others. Using your own judgement usually means just using common sense — few people have anything else — and using it can quickly make you just as 'expert' as the next person.

'Watch the market' is a good rule. The market might be trying to tell you something — although it might not always be right. 'When a company's share price drops sharply, the alarm bells start ringing for professional investors,' *Business Review Weekly* told us on 12 May 1989. 'The stock market has a much-vaunted grapevine that supposedly knows in advance of every important corporate event, favorable or unfavorable. It is unusual for a stock's price not to firm in advance of good news. Equally, a stock's price usually begins falling before bad news.' So watch the market. But don't follow its signals slavishly. Form your own judgements.

In any event, there's little alternative to substantial self-reliance by an investor whether in Australia, the United States or Europe. The Paris newspaper, *Le Figaro*, in its issue of 2 January 1989 published advice by three experts — Louis, Charles-Edouard and Max — on four shares listed on the Paris *bourse*. On the first, Louis said, 'Buy on weakness', Charles-Edouard said, 'Buy now' and Max said, 'Forget it'. On the second, Louis said, 'Forget it', Charles-Edouard said, 'Buy on weakness' and Max said, 'Buy now'. On the third, it was Louis 'Buy on weakness', Charles-Edouard 'Buy now' and Max 'Forget it'. On the last, Louis advised, 'Forget it', Charles-Edouard 'Buy on weakness' and Max 'Forget it'. So no two of them agreed on anything, except Louis and Max on the last. Whose advice should the investor take? You might follow Louis because you like the shape of his nose or you might average out their recommendations in some way or you might use a pin. The sensible approach would be to ponder the solid data each expert used and make up your own mind. There's no other route to sensible investment.

So, gather such advice and data as you can from stock exchange publications, company reports, financial journals and daily papers. As a world stock market has evolved in recent years, publications have begun to appear which give the investor an overall view of all the major markets. Such a book is the *Directory of World Stock Exchanges*[4] which appeared in London in October 1988, and which the publishers described as follows:

Global trading and internationalised financial markets make access to up-to-date information essential for brokers, financial analysts and investors...this comprehensive directory is the first book to bring together the latest data on 85 world stock exchanges, from the major exchanges in London, New York and Hong Kong through Europe and the Far East and including South America and the Middle East.
Detailed entries for individual exchanges include the following:
 * History, constitution and organisation of the exchange and its governing body
 * Membership details, including categories, rules and regulations, costs
 * Various markets operated — options, futures, unlisted securities
 * Procedural information on settlement, methods of quotation, new issues, takeovers and mergers, charges and commissions, publication of prices
 * Statistical data on the number and types of securities listed, turnover and price indexes
 * Technical publications produced by or about the exchange
   Also included are tables showing each exchange in such categories as variation in turnover and types of securities. The Directory provides business, financial and investment institutions with quick access to needed information.

Don't overwhelm yourself with reference books of this kind. Use them to help you to act efficiently; don't let reading and consulting them become a substitute for real action on the stock or other markets. And don't fritter away

---

4 The Economist Publications, London, 500 pages, £56.

too much of your investment money on them. Most can be consulted in public libraries. But select a few books to have at hand at all times and keep them up-to-date. You'll appreciate the convenience of having basic data for the conduct of your transactions.

Television and radio are also a source of up-to-the-minute data though mostly even more superficial and ephemeral than that of the printed media. Don't overload yourself with material — and learn to sift out the nonsense. Make a habit of quietly listening to what's going on around you. Make links between pieces of data that you pick up. What is cause and what will be the effect? If the Russians are forced to sell more gold on world markets to pay for bigger grain imports, will that depress the price of gold? Will it push up the price of grains — and will continuing drought in the United States jolt it up still further? What will the short-term and medium-term effect be on the beef industry? Will the dollar go up? The United States dollar? The Australian dollar? Be receptive to the advice of your stockbroker, your banker, your specialist investment adviser and others — but be ready to have a hard-headed look at all the advice you get to see whether it stands up; and check whether their advice fits the imperatives *of your own situation*. If you want income, let us say, and your stockbroker is recommending shares that offer long-term capital gains but not much money in your pocket now, does it make any sense to follow his advice slavishly? Or should you substitute for his good advice — and it might be good, in its way — something that better fits your cash flow requirements?

Sometimes, you might pick up more about share and other investment possibilities in the course of ordinary living than you will from more professional contacts. For example, it's always useful to have friends interested in the same things as you are. You don't need anything as formal as an investment club; although that might help. But, if you've got friends who play good tennis, your own tennis is likely to get better; if your friends like good wine, you're likely to appreciate a great vintage better; and if you've got friends who know their way around the stock market, you'll improve your understanding of the market, you'll get more fun out of it and both your friends and you will probably make much more money by informally pooling your information and experience, than you would have done alone.

'The auto market's too depressed,' I remember once saying to Charlie. 'I'm going to sell my shares in Repco.' (Repco specialised in making auto spare parts.)

'You'll be a mug if you do, mate,' Charlie replied. 'People aren't buying *new* cars. But they're holding on to their old ones. Old cars need spare parts — lots of them. Repco's going to boom.'

He was right. Against the general trend, Repco prospered, the price of their shares shot up, and I made a nice little profit.

Charlie wasn't an 'expert' or an 'insider'. But he was blessed with good sense, he was interested in the stock market and keen to make money out of it. He liked to talk about his investments, offer his assessment of trends, companies and their managements. Such friends are valuable. What did Shakespeare say? 'Grapple them to your soul with hoops of steel.' You'll enjoy their friendship and you might well make each other much richer.

Exotic Markets

However, the need to make your own judgements will remain. That reliance on your own judgement will be crucial to any decision you make to enter foreign, distant or 'exotic' markets. If you're to make a well-based decision, you'll need data about those markets and to have some feeling for the environment in which they operate. In the past, the New York investor invested in New York — or the United States; the Englishman in Britain; the Japanese in Japan; and the Australian in Australia. Today's investor can operate in a worldwide market, with the opportunities such a market presents and the temptations and dangers that arise from it.

Many investors are already seeking treasure-trove in far-off markets, more will probably try next year and the trend is likely to be reinforced throughout the 'nineties. Where will they go? Central and South America, Asia and the lesser known markets of Europe are likely destinations. Brazil, with dramatic gains in the past, could show up well in the future. It has great strength in raw materials, formidable investments already in industry and lively trade. But inflation, foreign debt and the uncertainties always present in highly volatile economic situations require the investor in Brazil, as in other Central and South American countries, to have steady nerves and the capacity to act and react quickly. As a neighbour of the United States, Mexico might be rather less nerve-racking, especially given its demonstrated capacity to cope with its recent economic woes.

The adventurous but not reckless might prefer those Asian markets travelling along a road with *some* similarities to that already travelled by Japan, Korea, Hong Kong, Taiwan, Thailand, even the Philippines. But do your homework before you commit your funds. For example, the impact of boom, bust or turmoil in China on the strong but sensitive Hong Kong market could be thrilling and rewarding, but devastating if things go wrong.

The less well-known markets of Europe might be worth a try too — but again mingle adventure with prudence. Portugal and Greece are already members of the European Community and that offers a measure of assurance — and possibly added dynamism after 1992. But monitor political and economic developments before you commit funds. That applies with even greater force to such a country as Turkey, outside the European Community but the recipient of a good deal of foreign investment which is moving its economy forward.

Austria, a candidate for EC membership which shares borders with eastern European countries on the brink of what could be beneficial change, has a whole raft of stable and reliable characteristics which could repay prudent assessment.

We don't want you to be a stick-in-the-mud stay-at-home. If you're going to be an active participant in the investor's world, you must live in the now, not in the past. We live in a world market, so you must be aware of its trends and the impact of developments in one part of the world on another. No single stock market is any longer an island. Wall Street will influence markets everywhere; so will Tokyo; and the commodity and financial markets in London, New York and Chicago will have their influence on most producers and consumers. Whatever your local or chosen market might be, you'll have to take account of what is happening in world markets at large and especially in those markets which dominate share and other economic and financial trends.

But it is quite another thing to be actively involved in share trading in faraway and exotic markets. Why should you do it? A reason often given is to diversify your investments. But diversification *per se* is no justification at all. The only justification should be that other markets are growing faster and offering more potential for secure profit than those at home. 'One of the more developed young markets' in Asia, South Korea, 'gained 72.4 per cent in dollar terms in the year to' November 1988 and 'the most fashionable emerging market [in 1988] was arguably Thailand'.[5]

That dynamism might be a sound reason for seeking out the exotic. But it's not living in the past to insist that you have enough data to make sane judgements. Some stocks such as IBM and Exxon are traded all round the world. Data on these multinationals are easy to acquire; but otherwise you need to know the market and you need to know the specific stocks in which you plan to invest. If you plunge into Turkish equities, you might — you just might — make a killing. But you *might* get slaughtered. If you're going to invest in Turkey, get to know as much as you can about the country, its economy, its prospects and the particular company whose shares you plan to buy. If you don't, you're gambling and that's not what investment is all about. You can take a risk — that's what investment *is* all about — but it should be a carefully calculated risk, reduced to the lowest possible minimum, and what you risk should be no more than you can afford. You should also bear in mind that, by the time you get round to being aware that, say, South Korea 'gained 72.4per cent in dollar terms' last year, the zip might already have gone out of that market. It might not; but check carefully before you invest in last year's bull market instead of this year's up-and-comer.

One way to minimise your risks, to delegate share selection and get a good spread might seem to be to buy into investment or unit trusts. Many investment houses

---

5 *Financial Times*, London, 5 January 1989.

offer units in South and Central American, Asian, North American, Australian and other markets. One of these houses claimed that 'a market comprising 592 listed companies representing the best of Brazil's private sector is excellent value at a total capitalisation less than that of RJR Nabisco [the American food giant]'. That may well be but, if you put yourself in the hands of such a fund, you surrender your own judgement. If your own judgement is good enough to confirm that of the fund, why not exercise that judgement independently? Investment and unit trusts handling foreign and exotic markets tend to launch a country or regional trust when it can already be presented as a sparkling investment with large gains already on the board. By that time, the life might be going out of the market and it might be about to stall or slump. Remember that the objective in all investment is to get in early, not when the boom is peaking or has peaked.

In summary, if you want to experiment with exotic markets, learn something about them first, get in near the ground floor on an upturn and think carefully before you take the easy way out of betting on someone else's judgement, whether through direct share purchase or via some investment, unit or other trust.

The Stock Market Down the Years: Charlie's Past Career

Now the time has come to look at how, over the years, someone might have accumulated a worthwhile portfolio of shares. You'll recall how Charlie made his coup on Happy Bounty. Shortly after that brilliant episode, he was idly turning over the pages of a Saturday newspaper when, in the financial pages, his eye caught an insurance company's advertisement proposing life insurance linked with a loan for the purchase of shares. Fascinated, Charlie could hardly wait for the opening of business on Monday and he quickly made a deal for $10,000. A lot of money. $10,000 insurance. $10,000 worth of shares. Much, much more than his annual salary. For a while, he thought he was Charlie the Brave, then, in a cold sweat, he revised that to Charlie the Reckless. What if the market were to collapse? Or his individual purchases turned out to be lemons? Of course, the insurance company retained the right to approve each share purchase; that would be a brake on outrageous foolhardiness.

Charlie spread his risks. The economy was doing quite well: manufacturing was expanding behind a favourable exchange rate; employment and consumption were high but not so as to provoke any great concern about inflation; investment was flowing in confidently but not excessively from overseas. Interest rates were low. New enterprises in such areas as motels, plastics and consumer finance were getting under way. Charlie bought a range of blue-chip and medium-quality stocks. He avoided speculatives — which the insurance company would have vetoed anyway. Some stocks he bought to provide income to service his loan and he looked to all his purchases to grow in value.

The scheme worked well. BHP made some new issues, enabling Charlie, through his rights, to acquire more BHP shares below market price. He benefited from other rights issues too, as well as from some bonus (scrip) issues, that is, he received additional shares for which he didn't pay anything. For the most part, BHP and the other companies paid the same rate of dividend on the new and bonus shares, thereby lifting Charlie's dividend income quite handsomely. A real estate agency and developer, L.J. Hooker Limited, made a rights issue of convertible notes, providing Charlie with a good rate of interest while at the same time conferring the right to change them into ordinary shares later on, should that turn out to be profitable.

Because Charlie had become such a good customer, his stockbroker got into the habit of 'phoning to ask if he'd be interested in a parcel of shares in some new float. These new flotations came along fairly regularly while the economy was growing and diversifying. Already Charlie had made some progress as an investor, but he still wasn't rich — certainly not rich enough to take up all the shares he was offered. Anyway, some didn't appeal to him and those with most appeal were usually in greatest demand so he was offered only minimum parcels. Most of the shares he bought went on the market distinctly above the face value Charlie'd paid for them. Sometimes he sold his allocation right away and took his stag's profit; but he held on to most, believing they'd continue to rise in value and pay good dividends.

There were times when he acquired shares more passively, for example, when one or other of his companies was taken over. Usually this was at a price above, sometimes very substantially above the prevailing market. The takeover offer was sometimes in cash, which added to Charlie's liquidity and enabled him to buy some other shares he'd had his eye on. At other times, payment was by way of a share swap: one share in the takeover company was allotted for, say, two shares in the company being taken over. Usually the market value of the new shares was greater than the market value of the shares surrendered; but Charlie sometimes had less faith in the takeover people than he'd had in the original company. In that event, he sold his shares in the new company quickly enough to take a profit.

By all these means and by purchase of some new shares from time to time, his portfolio grew steadily, his holdings after a year or two being more than double the value of the $10,000 he'd borrowed from the insurance company. As and when he had a surplus of funds, he reduced his indebtedness to the insurance company, so that his ratio of liabilities to assets steadily improved.

That didn't mean he didn't make mistakes. Some companies were shooting stars: they blazed across the heavens for a year or two and then suddenly, their life and sparkle gone, crashed into receivership. One such company, Latec, formed by the brothers Catel, had brilliant growth in motels and finance but overreached. Put into receivership, it later recovered and is still listed on the Australian Stock Exchanges. But Charlie lost a few dollars.

Another company, Mainline Corporation, grew quickly into one of the most dynamic companies in the construction industry, building a good proportion of the biggest and grandest buildings going up in the capital cities. Then the Australian Government, afraid that growth and imports were getting out of hand, imposed a credit squeeze. Mainline had cut its margins too fine. When the market for office buildings in the central business districts contracted sharply, it faced disastrous losses. Put into receivership, its assets sold off to satisfy creditors, the mighty Mainline joined the dinosaurs. Charlie learned a lesson. He'd originally acquired his Mainline shares through a takeover; then, when they'd done well, he'd bought some more. The collapse came so suddenly that he couldn't get out without suffering losses. He'd spread his shareholdings widely so that Mainline didn't endanger his overall position but it was a chastening experience. He realised that even the highest flyers could suddenly crash and that he was as capable as anyone else of making poor judgements or, what was more to the point, allowing his judgement to be distorted by the excessive optimism of the market and the charisma of a particular company.

Mainline fell to a government-engineered slump. Charlie had divested himself of some of his other holdings to buy some property before that general market slump arrived. He'd been lucky in that he'd needed to put some money together to buy a particular house and that had forced him to reduce his exposure in the share market at just the right time. However, he kidded himself that he'd known some of his holdings had become overvalued and that he'd have got out anyway, whether to diversify into other assets or not.

For a couple of years after that, Charlie did very little on the stock market. He said 'Hello' to his stockbroker on social occasions, even played cricket with him, and maintained his other contacts; but otherwise he sat out several waltzes, waiting for livelier, more promising tunes. Gradually, he sensed the good times returning. The world economy was booming as never before. Consumption and investment were high. Unemployment was virtually nil in the developed countries. And above all, government expenditures — on social welfare, education, economic and social infrastructure, defence — were racing ahead as though the sky was the limit. In the midst of this, the first man landed on the moon.

The effect on commodity prices, including metals and minerals, was unprecedented. Suddenly, there wasn't enough of anything. Stocks were low and order-books full. A spectacular market developed for nickel, of which Australia had not previously been known to have significant deposits. But, just as, some years earlier, everyone had started to look for uranium, so now everyone began looking for nickel. And they found it. Indeed, in the end, they found some of the biggest low-cost deposits in the world. But, although some finds were necessary to ignite the boom, it wasn't the biggest and best finds that caused the brightest blaze. WMC found nickel at Kambalda but the market took that with relative calm. Then a new small company called Poseidon found nickel also in Western Australia. Especially in the early days, it was unclear just how much nickel Poseidon had or what its cost of extraction would be. But those boring facts scarcely mattered. A little company with a lot of nickel could deliver a lot of lovely lucre. No one did many sums. Few had enough data to do their sums anyway. But the price of Poseidon soared from about 60 cents to a staggering peak of $287! A speculator who'd invested $100 in Poseidon at the low point would have emerged with nearly $50,000 if he'd sold at the peak.

Of course, not many people made profits as enormous as that. But many did make big gains as the market galloped upwards. It wasn't only Poseidon; virtually every stock on the market soared.

Charlie never held any Poseidon shares. When it was all over, he boasted he was glad he hadn't; he'd known, he said, that Poseidon was too dangerous a punt. But that was when Poseidon, having teetered on the $287 peak, had already collapsed with its backers into a dark valley, before slowly and painfully picking itself up to become a quietly profitable company, still listed on the stock exchange.

Charlie had ridden the buoyant market much more comfortably on the backs of more solidly based shares of less speculative interest. He'd had WMC, as well as quite a holding in MIM which hadn't found nickel but whose copper had done very nicely. He'd been in and out of a few speculatives which were quickly forgotten but which gave him modest profits through purchasing low and selling before they slumped too heavily from their peaks. By the time the nickel boom died, he was holding only some blue chips and he'd sluiced off his stock market profits into some modest property acquisition.

That didn't mean that he got right out of the stock market. He stayed in, buying and selling as profitable opportunites arose. The oil crisis focused attention on energy stocks. He'd bought some oil and oil-related shares earlier. He'd made some boo-boos too. At one stage, he'd bought some shares in a company that was active in the area of one of the first commercial flow-oil discoveries in Australia at Moonie, near Roma in south-east Queensland. That was good thinking. It was like investing in a company that was selling picks in a gold-rush town. But this time it didn't work out. When he visited Moonie later, he knew why. The exploration and drilling for oil hadn't done much for the district and, when production started, a pipeline took the crude to a faraway refinery, requiring only a handful of people to monitor the operation from a lonely paddock way out in the bush. No boom town there. So Charlie learned another lesson: by all means do some thinking about flow-on benefits from mining and other developments, but don't let your assumptions too readily carry you away.

Charlie had added to his BHP holdings too, especially because of the company's discovery of a major oil domain in Bass Strait. Some of the Big Australian's shares he'd picked up at good prices but some, in the euphoria of the Bass Strait bonanza, he'd bought too high — a lesson which he should have learned long before. But he held on to them for what he knew would be continuing good times for the company ahead. Otherwise, he didn't plunge into the market for any dramatic gains until the second oil-price hike in 1979 focused attention on gold.

Charlie had held WMC almost as long as he could remember. He'd had a temporary dalliance too with one or two other more specialist gold companies from time to time. But, in 1979, he saw that something special was on the way. The world wide surge in prices to which oil hikes had imparted extra momentum had already caused a rapid decline in the value of paper money. Now there had to be another huge leap upward in the value of gold as expressed in paper currencies. So Charlie reasoned. He wasn't alone in this belief but he was ahead of most people in acting on it. And, as he knew by this time, that's all you need — to be a short head in front of the market.

Almost all the specialist goldminers on the Australian market were cheap. You could pick any one — or half a dozen — put your money on and wait for the gold price rise to earn you a nice little profit. Charlie put his money on three: Wattle Gully, North Kalgurli and Australian

Development. They all had gold, although they certainly weren't among the big miners. They were producing at a profit at the relatively low prices of 1979, so, if the gold price soared, all the gain would be pure profit. But, as Charlie knew, rational arguments like those weren't really decisive. If the gold price took off, the price of gold shares — or of any companies that said they were looking for gold or thinking about looking for gold — would shoot up like a rocket.

Charlie bought Wattle Gully at 8 cents. From $300 an ounce in July 1979, the gold price moved to $400 a few months later and $875 early in 1980. The demand for gold was frantic. 'A dentist brought [to a gold exchange] a pile of gold inlays and silver fillings he had removed from teeth over five years [and made] a $3,000 sale.'[6] Wattle Gully touched a peak of $1. Charlie unloaded at 95 cents. He'd bought North Kalgurli for 15 cents. He sold out at $1.95. Australian Development was his most expensive buy at 40 cents; those he sold at $2.40. Already middling rich, Charlie was much richer by the time the gold price retreated to levels around $400 and took gold share values with it.

After the gold boom, he kept a well-tended portfolio but was relatively inactive through the recession of 1982–3 and the severe commodity slump of 1985–6.

Black Monday: 'What Goes Up ...'

But slumps don't last for ever any more than booms. As the commodity depression bottomed out, stock markets began to lift. During 1986, a widely based surge began, gradually incorporating most market sectors. Around the world, from Wall Street to the City of London, to Frankfurt, Amsterdam, Tokyo, Hong Kong and Sydney, share prices rose, at first steadily, then strongly. Good growth in the United States, Japan and most European countries was reinforced by deregulated financial markets which encouraged a wide spread of investments, including bond and stock trading and highly leveraged takeovers. The boom was further fuelled by the junk bond craze and the enormous profits it generated. As 1987 entered its third quarter, stock

---

6 Greider, *Secrets of the Temple: How the Federal Reserve Runs the Country*, p.83.

exchange indices were reaching towards levels about double those of a year earlier. On 25 August, the Dow Jones index in New York peaked at 2722, Sydney a little later at 2400. Then most exchanges began to move sideways or edge down. Rallies kept markets within spitting distance of their peaks. But the warning signs were there.

Nevertheless, few investors were deterred. As in most booms, not only the janitors and the taxi-drivers, but even the institutional investors and trust managers behaved as though the boom would never end. They continued to buy although such rational indicators as price/earnings ratios proclaimed most shares already over-bought. As early as June, one big and canny British investor, James Goldsmith, had got himself safely out of the market; but he was an exception. Few others showed any anxiety or even reasonable caution. The big players — many of whose names were associated with a great and glorious capacity to play the market like their personal violin — showed no more prudence than the little fellows.

But, by August, our cautious Charlie was getting edgy. He'd seen it happen before. What goes up as far and fast as this must come down with a thud. The saga of Happy Bounty and Poseidon kept nagging at him. But when would the market arrive at the moment of truth? He knew it must be soon. Few commentators shared his anxiety and fewer still concurred with him on early timing. But the gut feeling that he'd been here before, that the market had peaked and that a crash of some kind had to lie just ahead, refused to go away. He had no idea of the dimensions of the crash. It might be a relatively mild correction or a slow retreat from unsustainable highs. But he knew the bull market was just about over.

Where would the 'correction' or the 'retreat' or the 'crash' start? He didn't know. It could be Tokyo, London or New York; or the crash could be related not so much to a place as to an event. Perhaps a bank failure or a collapse in still not-very-robust commodity markets or something no one had really yet focused on.

Anyway, in the middle of August, nervous Charlie began to sell. He gave his broker orders to sell those shares in which he had least confidence — or which he was most confident had reached their peaks. In September, he sold a second line of stocks, some of which he would have liked to keep in a more stable environment but which would undoubtedly qualify as overpriced once the runaway bull market began to stagger. (Indeed, he saw that it was staggering already, although few people were acting on the signs.) By the second week of October, he completed sales of everything he had left. Then he sat back and waited.

Had he, this time, been a too-cautious Charlie? Had he, he wondered, dipped out on the greatest bonanza of all time? Would he, if he'd waited just a couple more months, have enjoyed his best Christmas ever? All he could do was wait and draw solace from what Nathan Rothschild once said: 'How did I make my fortune? By always selling too soon. Sell, regret — and grow rich.'

Charlie didn't have long to wait. On 19 October 1987, the Dow Jones index fell 508 points. Investors lost $500 billion in a single day's trading. 'What began as a routine stock market correction [in August] and last week developed into a terrifying rout', the newspapers reported on the morning after, 'yesterday became the stock market crash of 1987, the worst in history and maybe not over yet.'

It was a classic situation — the bursting of an unsustainable bubble — but intensified by the scale and techniques of modern stock trading. Once the market began to fall, stop-loss limits were triggered. The momentum of the fall became not only irresistible but also automatic. Computer trading and programming compounded the speed and scale of the collapse. And the market was weighed down by a multitude of institutional traders operating on a massive scale. Blue chips fell like a stone along with the dogs. Little attention was paid to quality or fundamentals. In a market driven by panic, everyone wanted to get cash and get out. The next day, stock markets around the world began their own decline, each according to its own character and — fortunately and surprisingly — at its own pace. Hong Kong closed. Sydney dropped about 30 per cent. President Reagan declared the American economy fundamentally sound. 'His comments sounded eerily like the things [President] Herbert Hoover had said in the autumn of 1929.'[7]

---

7 Ibid., p.716.

As it turned out, October 1987 did not herald an economic disaster of the dimensions of the Great Crash of 1929. But, for months, Charlie held his breath. He had got out in good time; but millions hadn't and he knew that those who'd avoided the agony of the first phase would not necessarily be permanently immune. Anxiously, he observed the shambles of the stock markets around the world. Most were like terrain stricken by an earthquake, with periods of relative calm followed by painful after-shocks. Only Tokyo resisted and soon began a climb to what would be new and ever higher peaks, largely unaffected, except in an upwards direction, even by the final illness and death in mid 1989 of Emperor Hirohito.

But, if most other markets remained cowed, the world economy did not sink into depression. Unlike the experience after the Great Crash of 1929, governments pumped enough money into the system to ensure that the real economy kept going at a high level. As early as the morning of 20 October, the Federal Reserve Bank in Washington 'affirmed...its readiness to serve as a source of liquidity to support the economic and financial system'. A shaky confidence slowly returned. Rates of growth in the United States in 1988 and 1989 were good; so they were in other major economies. Commodity prices made a dramatic recovery. Signs of inflation began to reappear. Stock markets climbed back.

But, for the moment, Charlie wasn't tempted. He could see that shares might recover most of their October losses. But the recovery would be hesitant and choppy. Money could be made by buying in short-term troughs and getting out in a rally soon after. But that wasn't for Charlie. The sustained bull market was over, for the time being; and he opted to stay out until he could go in again with more assurance, perhaps in a few months, perhaps in 1990 or later. He'd watch and wait until he felt the time was ripe.

In the meantime, he had cash in his pocket. Governments having made money easier, interest rates had fallen. Through sale of his shares, he'd been able to pay off his overdraft at the bank and was still able to get a reasonable return on the little surplus cash he now had parked there. But, as time passed, Charlie could see other opportunities coming up. Despite the stock market losses, many people still had money but, like Charlie, they'd be drawn back to shares only slowly and hesitantly. Even lower interest rates wouldn't tempt many back. They'd look elsewhere for profitable investment.

Charlie pondered the situation long and hard. By early 1988, he could see a property boom was a reality or just up ahead. Not in England: there the boom had gone on too long already and was due for a correction, even possibly a slump. But in some other countries and/or areas values were still low and likely to rise.

Having put the stock market to one side, Charlie kept his eye on commodities, which stayed encouragingly buoyant, and on currencies, which were no less volatile after the October crash than before. But, he told himself, the safest and most profitable place to entrust his cash could be property. All he needed was a promising project.

3
The Worst House in the Street

Bricks and Mortar: The Wise Investment?

Long before Charlie did his post-crash soul-searching, another good man had told me, 'Put your money into bricks and mortar. They last for ever!' That wise old fellow ran a caravan park. He owned no bricks and mortar. So he was handing out advice he hadn't followed himself. Still, he was right. But was he *inevitably* right? Were there no circumstances in which he could have turned out to be wrong? The answer is that there's no 100 per-cent sure thing, not forever anyway. In property as other investments, you have to show good sense and follow a few simple rules. But there's nothing complex about property investment — nothing that's beyond your capacities or that will require you to give all your time to it in order to make good profits.

As with every investment you'll ever make, so with property, you must choose your moment wisely. Most things in life depend for success on good timing. In investment, timing isn't everything — other things must be watched too — but timing is a fundamental you must get right.

Provided your timing is right, there's one special justification for putting part of your resources into 'bricks and mortar' — or land which, as everyone knows, they aren't making any more, except in one or two places like The Netherlands! The special justification for buying property is that it's *the* investment above all of which most people have direct, personal experience. Most people — the percentage varies among countries and over time — buy at least one house or apartment, for their own use, in the course of a lifetime. Therefore, most people go through the whole process of choosing a place they like, deciding whether it is better to buy than to rent, assembling the funds for a deposit, borrowing the rest from a bank, building society or other loan source, hiring a lawyer for the conveyancing and so on. This basic investment in real estate — to provide 'family shelter' — isn't quite as inevitable as death and taxes; but, for most, it's a normal episode belonging usually to the earlier years of adult life. Is it an episode that can profitably be repeated?

I said investment through the stock exchange can be the lazy person's race-track to riches. Certainly the stock market *can* open up a fast lane. But only sometimes. No one can guarantee that opportunities will turn up constantly on the stock market and that you'll always succeed when you reach out to seize them. Remember I'm not talking about gambling your way to riches. I'm talking to the cautious person, suggesting how you can prosper without risking an almighty crash. One good risk-reducing rule is never to put all your investment eggs in one basket. 'Spread your risks' is a corollary you should repeat quietly to yourself until it becomes a creed to live by. Spread your risks on the stock market by buying a variety of shares, preferably in several high-potential economic sectors. And spread your risks *away* from the stock market through a variety of other investments. Create several investment packages to be utilised in case of need, so that, if the stock market turns sour, you might recoup your fortunes elsewhere. Real estate is one such risk-spreading package, offering gains in good times and a refuge in bad.

So let's suppose, having started with almost nothing, you've now made some profits on the stock market. You've made just enough to put a deposit on a modest house or apartment, to live in yourself or buy as an investment. You'll have to sell some shares to get the deposit. That might not anyway be a bad thing. You'll be forced to look closely at your holdings to decide which have been performing well and which should, in any event, be discarded. That's a review exercise you should undertake frequently. If the stock market has had a long upward swing, seems to be overheated and could be heading for what the jargon calls a correction, you might be wise to take your profits anyway, while the going is good. Never forget that you should be as ready to sell at the right moment as you were to buy. So if the market shows signs of turning down, a well-chosen property purchase could oblige you to convert shares into cash at a propitious moment.

All that is simple enough. But what is a 'well-chosen property purchase'? How should you go about choosing the right house or apartment — or land, for that matter? Up to a point at least, the same criteria will apply whether you're buying a place to live in yourself or to rent and sell at a profit later on. There are some differences. A place to rent might be lower-priced than a house to live in yourself. Or you might buy in an area you know is popular but which has little appeal to you personally and is inconveniently located for your work or other interests. But these and other considerations will fall within the principles and practice governing sound real estate investment.

Location, Location, Location

The first consideration is location. Some say wise real estate investment consists of location first, location second and location third. The land itself is often — perhaps always — more important than what stands on it. Whatever is built will deteriorate and have to be rebuilt or reconstructed at some time. The land will always be there. You can't move it. You can't decide it would be more convenient elsewhere. Perhaps it would but there's nothing you can do about it. If you choose well, the land might turn out in time to be worth a million or ten million dollars while the house on it might end up costing you money to remove. If you choose badly, you might find that, in a few years' time, you'll hardly be able to give the property away — house, land and all. A palace isn't much use in the midst of a trackless desert or surrounded by freeways, heavy industry and residential slums. On the other hand, a tumbledown hut might be worth a fortune if it's within a few steps of the white sands of Surfers Paradise beach. A pocket-handkerchief apartment will be worth a million dollars in the central business district of Tokyo. So will a quite small place in Fifth Avenue, New York, or Mayfair in London. It's the location that confers value, more than the dwelling.

So choose your location with great care. What does a good location mean? First, it means a spot in a city that people are coming in to — not going away from. Have a good look at business and demographic trends. Is the baby-boom over? Is a rush of tourists coming up? A city growing quickly will attract more and more people to it. There's a multiplier effect. They'll want to or have to come to the city to find work or do business or enjoy themselves. However, even within a fast-growing city, you need to look for a location that is in demand — an area that people are flocking to rather than one they will live in only as a last resort. Then, within that sought-after area, look for the good streets, the good views, the high points that can't be built out. Are you going to build a single-family house? If so, is there a danger that your single-family house will have its amenity spoilt by high-rise buildings nearby? Is the area strictly residential or is it zoned also for shops, offices and factories? Is a never-to-be-built-on park nearby to add to the amenity of your street? What are the city plans for freeways? You wouldn't be the first to buy a house only to find that next year's view from the front porch will be of cars and trucks flashing by and the prevailing breezes will waft petrol fumes instead of the perfume of violets. So check carefully whether the value of your property could plummet because of possible changes in its environment.

Remember you might lose but you might also gain from changes. Is the area zoned for high-rise apartments in an attractive spot close to a commercial centre? Can you get a big, but old and ramshackle house on a large block, at a low price, demolish the house and construct a large apartment building? Are schools and shopping areas handy? If you're building high-rise apartments, will the foundations be sound or will the costs of those foundations be excessive? Is there any threat of natural disasters, such as flooding or beach erosion? These and other questions will need to be answered to be sure you're buying in a good location. Don't be afraid to ask questions. They'll be well worth the trouble. If it's a good location, you can do a lot with it. If you buy a lemon, you can't do much about it, except find a buyer as inattentive as you've been, or take your losses and go. Remember a bad location can't be regarded in the same way as a bad house. A bad house you can pull down. A bad location you're stuck with. You can only try to get out with a minimum of loss.

So, let's suppose you've found your good location and the street in which you want to buy. Which house should you buy? The answer is, 'The worst house in the street'. That's right, the worst. If the worst house in the street also occupies the best individual site in the street, has planning permission for the erection of high-rise apartments and is priced according to the condition of the house rather than its location, site and zoning, grab it. You've got a bargain.

Of course, the worst house in the street won't always be for sale. If that's the unhappy fact, look for the second worst, then the third and so on. Never buy the best house in the street, unless you're cornered and it has offsetting advantages. Generally speaking, a street will, within the intrinsic worth of its location, give value to individual houses within it according to their individual quality. The best house in the street will probably be fully valued for the land itself and the building on it. There will be little prospect that the building can be profitably upgraded or can be demolished and rebuilt at a profit. If it's selling below its potential, that could be because the environment created by other, inferior houses in the street is dragging its value down. You can't improve this environment by buying the best house; but you can by buying the worst. Moreover, you'll probably get the worst at a cut price because it compares so poorly with its neighbours. The cut price will probably undervalue both the house and the land on which it stands.

Let's take an example of this. Some years ago, Charlie bought a house in an outstanding residential area. Its foundations and outer brickwork were sound but it qualified as the worst house in its very long street. No one wanted it. Charlie bought it for a mere $16,000. He then reconstructed and enlarged it for about as much as he'd paid for it. His total outlay was therefore about $32,000; but, before he'd even completed the remodelling, he was being offered $80,000 for it — a profit of more than 100 per cent. During the remodelling, the value of the better houses in the street hardly changed; and since then, Charlie's house has more than kept pace with the upward price spiral in that first-class area and, I reckon, could now be worth more than a quarter of a million.

Don't forget that your house, whether you buy it to live in or rent to others, is an investment and, at the beginning of your investment career, it's a big one. You might want to sell the house one day or you might want to borrow against it. In either case, you want its value to rise as far and fast as possible. That means you should buy it for as little as possible, preferably as close as you can manage to the bottom of the residential property cycle in the area. You should choose a street in that area with the best prospect that property values will rise fastest over the medium and long term, taking account of the property cycle. If unrealistic premiums have already been placed on future values in the area and the street, then forget that location, at least for the moment, and either look for a bargain in another good location or wait for prices to come down. If the best house in the street is already valued at a price that accords with what other houses in the street would bring if they were upgraded, then keep away from it. If the worst house in the street is valued at or below its site value and the property cycle and other factors are such that that site value is likely to rise rapidly, then it's a good buy.

I'll give you an example from my own experience. Some years ago, I heard of a house for sale in a very good area and street — an 'excellent address'. When I looked at it, I found it was on the high side of the street, with great views that couldn't be built out. At the back was a small, quiet, enclosed park. Perfect. But the house was lousy. The owner was a corporation, anxious to get rid of the house because it no longer fitted its plans for staff housing. The residential market was poor — pretty near the bottom of the cycle. Interest rates had just gone up and sales and prices had slumped. The price of the house I was offered was less than the value of the land on which it stood — way below the replacement value even of the existing 'lousy' house.

How did I calculate the value of the land? That's not easy to do — and it varies with the market. You can take the unimproved capital value used by the local rating authorities; but that's usually outdated and well below the market value of the land. You can take the prices paid for 'equivalent' land at auction or by sale nearby; but built-up, inner-suburban areas usually don't have 'equivalent' land, without buildings, whose sale or auction provides much guidance. You can take the price of houses in the area and deduct the replacement cost of the house currently built on the block. The difference should be the value of the site — but once again, it's only an approximation. Or you can get a licensed valuer — but it's surprising how wrong they can be, erring usually on the cautious side.

However, I made what calculations I could and they all persuaded me that the price of the house I was being offered was well below the value of the site alone, certainly well below its value as soon as the housing market livened up. But I still thought I might do better. The house was being sold by a corporation not normally in housing and real estate. They weren't real-estate experts and were keen to sell: they wanted to be shot of the house quickly. So I had a keen seller and could offer myself as a don't-care-all-that-much buyer. My bargaining position was strong. Their asking price was already low, but I made an offer 15 per cent lower. Keen though they were to get rid of the house, they winced at that but they made a counter-offer 10 per cent below their original asking price. I accepted immediately. I had a bargain. The basic design and construction of the house was sound, so I was able to renovate and extend. Before I'd finished, the market was on the way up again, and I could have sold it for much more than I'd paid for it. But I didn't. I knew that, over a longer term, I would still be on a good thing. Why sell until I'd squeezed all I could out of the bargain? I still own the house: it's now worth more than ten times what I paid for it.

A couple of features deserve elaboration. First, as I've said, the 'worst house in the street' was basically well designed and well constructed. It had good foundations and solid brick walls. Its position on the block, though not perfect, allowed easy, economical reconstruction taking full advantage of the site, including a good outlook from high ground. These were very simple considerations. They didn't call for any expertise. But often buyers turn down outstanding opportunities because they see only the lousy house and fail to visualise what it could become.

Second, the area and street weren't going to get any

worse. On the contrary, they were already first-class and likely to be even more highly regarded as time passed. It was 'quiet residential' but close to schools, shops — all the facilities you could ask — and the address was prestigious. More and more people were going to want to live there. All that was needed was to make the worst house in the street presentable. I was going to have to do some organising and managing, all of it part-time — and, inevitably, make some financial outlay. But I wasn't taking any risk. I was outlaying a minimum amount of money in a market which, I assessed, was at or very close to the bottom. Any circumstances in which I'd be putting the house back on the market would almost certainly be better than those in which I'd acquired it.

Timing

There's a lesson too in that appraisal of the market. I spoke earlier of the dangers of buying shares when the stock market has already taken off and particularly when the bulls are roaring. You don't want to be the one holding shares bought at peak price when the market starts to tumble. Your timing needs to be good and your footwork spry in any investment situation. After the First World War, John Maynard Keynes, probably the outstanding economist of this century and an investor of rare skill and sensitivity, backed

> his by now widely advertised judgment that the Versailles requirements were far beyond the capacity of the German economy by speculating heavily on margin against the mark. He narrowly escaped financial ruin, was saved by loans from his publishers and a friendly financier.[1]

What did Keynes do wrong? His

> error was only in timing. In the summer of 1921, prices began again to rise...By November 27, 1923, [German] domestic prices stood at 1,422,900,000,000 times the pre-war level...At the time of momentary stability in 1921, the mark was around

---

1 Galbraith, *Money: Whence It Came, Where It Went*, p.155.

81 to the dollar...in July [1923] it went to a million to the dollar.[2]

This underlines the point that, in any market, your timing has to be good. In a peaking market, it has to be brilliant if you choose to be a bull right up to the last moment. If you're not spry enough, you'll get caught by a price collapse before you can resell. That means you'll get caught with losses, perhaps very sharp losses, instead of gains.

This can happen in the housing/real estate market, as well as in the share, currency or any other market, so a clear warning should be heeded about buying too late into a housing boom. For example, during the later 1980s, the housing market in south-east England, including especially London, rose dramatically as a result of rising incomes, easy credit and speculation. Each year the market went higher, with average house prices rising by 25 per cent in real terms in 1988. Huge sums were invested by a multitude of ordinary people buying their own houses, upgrading to bigger and better ones, investing in rental and resale real estate. Borrowing from banks and other credit institutions reached record levels; indeed, on the financing side, nothing of the kind had ever been seen before.

For a time, interest rates trended down, making mortgage payments easier. But, in the latter half of 1988, they rose sharply. What happened? Did the interest rate rises herald a collapse of the housing market? In the first quarter of 1989, prices began to level out, some to fall. Any dramatic fall seemed to be delayed, at least, by potential sellers withholding their properties from the market. But how long could that continue?

There's always a lag before higher mortgage charges really begin to bite. The reasons are partly technical: some mortgage rates change only at the end of each quarter or half-year or year. But technical and other restraints tending to allow a soft landing for a property market are temporary. A boom doesn't go on for ever. The historical experience suggests that the only alternatives are a sharp collapse of a kind that, in England, occurred in 1974 or a more gentle

---

2 Ibid., p. 155–6.

easing of the market on to a high plateau. The question is when one or other of these alternatives will emerge.

Much of the 1980s boom in England originated in tax breaks on mortgage payments. Will the market collapse if and when these tax advantages are removed or reduced? Is the government likely to do such a thing? If so, when will that be? Will it be next month or next year or several years ahead? We don't know. We can only guess. One view is that already 'the cut in the top rate of tax on investment income, from 98 per cent in 1978 to 40 per cent now [1989], has greatly reduced the attraction of investing in housing as opposed to shares or gilts'.[3] This might mean, for example, that older people will trade down sooner to a small house after their children leave home and that they'll think twice about investing in a second house. Though more people will inherit houses from the generation of postwar owner-occupiers, they might want to sell their property inheritance and invest the proceeds elsewhere.

These might not be the most important elements depressing the housing market in England. 'More than half of the increase in demand for houses in the 15 years to 1985 was due to demography.'[4] But the smaller numbers of those born since the early 1960s will cause the numbers setting up house to fall and the future demand for residential property to decline sharply. From a net increase of 200,000 a year in the 1980s, formation of new households will slow to 100,000 a year in the 1990s.

What will be the result? In three decades from the 1950s to the 1980s, house prices in England did not fall in any one year in nominal terms; and even 'after adjusting for inflation, the typical house is now worth almost three times what it was thirty years ago'.[5] There have been severe blips in the trend: prices fell in *real* terms in 1974–5 and 1980–81. They did too in particular parts of the market, which again emphasises the need to look not just at average trends, but also at what is happening in particular regions and in particular sectors of the real estate market. In 1974–5, housing prices were flat in nominal terms but, taking

---

3 The *Economist,* London, 18 February 1989.
4 Ibid.
5 Ibid.

account of inflation, fell by 25 per cent in real terms. If that experience were to be repeated over the next couple of years, the drop in housing prices even in nominal terms, on the assumption of 8 per cent or less inflation a year, could be of the order of 15 per cent and more severe reductions could be on the way. 'If the past link between demand and prices continues,...real house prices will fall by 3% a year over the next 20 years, or a total of 50%.'[6]

Quite apart from these future prospects, while housing prices in England have stood up, in nominal if not real terms, for about three decades, they have suffered sharp falls elsewhere, including continental Europe and the United States. The end of the baby boom and the advent of the baby bust generation in the United States, by reducing the formation of new households, is in process of halving the rate of increase in the demand for housing from 1.3 to 1.7 per cent a year in the 1970s and 1980s to only 0.6 to 0.7 per cent a year in the 1990s and the early years of next century. In the Netherlands, in the early 1980s, prices fell heavily in both nominal and real terms, sales were difficult and rents plunged. Similar experiences were noted in other markets, for example, in Canada and Australia at other times and in varying degrees.

So the housing market can not be relied on *inevitably* and *invariably* to be a sound investment. You must choose your time and your market and be sure you buy into sectors that have a good demand future. Location will always be a prime consideration. But, whatever you do, avoid buying into any market in an advanced phase of a boom.

Two dangers must be guarded against, one serious, the other critical. The serious danger is that you might buy a house — or apartment or other property — at more than you really need to pay. If the market has been rising for a long time, a house worth $100,000 two years ago might now be worth $175,000. If your intention is to buy and sell a house quickly in a buoyant market, you might still stand a chance of making gains. That house worth $175,000 might touch $200,000 before the boom busts so that, after conveyancing and other costs, you might still make a small profit. (The Taxation Office would of course be interested

---

6 Ibid.

in any rapid turnover of your assets in a way that would turn you into a trader or developer; and that would reduce your after-tax profits.) But, unless you're very spry — and a mite lucky — even a small profit could elude you. The steam can go out of a boom property market very quickly.

What is it that takes the steam out of the market? There are several possibilities. A rise in interest rates. A government decision to disallow negative gearing. The introduction of a capital gains tax — or a change in the rates or conditions that make a property owner liable for capital gains tax. The threat or, without prior warning, the sudden imposition of a wealth tax. Disallowance of mortgage payments as tax deductions — especially if that tax subsidy has been responsible for the preceding boom in house prices. And, of course, a shortage of houses and flats might, quite suddenly, become a glut, even though monetary and tax conditions remain constant. Demand might have been satisfied or market sentiment might change quite abruptly so that investors or home-seekers or both now see a downturn ahead.

Under the impact of any of these changes — and others — buyers can vanish like the dew and sellers suddenly pop up everywhere. So it may very well turn out that, before you put that $175,000 house back on the market, the price will have rocketed up to $200,000 and then slumped back to $150,000 — still a huge advance on its price a couple of years ago as the boom was starting, but — and this is the important thing *for you* — a big discount, of about 15 per cent, on the price you paid for it. If you are then to make a profit on your investment or even get your money back, you might have to wait until the cycle turns through almost 360 degrees again — a process that might take three to five years or longer. In the meantime, you might recoup some of your losses — or get just about enough to pay your interest charges — by renting the house, instead of selling it. But whatever the rents, they'll give you a much poorer return on the $175,000 you paid for the house near the top of the boom than on the $100,000 you would have paid if you'd bought as the recovery was starting.

What you should look for is an experience similar to Charlie's in Canberra about ten years ago. He bought a house in a good but not dress-circle suburb, cheaply, at about $38,000. Then prices fell. He could have bought it a year or so later for only $34,000. If he'd put it back on the market then, he'd have lost money. But anyway, he'd rented it. He'd bought cheaply, so the rent gave him a fair return on his outlay. Not brilliant but enough to meet essential costs, including interest. The price of that house — and of houses more generally in Canberra — stayed down for the next four years or so. Then they surged. Quite suddenly, the house was worth about $95,000. Charlie could have sold for more than twice as much as he'd paid for it. A short time later, prices slipped — or, more accurately, stabilised on a high plateau before starting another advance in 1988 after negative gearing was restored as a tax break. So the times to buy were from about 1979 to 1984 and 1986–7. The times to sell, if you needed to, were 1985 and 1988. If you acted within this pattern, you made money. If you bought in the seller's market and sold when the market slumped, then you lost.

That is the serious danger that confronts the property investor. The critical danger is more terrifying. That arises from a process whereby, on payment of a deposit, you buy from the plans, with the idea of selling before you have to come up with the full purchase price. In the housing market, it's rather like buying shares on margin, a practice that nearly ruined John Maynard Keynes in 1920–21 and contributed to the tally of bankruptcies when the New York Stock Market crashed in 1929. The risk arises especially from a runaway boom. Indeed, a prerequisite is that there should be a strong sellers' market for the process to operate. How does it work?

An investor, developer or speculative builder decides to erect, let's say, a block of apartments. Before he turns a sod, he begins selling apartments off the plan, on the basis of a deposit of about 10 per cent of the full purchase price, the balance of 90 per cent to be paid when the building is finished. It's a firm and enforceable contract to buy. Although only a 10 per cent deposit is demanded, the full price must be paid when the apartments are delivered. That causes no difficulty so long as a sellers' market persists and prices continue to rise. In the course of construction, the apartments might change hands several times, each 'owner' taking his profit in turn. That profit might be pretty large, especially if the developer, anxious to cover himself, has discounted his off-the-plan prices and the market rises sharply to a peak as building proceeds.

However, if the market turns down sharply *before* building is completed, the result can be disastrous for that 'owner' who is left holding the new-born apartment(s). Let's suppose you contracted to buy for $1 million and paid a deposit of $100,000. Then the market falls, slicing something like 20 per cent from values. Your $1 million purchase becomes worth only $800,000. That's all you will now get if you sell — and if you hang on, the price might slump further to $700,000 or even $500,000, if many people are forced to sell to get cash quickly. But you must still pay $1 million for your purchase. That means that, if you sell right away, you will lose $200,000 and, if you hang on, you could lose much more, perhaps half a million dollars. If you decide to get out, you will, by your own action, accentuate the market slide; others who have been playing the market could decide to get out too and start a stampede. So prices could fall far and fast, way below cost of construction. Those who don't get out quickly enough might suffer losses of hundreds of thousands or millions of dollars. This is not an imaginary tale of disaster; it is an account of an actual scenario that played itself out, for example, along the Gold Coast in the early 1980s. No doubt it will play itself out again at other times and in other places.

But isn't there a way out if you bought from the plans? You paid only a deposit, which we've assumed to be 10 per cent. On a $1 million investment, that's $100,000. Can't you cut your losses, declare all bets off and retire from the affair, wincing from the loss of $100,000 but at least not losing, say, half a million? Unfortunately, it's not as easy as that. If you'd bought and paid in full for shares in a limited liability company, your liability would have been only what you paid for your shares. But that's not your position now. It's more like that of a share trader who bought on margin: he has paid only 10 per cent of the value of his purchase but he has *contracted* to pay the full price — his liability extends to the full 100 per cent of the purchase price.

So you have contracted to buy an apartment or apartments for $1 million. The developer has a contract entitling him, on completion of the building, to that amount. A mere $100,000 wouldn't be acceptable to him, if he can now sell the apartments for only $500,000. He'd be losing $400,000 on his contract and the low price mightn't even cover his building costs. So he'll insist on the buyer meeting the contract. The buyer must pay and, if you can't, you face bankruptcy.

So here is a real, critical danger. It's a good example of the risks of over-reaching and allowing too many unknowns to enter into the outcome of any financial transaction. If you buy on deposit, in a rising market, too far into the boom, the boom might collapse, causing you acute distress. Although you stand to make major gains if the market surge continues, you'd be well advised to avoid buying off the plan for early resale unless you're very sure of market trends. If you do buy in this way, then buy in a slump or before the recovery has gathered momentum — and don't commit yourself to payments which would be too much for you if the market falls.

If you can buy at the bottom of a slump — and bear in mind that defining where the bottom is will not be easy — then your chances of substantial loss — what the experts call your 'downside risk' — is small and your chances of substantial gains high. As with other investments, so with real estate, buy when everyone else is selling — or has sold — and sell when everyone else is buying. Pick the trend of what everyone else *will soon be trying to do* but is not doing now — and then opt to be the odd one out. If you join the crowd and buy with everyone else, you could be the one left standing when the music stops. If you sell when everyone else is selling, you risk unloading a valuable property at a price far below the value the market put on it a short time ago and will put on it again a short time hence.

So buy when everyone else is selling and sell when everyone else is buying — provided you're sure the market will turn round fairly soon. You must be convinced the fundamentals are there for a turnaround. It's no good buying up big in a goldmine town whose lodes have run out for ever; the odds are that the town will never boom again and that property values will be depressed for evermore. But, if the long-term fundamentals are good, and you know you're dealing only with a dip in a long-term trend, then buy as close to the bottom of the dip and sell as close to the top of the recovery as you can.

That leads to the very important point that you should sell at a high point of a recovery, avoiding like the plague a situation in which you might be *forced* to sell. The technique of buying off the plan on deposit, in the course of a runaway boom, carried this danger. Always be sure you've got enough funds to carry through a transaction to completion and that your credit is relatively long. Short-term credit can be useful but don't let yourself be caught. If the short-term credit runs out and replacement credit is unavailable or expensive, then you might be forced to sell on a market that has moved down. If others have been caught and want to sell too, you could suffer heavy losses. Again, the answer is to buy as close as you can to the bottom of the market. Then the only way for the market to go is up and, if you have to sell, you'll probably sell at a higher price anyway. A forced sale will cut your profit but at least you won't go broke.

Again we come back to the vital importance of timing. Timing isn't everything but it *is* a great part of the battle. Correct timing allied to careful judgement in choice of location is a winner. Not all real estate markets in every city boom and slump at the same time. Nor do all types of real estate — houses, apartments, commercial property, country property — move in step. The various markets rarely move at the same pace or even in the same direction at the same time. Apartments might be selling at give-away prices in Waikiki while they're bringing a king's ransom in Surfer's Paradise. While houses are selling at peak prices in Sydney's harbourside suburbs, the office accommodation market in the city might be in heavy over-supply.

Just the opposite might be the case in Canberra. For example, in 1986–7, a boom in commercial building accompanied a major depression in residential building in Canberra. This sort of situation needs close examination. Which of the two markets gives the clearest guide to property trends in the national capital? Does the runaway boom in office blocks suggest that office workers are about to flood into the national capital and spark a boom in the residential sector? Or does the residential slump give the truer guide? Is it a warning signal? Will the office sector be over-supplied and will the potential investor in offices be well advised to keep away from that sector — at least until you are clearer about residential trends? If you need office accommodation for your own use, should you defer purchase and rent instead, pending the arrival of the slump which you foresee just over the next property cycle hill? These are the sorts of questions you should ask yourself. Relate your timing to each specific location and each category of real estate you contemplate entering or leaving.

Sidelining

There will be times when you should simply be inactive — do nothing. That applies right across the various categories of investment — share or bond purchase, residential, commercial and country property, stamps, diamonds, anything. There are times when you should withdraw to the sidelines and watch the world pass by. That might not mean you will be sidelined for all investment at the same time. It may be that you'll withdraw from, let us say, residential property in Perth, but see opportunities in a coming bull market in gold shares on the stock exchange. Or you might see no immediate opportunities. However extensive your sidelining, don't be dispirited by it. Don't feel you're losing your vigour. All it means is that you're being intelligent. Taking a holiday from an unpromising market is the right thing to do.

Remember that, when you started on this enterprise of becoming a millionaire, you didn't do so just to have something to occupy your time. You already had plenty of things to do — or planned. Making money was your purpose but not an end in itself. You wanted to make life more comfortable, satisfying and enjoyable. So, if there's no profit to be made, sitting on the sidelines — and enjoying yourself with the money you've already made — makes sense. Of course, because one real estate market has ceased to offer any immediate prospects, that doesn't mean you should take your eye off other markets of opportunity. You might be wise to sell out of apartments — or borrow against them — so as to buy a rural property. The Australian

Bureau of Agricultural and Resource Economics calculated that the return on rural properties, including capital appreciation, was 14.1 per cent in 1987–8 and would be 11.1 per cent in 1988–9. Not spectacular returns; but many believe rural investment to be sound for the long term. One well-qualified assessor claimed that values of good-quality rural investments had grown 1.5 times more than the Consumer Price Index between 1974 and 1989. That sounds good; but the emphasis is, as it must be, on buying the right rural land at the right time. Among other things, don't buy a rural property just because it makes you feel good — although that can be one of life's 'profits' too. Rather discipline yourself to wait until you can combine pleasure with financial profit in buying rural — or any other — property.

Building a Property Portfolio

Let's now run through a scenario of building up a property 'portfolio'.

Well-organised — and fortunate — Charlie had bought some property just before the collapse of Mainline. A few years later, for family reasons, he had to change his residence, but he kept his old family home. It was well located and would gain in value without any effort on his part and bring in a high and steady rent.

He did a lot of scouting before deciding on his new home, enquiring at most local real-estate agencies and carefully scanning advertisements, including the specialised real-estate press. He must have looked over more than a hundred houses before finally deciding on the one he wanted: a house in a good location suited to his family needs and meeting his criteria for a sound, long-term investment.

While going through this laborious but rewarding process, he came across a 100-carat bargain. The house didn't suit his personal and family needs: it was too small and not in quite the right location. But the location was nevertheless good: close to the city, in a quiet residential area. Most amenities — schools, shops, playgrounds, sportfields — were within easy walking distance. The house was architect-designed, well built in full brick and tile, and set in a large, well-established garden. Although it had just about everything, the owner, desperate to sell, had put it on the market for a modest $14,000. Charlie offered $13,000.

Then he had a stroke of luck. The real estate agent took his deposit with the proviso that another buyer might already have contracted to buy, 'subject to finance'. Late that night, Charlie got the bad news: the house had been sold, as the salesman had feared. Charlie swallowed his disappointment and went on looking for his new home. Then, two days later, the salesman rang again: the buyer hadn't been able to get finance and had had to withdraw. Charlie could have the house if he wanted it. What price? The other buyer had offered $12,000. Charlie could have it for that. He grabbed it before it could get away.

Now Charlie had another problem. He needed money for his new family house. He could also see a stock market boom coming up and he'd already committed himself heavily to what he regarded as assured profits. This bargain house wasn't expensive but he'd pressed his bank hard enough for the moment. Life would be easier for everyone if he could get $5,000 or so from somewhere else.

Charlie had got on to good terms with his solicitor who, *inter* not very much *alia*, did his conveyancing. He knew the solicitor had many pastoralists among his clients and that some of them entrusted funds to him for safe investment. Charlie asked him for $5,000, secured on the bargain house. 'No worries,' the solicitor said and drew up the mortgage documents forthwith. Charlie was beginning to feel like a real landlord-capitalist. He furnished the house and rented it well enough to pay interest to his solicitor's squatter-client and have a useful margin on the side.

While he was digesting this, the stock market took off on the Poseidon boom. Charlie had no Poseidon — or Tasminex or any other of that boom's more spectacular issues — but everything he did have nevertheless zoomed upwards in price. Charlie sold in good time but not everything. In retrospect, he held on to rather too many blue-chip BHP shares. He'd allowed himself to buy too many of them at too high a price in the euphoria that had followed major oil discoveries in Bass Strait. But, if he made some mistakes, Charlie emerged with cash in his pockets.

What to do with it? The stock market had now dropped dead. The wool market was pretty moribund too. A series of body blows, including substitution of artificial fibres, had driven the price of wool down disastrously, to reach a low of about 30 cents a pound in 1971. Most woolgrowers survived by courtesy of their banks or by diversifying into cattle and crops. Sheep were at giveaway prices. The price of grazing land was dismal.

Charlie shared the desire of most Australians — indeed, of most humankind — to call a few of God's green acres his own. He now saw his chance. But, over the years, Charlie had become pretty hard-headed. He wasn't a man to be carried away by expensive pretensions. He wanted cheap land that was a 100-per-cent sure-fire good investment. The wool market had collapsed for reasons that could be long term. Artificial fibres were here to stay and would probably hit wool even harder in the years ahead. Beef wasn't doing too badly, although agricultural protectionism around the world allowed no guarantees about the future there either. But there was something that would give Charlie more security than farming. He could buy a place that would be good for sheep, cattle and horses, that would grow some oats and maybe a bit of wheat but that, above all, would be within commuting distance of Canberra, say, up to a half-hour's drive, so as to appeal to the Pitt Street farmer. If he could find such a place, he'd be on clover.

Charlie found his place: 2,000 acres within thirty minutes of Canberra City Centre, for a price he negotiated down to $35,000 — a little more than $17 an acre. He bought 2000 Merino wethers from the desperate former owner at $1 each and 100 Hereford heifers at $30. He needed a shearing shed — he got it at a knock-down price — and a weekender to relax in with his family. He managed the whole deal for not much more than $45,000.

Charlie always said that being poor had taught him a lot. 'I know the value of a dollar,' he'd say.

'So do I,' I'd reply.

'I had to know.'

'But you've been lucky.'

'Like a golfer: the more I practise, the luckier I get.'

He proved to be pretty right: if good luck goes with a disciplined lifestyle, that was the way it continued to turn out for Charlie. Almost from the moment he bought his rural retreat, the price of wool began to rise and, with some hiccups, kept rising until, in the 1988-9 season, the indicator passed 1000 cents a kilogram. Beef also did well for the first few years but then the European Economic Community put a virtual ban on beef imports, and the markets in Japan and the United States became more difficult. Prices plummeted. The Herefords Charlie had bought for $30 a head peaked at over $200 a few years later and then dived almost overnight to about $20. Some farmers who'd bought near the peak were ruined. But not Charlie. He'd bought low, enjoyed the boom and rode out the beef depression without pain. Anyway, wool by then kept him liquid. He'd also bought a couple of palominos for the kids. Two of the mares foaled and Charlie started talking grandly about his 'stud'.

Charlie still had some debt, mostly to his bank, but the high inflation of the 1970s and early 1980s cut his debt in real terms without any effort on his part and the ratio of assets to liabilities improved. As an example, one of his houses in 1972 was worth $50,000, with a mortgage of $40,000. Ten years later, it was worth about $250,000. It's value hadn't increased much in constant dollars; so that, in real terms, he'd made little profit. But in 1972, his equity in the house had been $10,000 or 20 per cent of its value. By 1982, his equity was $210,000 or 84 per cent of its value. He still owed the bank $40,000 but now, in real terms, it was only about a fifth of what he'd borrowed, even though he'd paid nothing off the mortgage.

So Charlie became richer even sitting around doing nothing.

'That's the way it's always been,' he told me. 'The poor work their guts out and get poorer; the rich get to own the world by doing bugger-all. The only difference...'

'Yes?' I prompted him.

'...is that now *I'm* one of the lucky poor — which is just another name for the undeserving rich. I've managed to get myself off the treadmill and on to the escalator.'

In fact, Charlie had never sat around doing nothing. He'd never been more than a part-time investor. He'd always worked hard at his career. And, when opportunities offered, he'd invested what he earned — or what he could manage to save or borrow — as profitably as he could.

He made some mistakes. Once he got a proposition to buy some apartments on the other side of the country. He had no chance to inspect them personally. So he bought sight unseen. Not quite unseen. The vendors provided a video which he studied carefully. He decided the price was low enough, the location good enough to make the purchase worthwhile.

He was wrong.

There's a lesson in that. Particularly in the purchase of property, you should always inspect what you're buying. There are many advertisements for a 'ranch' in Texas or a castle in Scotland or an island in the sun, whether in the Caribbean or off the Queensland coast. Some might — just *might* — be good buys. But most are of such quality that they could be sold, at the asking price, only to people who've never set their disappointed eyes on them. The locals wouldn't touch such property. Much of it might be desert or bog or otherwise unsuited to business or recreational use. As a general rule, never buy any property without examining it carefully in its own environment.

About the same time as he bought in error, Charlie was offered some units in a major international development on Hamilton Island, off the central Queensland coast. The offer included a free air trip to inspect the development on the spot. Charlie turned it down. That was another mistake.

But he had some successes too.

Some years before, he'd bought an old house at the coast for family holidays. Old it really was: timber, fibro, poor brick foundations, the typically cheap vacation house that was about all earlier generations could afford. Its remaining life couldn't be more than a few years. But the location was superb. Right next to a golf course, looking over the Pacific, with a splendid beach only a few metres away. And the street was zoned for units (apartments).

But there was a problem — and an opportunity. The old house now had to go; its life expectancy was almost nil. But the land on which it stood, though large for a single family house, was rather small for units. Then Charlie had a brilliant thought. Between his house and his neighbour's to the south was a strip of unused land. Presumably it belonged to the Council — or the Queen. He looked it up on the Shire plan. Sure enough it was reserved for a road; but the plan had never been implemented and he couldn't see any value in constructing a road there now.

He put a simple proposition to the Council: 'How about letting me take that useless strip of land off your hands?' The Council demurred. They demurred for twelve months but then yielded to the inevitable. 'Yes, you can have it,' they told him, 'for $12,000'.

That was only the beginning. Plans had to be drawn up. The Council had to approve the development and, after that, the building plan; and it was careful to squeeze as much money as possible out of Charlie along the way. He had to find some builders, compare their quotes, and make up his mind which of them he trusted most. Then, when building started, the money flooded out. He spent sleepless nights wondering whether the flood would ease before he went broke.

But it was all worth it. He ended with a modern apartment for his family and the rest to rent or sell. He'd made the most of what had originally been just a holiday home asset for his family.

'You know', he confided in me, 'the simplest things can work out profitably. Who'd have thought that tumbledown old house could be converted into a fine, modern apartment building like this?'

'You always were lucky,' I reminded him.

He grinned. 'I keep practising and — like I told you — the more I practise, the luckier I get.'

Buying Overseas: Foreign Currencies

There was more to come. After gaining power in 1983, the Labor Government turned expectations upside down by 'deregulating' — as the buzz word put it — wide areas of economic activity. One area was finance, including movement of funds across the national frontiers. For the first time in decades, Australians could buy and borrow overseas, invest in overseas companies — take them over, if they were so inclined — and buy overseas property, without limit. Before that, Australians could buy a house or apartment for personal use only up to a certain maximum value, generally less than $100,000. For all such purchases, they had had to get exchange control approval through the Reserve Bank. Now all that was over. If he wanted to, Charlie could buy himself an elegant place overseas — if he had the money.

'I'm not sure this freedom to buy overseas isn't going to get us into trouble,' Charlie confided to me.

'You mean trouble for you and me?'

'Not right now, but eventually. You remember when Menzies abolished import restrictions?'

'1960, wasn't it? Nearly cost Menzies the Prime Ministership. We all started buying everything like crazy — all around the world.'

'That's right. Then he had to crack down with a credit squeeze. To stop the imports. He ended up stopping just about everything. That's what cost him votes. But what I'm getting at is this. When they freed imports, we bought like crazy. Now we're freeing foreign exchange, Australians are going to buy like crazy too. They'll buy overseas property — for profit and pleasure, they'll invest and takeover wherever they see an opportunity. Some of it will be good — like the overseas investments of the old countries, Britain, the United States and the rest. But a lot'll never have Buckley's chance of earning any foreign exchange to service it. A big part of it'll be pure consumption. And they won't be able to stop it. Not the Treasury. Not the Reserve Bank. No one.'

'How's that?'

'Look, mate, it's easy enough to take controls off — to deregulate. But you try putting 'em back on. That'd be a real crisis. Foreign exchange crisis, payments crisis, crisis of confidence, the lot.'

'They could shut down the local economy, though. Put on a credit squeeze. Raise interest rates.'

'Like Menzies? That scares me, too. Suppose domestic interest rates go up — and overseas interest rates stay low. Will there be a lot of people and corporations that get into borrowing big overseas? What used to be local borrowing, using local savings, will become foreign borrowing and the local savings — what there are — will be used for something else. Perhaps they'll just go to boost consumer credit. Plastic money and the rest.'

'Could be.'

'Why pay 20 per cent at home when you can get money for 8 per cent overseas? The currency risk might seem to be worth it. I'm telling you, mate, there could be dangers ahead. Freedom's fine but it could cost us...'

Despite his misgivings, Charlie bought himself a place in London almost as soon as the ink was dry on the new regulations.

'Wonder how many other Australians are going to be as irresponsible as I am?'

'I would be if I could,' I confessed.

There was a lot of sentiment in Charlie's London buy. A fifth-generation Oz, his ancestors had come from England. Strictly, that wasn't even half true. A great-great-grandfather had started life in Devon; but the rest of his forebears had been dour Scots. Still, there might have been a certain logic in what Charlie did: the finest prospect a Scotsman ever sees is the high road that leads to London.

The housing boom hadn't really started in the south-east of England then. But a more important factor made property in England cheap for Charlie: the coalminers had called a strike that was doomed from the start but that hit the British economy and the pound sterling hard. At one stage, the pound faced the prospect of parity with the American dollar. That was when Charlie bought: a fine old house overlooking Regents Park. It was too big for him and his family, especially as a place to live in only occasionally. But he could convert it into a couple of apartments and, provided you knew your way around the tenancy rules, rentals were good. So sentiment was satisfied in the profitable way Charlie always found most pleasing.

But, if England was the greenest place Charlie'd ever seen, he soon realised that the greenest places in this world are always the wettest. After a while, Charlie thought he'd like to have his overseas joint where the sun shone more frequently.

It was about this time that he'd torn down his dilapidated holiday house at the coast and begun building apartments. So he was feeling a bit strapped for cash. Then came the stock market crash of October 1987, from which he'd extricated himself by the skin of his teeth. The timely extrication blessed him with a little bit of money in the bank. He knew it wouldn't last long as the apartment building went ahead, but at least it relaxed a bit of the pressure.

On the way back from a trip to London — Charlie could afford it these days, though he still chased after the cheapest fares — he and his wife stopped off at Nice in the south of France to look at some villas with a view of the Mediterranean. In the end, they didn't buy a villa. They decided that an apartment, not too far from beach and marina, with a commanding view of the Med was more to their liking.

One way and another, Charlie learned a lot from these overseas transactions. One thing they did was make him acutely aware how crucial fluctuations in exchange rates could be. He'd bought the London place when £100,000 was worth about $A140,000. After May 1986 and Treasurer Paul Keating's 'banana republic' interview, every £100,000 worth of value in his house became worth $200,000 to $250,000. In Australian dollars, he'd made huge paper gains, even before the London housing market made its most dramatic upward surge. Every £100,000 of value, originally equivalent to $140,000, then became worth about $400,000 to $500,000.

The purchase in France was different. He'd contracted to buy when the Australian dollar was worth little more than four francs. By the time he completed the purchase, the Australian dollar was worth more than five francs, so he'd saved about 20 per cent: what would have cost him about $500,000 on signing the contract cost him only $400,000 to complete.

'Of course, you've got to remember that, if I ever sell the place, I'll get fewer Australian dollars back for it.'

'Unless the dollar falls again,' I countered.

'You could be right, mate. So I've hedged my bets. I took out a local loan — in francs. Interest rate a lot lower than at home. I get more for money on deposit in Australia than I pay interest in France, so I've got to come out in front...'

'Unless the dollar collapses.'

'Right. If the dollar falls, the interest costs me more in Australian dollars. But I can pick my moment to repay the franc loan. If the dollar really picks up or the franc falls or both, a rate of eight to ten francs to the Australian dollar wouldn't be unrealistic. It's been there before.'

'Then a debt of $200,000 would be cut in half — at ten francs to the dollar instead of five. But what about your theory that freedom to spend foreign currency could cost us...?'

'That's why I've hedged. I could be picking up the apartment dirt cheap. On the other hand, I could hit trouble with a collapsed Aussie dollar. That's why I've paid out most of it and used the franc loan only at the margin. I just hope it works out.'

'At worst, you *could* let it to a starlet for the Film Festival . . .'

Charlie leant back reflectively in his chair, stretched out his legs. He'd given up smoking — 'Not because it's a health hazard. It's just too expensive for the bad it does.' If he hadn't, he'd have puffed on his pipe.

'You know,' he said finally, 'there's a lot of money to be made out of this currency racket.'

'Why don't you squeeze it for all it's worth?' I suggested.

'Getting scared, I suppose. It's a dangerous game. Some people have done a lot of money on it; and this dog might be a bit long in the tooth to be trying flash new tricks. When you're dealing with currencies, you need to think fast — and move yer bloody boots.'

'You just need practice.'

'Could be.'

'And the more you practice, the luckier you get.'

'Haven't I heard that somewhere before?'

'I'm quoting the maestro.'

'Perhaps I'll think about it...'

He thought about a lot of things while lying on the Mediterranean beaches and drinking Provençal wine — which, he insisted, wasn't half as good as Australian but light and pleasant nevertheless. He read about the 200 richest Australians:

> Above all...the seriously wealthy possess property. The primary source of wealth for 31 of the 71 [Australians] worth more than $100 million is property. [In 1988], 37% of those with fortunes worth more than $100 million made their money on property. [In 1989], the trend has intensified: for nearly 44% of the $100 million club the primary source of wealth is property. [7]

---

7 *Business Review Weekly*, Melbourne, 12 May 1989, p.51.

He pondered currency movements, commodities, art auctions at Christies and Sothebys in London — and in Paris and Amsterdam. On a trip to London, he took in Stanley Gibbons' stamp centre. After all, he told himself, he ought to keep his mind active.

The rural property market in Australia was attractive too. Should he sell what he had? Or add to his rural empire? From 1987, rural commodities had done well. Wool had gone to a peak of 1257 cents a kilo in April 1988 and, although it had since 'stabilised' at lower levels, prices were still good. Drought in the United States had helped grains and beef was in a good phase: the Japanese and other markets, such as the Korean, were opening up. If the Aussie dollar fell, rewards in the local currency would go up...

Even so, despite some headlines about Japanese acquisitions, there hadn't been all that much buying of rural land, so Charlie still had a chance, in the autumn of 1989, to pick up a country estate or two. (He loved the sound of 'country estate', made him feel like Lord Charlie!) He could still buy at reasonable, if not giveaway, prices. Of course, it would have been better if he'd got in before the market had moved up at all, but good rural land still looked like a good investment as compared, for example, with commercial property in the oversupplied central business districts in the big cities. Perhaps now was the time, he pondered, to go rural in a big way. Long term, of course. The future fundamentals looked sound — growing demand for rural commodities, some prospect of freer markets in Europe and North America, bigger purchases by Asia if things went well. But, Charlie thought, he'd have to act smartly; it'd be no good buying big if and when a runaway rural boom was already under way.

But then again, he wondered, why do anything at all? Why not just be bone lazy? Why not sock away whatever money came his way? He had enough property — all he'd ever need — and he didn't want to mollycoddle the kids. Enough of nearly everything. Why not just cash up for a while? Inflation was down. Perhaps it'd stay down — although in most places it wasn't all that steady. He watched gilt and junk-bond rates carefully. Even cash in the bank, if placed right, would pay a solid 4 per cent over inflation, indeed, in Australia a great deal more...

4
Saving Your Money:
Socking It in Banks
or Banking It in Socks

Apart from anything else, Charlie pondered, the simplicity of being cosily cashed up has its appeal. Millions of other people, at other times and places, have thought the same.

Why bother going through all the hassle of buying shares or property? Isn't it all a bit of a bind? Why not just save your money — in notes and coins — and put it away somewhere safe? Indeed, a lot of people still do this, week after week, year after year. It's one of those wise things that the elders of most tribes tell us we should do. Banks, insurance companies and other financial institutions, less disinterested than our tribal elders, tell us much the same thing, assuring us that that's the way to grow rich, though the commandment they recommend for us is not a commandment they choose to follow themselves. Banks and similar institutions, which borrow other people's money to relend, have a special bonanza when the monetary authorities raise interest rates to 'damp down the economy'. Much of this is achieved by a lag in the level of rates at which they borrow while there is a prompt and sudden surge upwards in the rates at which they relend. In other words, it becomes an even more mouth-watering temptation for banks and similar institutions to seduce people into handing over their dollars and cents. The 'damping' and the consequent pain to others can then be used to push financial institutions profits to new record highs.

Nevertheless, there is some superficial validity in what the tribal elders say: those who do save regularly can end up with quite a hoard and for those who prefer the simplest, most undemanding way of handling their personal finances, it has its virtues. Cash is immediately convertible into real goods and services. It's a store of perceivable value, to be seen, admired and counted. In addition, if advantage can be taken of a sudden hike in interest rates, current income will be boosted. However, as we shall see, that means grabbing the hike when it comes, not holding cash in interest-bearing paper beforehand which will then lose value when interest rates rise.

The Mystique of Money

Notes and coins have emotional values. The man with a roll of notes in his pocket feels rich. The man who can throw such a roll on to a gaming table or to a bookmaker at the racetrack seems powerful — a big man. A child gets a much greater thrill out of holding coins he has saved than from reading a credit balance in his savings account. Perhaps its attraction goes beyond this:

> The mind confers real value and elaborate power on these mere scraps of paper [banknotes]. It infuses money with potent psychological meanings, a surrogate for mortal anxieties and yearnings that lie deep and unexpressed in everyone. The psyche insists that money has meaning. And so does the society...The money illusion is ancient and universal, present in every transaction and absolutely necessary in every exchange. Money is worthless unless everyone believes in it. A buyer could not possibly offer a piece of paper in exchange for real goods — food and clothing or tools — if the seller did not also think the paper was really worth something. This shared illusion was as old as stone coins and wampum, a power universally conferred by every society in history on any object that was ever regarded as money — seashells, dogs' teeth, tobacco, whiskey, cattle, the shiny minerals called silver and gold, even paper, even numbers in an account book. [1]

Money has uglier and more sinister connotations, too: 'rural peasants in Colombia, as they were drawn into the commodity-exchange economy of modern capitalism, would devise their own devil legends to explain the dreadful

---

1 Greider, op. cit., p.226–7.

power money and commerce now held over their lives'.[2] More generally, 'when Freud was first attempting to chart the geography of the human psyche, he kept encountering an outrageous association — money and excrement. Gold stinks. Miserliness is "dirty". Faeces are the infant's coin.'[3]

But, while money has these repulsive connotations, its virtues are more obvious to those in a modern society, whether it takes the form of physical cash — notes and coins — or credit entries in bank ledgers. These virtues are dominant for most of us. But we must be clear what they are. We must also be clear about its vices: for example, the process of socking your money away somewhere might not prove, in many situations, even to be safe. Let's take an example.

Watching It Dwindle

Nearly twenty years ago, Charlie had a mate who owned a range of properties, including a couple of small country hotels. Though still young, he decided to retire so as to rid himself of the burdens and irritations of running one hotel directly and finding people to manage his other properties. The market was healthy, indeed robust, prices for his properties being at an historic peak. So he sold everything. He got a great deal of money which he promptly put in the bank. So far, so good. He took advice from his bank manager. As a result, except for a working balance in a cheque account, he salted his money away in fixed-interest, medium- to long-term securities. He got what then was a good rate of interest ranging between 6 and 8 per cent. With a sigh of relief, he settled down to live on his interest, earned trouble-free. It looked like the most brilliant move in a successful business career. He had an income of about $30,000 a year — several times average earnings in 1970, when a yearly income of $10,000 marked you down as a distinct success.

Then the rot set in. A man who had been earning $10,000 a year in the early 1970s was getting more than $50,000 a year for the same work about a decade later. The

---

2 Ibid., p.231.
3 Ibid., p.231.

high-income $30,000 a year of Charlie's mate was now no better than a middling income — and its real value was declining all the time. Not only that, but also the capital on which he relied had sagged badly in real terms. He had had almost half a million dollars in 1970 — then a considerable fortune. Ten years later that sum had been eroded in nominal terms because of his need to supplement the declining value of his real income. Nevertheless, he still had capital to a face value of about $400,000. But its power to purchase had lost about four-fifths of its 1970 clout. Not only that. Interest rates had soared. So his fixed-interest securities had declined tragically in value. If he sold them, they would bring him, even in money terms, only a fraction of what he had paid for them in the early 1970s. Fortunately, some of his securities had matured and been renewed on more favourable terms; but even so his capital losses were enormous.

He was by no means the only one whose financial performance was unsound.

Not very long ago [wrote the economist J.K. Galbraith in 1975,] one of the investigations into the typically intricate affairs of the 37th President of the United States turned up a more than normally interesting transaction. Mr Charles G. Rebozo, Mr Nixon's good and reticent friend, had received for the then President's benefit, political or personal, $100,000 from the even more reticent entrepreneur, Mr Howard Hughes. This considerable sum, it was claimed, had thereafter been kept in cash in a safe-deposit box for rather more than three years before being returned to Mr Hughes. The curiosity concerning this transaction was not over why anyone should return money to Mr Hughes, which is something like returning salt tears to the ocean. Rather it was why anyone should leave so much money in storage. So left, as everyone knew, it lost radically in value — a dollar of 1967 had the purchasing power of only 91 cents in 1969, the year Mr Rebozo resorted to storage, and of less than 80 cents when he retrieved and returned the money. (In early 1975, it was down to 64 cents.) The impact of this trend could not have been lost on the two gentlemen. The partial compensation for this loss in the form of interest, dividends or, one might even hope, capital gains, which a minimally prudent man would have been expected to collect, was foregone. The most retarded of the borrowers in the Parable of the Talents had incurred rebuke for coming back with only the original advance. Neither Mr Nixon nor Mr Rebozo was thought indifferent to pecuniary concern; both had fallen well below the Biblical minimum for financial performance. There was general disbelief and shaking of heads that they should have been so bad... Everyone expects [money] to depreciate in value...Everywhere the tendency in these years was the same — for prices to rise, the purchasing power of money to decline and at an uncertain, erratic rate. Nothing is forever, not excepting inflation. But to many it must have seemed that this tendency was distressingly persistent.[4]

It was this erratically persistent performance of money in the 1970s and 1980s that caused Charlie's mate such acute distress.

To recapitulate, the half-million dollars he had put away in the early 1970s had, *at best,* not increased even in nominal terms a decade later. The money he had 'invested' — in government bonds, commercial debentures and other fixed-interest forms — had been repaid, on maturity, in the same nominal amounts he had lent. Such long-dated securities as he still held, paying a low rate of interest, had declined enormously in *market* value, being worth perhaps no more than half or a third of their face value. Even when he got their face value back on maturity, they'd lost most of their real value. Inflation had been high in most years — sometimes over 20 per cent and often more than 10 per cent. The cost of living had consequently increased several times in the course of the decade. A family house which might have cost less than $20,000 in the early 1970s was worth more than $100,000 and perhaps up to $200,000 a decade later. In dollar terms, he would have received several times as much for his property in the early 1980s as he had in the early 1970s. A conservative estimate would be that he would have received $2.5 to $3 million in the early 1980s compared with the $500,000 he had received in the early 1970s. He had saved his money and put it away carefully — and at least three-quarters to four-fifths of it had disappeared before his eyes.

4 Galbraith, Money: *Whence It Came, Where It Went,* pp.1–2.

Holding Cash and Renting It Out

So we need to reflect when we talk about the 'safety' of an investment. We need to consider what is likely to happen when we put our money away in some sort of 'sock'. Some insurance companies are still urging 'investors' to put their money away safely for retirement in much the way Charlie's mate did. As late as November 1988, a reputable Australian life insurance company was advertising savings bonds with an initial investment of, say, $1,000 or $5,000 to be topped up by $2,000 each year until the bonds matured after ten years. The 'investment' could be split between cash and managed units. The advertisement — which lacked explicitness — suggested, especially through an illustration, that retirement in conspicuous luxury would result. But would it? Or was it more likely that the return on the bonds, and more particularly the cash element, would do little, if anything, more than keep pace with inflation and that the capital sum, when returned to the bondholder, would be worth half or perhaps much less than the real value of the money paid for them? If the inflation rate averages 7.2 per cent between 1988 and 1998, a cash investment of $5,000 in 1988 will be cut in half to only $2,500 ten years later.

Generally speaking, the proposition put forward at the beginning of this book is valid: to make a fortune you need to get your hands on other people's money and put it to good use. A corollary is that it is wasteful and unproductive for you to hand over your money to someone else for him to make the gains you should be making yourself. But, apart from that general position, are there any circumstances in which the simple saving of money — holding it in cash form or in interest-bearing instruments — may be justifiable?

In the short-term, you will need *some* cash. Sometimes, you will need rather more cash — you will want to increase your 'liquidity' — in order to be able to take prompt advantage of some opportunity on the stock or property market. This short-term cash will normally be held in a bank or in some slightly more sophisticated form, for example, commercial bank bills.

What about longer-term savings? You can, if you wish, hold all your savings in cash — in notes or coins. This has the disadvantage noted of Howard Hughes' $100,000: it earns no interest or dividends. Galbraith claimed that it also made no capital gains — true enough for the period he was talking about but, as we shall see later, not necessarily the case if deflation confronts the economy. In recent years, we have been more accustomed to inflation than deflation, sometimes at the relatively modest rate of 3 per cent a year, sometimes above 20 per cent even for leading Western economies. In some other economies in Asia, Latin America and Africa, the inflation rate has been more than 100 per cent for fairly long periods. To hold your savings in cash — in your pocket or a sock or under the bed — would in these circumstances be to invite a steady or precipitate erosion of your real wealth.

One exception to that steady erosion is, as we have noted, a deflationary situation. Another is to hold your wealth in gold. If you had converted $100,000 into gold in 1970, you would have received about 3000 ounces for it. If you had kept it under your bed ever since, those 3000 ounces would now be worth about $US1,300,000 or more than $A1,500,000 — about fifteen times greater. Even allowing for inflation, you would be comfortably ahead. Your gain would of course have been in capital growth; you would have earned no income from the gold. You would have held gold, not as cash, that is, notes and coins of little intrinsic value, but as a commodity, something we shall discuss later.

Holding cash — and even gold — would have had the disadvantage that security would have been poor if it had been under your bed or in a sock. This might have been modified if you had held it, as President Nixon did his $100,000, in 'a safe-deposit box'. Galbraith didn't say whether the safe-deposit box was under Nixon's bed, in a safe in his Oval Office or in a bank. Most of us would most likely keep our safe-deposit box in a bank. There we would assume it to be secure.

But would it? The short answer is, 'Yes — in so far as anything can be secure in this world'. There could be a bank robbery — and your safe-deposit box could be part of the loot never to be recovered. Then unless there was insurance, you would have lost your hoard. But, leaving aside such acts of larceny, your money would be secure. Indeed, it could be rather more secure than if, instead of keeping it in a safe-deposit box in the bank, you deposited it in some account with the bank.

That brings us to a second way to hold your savings: in the form of various interest-bearing instruments. When you deposit money in a bank, you normally receive some form of 'price' or 'reward' or 'payment' from the bank for using your money. This is called interest: a payment for use, incorporating a mostly small risk factor.

In the past, banks have not been invariably secure. In the United States in 1929, some 659 banks collapsed; in 1930, the number increased to 1352 and in 1931 to 2294. Although bank failures are fewer today, they still happen — even to large and reputable institutions. By the nature of their business, banks create credit and their liabilities are always far greater than their immediately liquid resources. If depositors lose confidence and mount a run on a bank, it may not be able immediately to return to its depositors the cash it has been holding for them on call and the bank risks collapse. If it can restore confidence, then the run ceases: 'however desperately people want their money from a bank, when they are assured they can get it, they no longer want it'. [5] To cover the contingency that depositors might not be able to get their money when they want it, modern banking practice requires that insurance or some other guarantee arrangement secure depositors' money. Australia has not had as many bank failures as the United States; but there have been some and the 1988 collapse of Rothwells merchant bank reminded us that even a reputable financial institution, supported by a state government, is not immune.

But this is not the most serious source of insecurity in holding your savings in a bank account. A more serious insecurity stems from fluctuations in the value of money and in the rate of interest. Fluctuations in the value of money can take two broad forms: fluctuations in *domestic* prices and in the external value of the national currency. The first causes a decline in the real value of your money in your daily life if prices go up or, rather less likely in recent times, an increase in the real value of your money if the

---

5 Ibid., p.81.

spectrum of local prices declines. The second means that expenditures outside your own country or on imported goods and services will cost you more in local dollars if the national currency depreciates or less if the value of the currency rises.

We have had plenty of examples of the effect of inflation on our holdings of money in the last twenty years or so. However, there have also been massive fluctuations in the external value of the national currency. The most widely publicised fluctuations have been in the United States dollar, either in terms of gold or other currencies. Over a period of just a few years, the United States dollar has been worth as much as 250 Japanese yen and as little as 120. It has been worth 2.80 German marks or only 1.60. Other currencies have undergone similar fluctuations. From the early 1930s until 1967, the pound sterling was equal to 2.5 Australian dollars. Since then it has fluctuated, being at one time worth only $A1.40 then returning to 2.50 and more recently (1989) swinging between about 1.95 and 2.35. Against the German mark, the Australian dollar has moved between about DM2.60 and DM1.30; against the Austrian schilling from about 18 to less than eight; and against the Dutch guilder from 3.25 down to about 1.40. So if you hold your savings in cash, even for relatively short periods, you must be prepared for significant changes in its value both at home and beyond the national frontiers.

As one homely example, if you estimate you will need the equivalent of $10,000 for a holiday overseas and the value of the dollar falls, you might find that your $10,000 will support you for only two weeks instead of the three or four you had planned.

Of course, the dollar might not fall against all currencies at the same time and you might be able to change your holiday destination rather than be forced to curtail the length of your exotic safari.

Can this potential loss be offset? In the early stages of the inflation of the 1970s, it could not. Capital losses were incurred, both in domestic currency and in its foreign equivalents. As experience was gained, interest rates tended to move upwards and to be calculated in real terms — that is, a price for the use of money was added to the inflation rate and interest rates, for any given transaction —

mortgages, consumer credit and so on — were made flexible over the period of the transaction, that is, you did not borrow money over a long term at a fixed rate of interest but at a rate subject to change according to the market for money at any given time. Capital losses could not necessarily be avoided by these arrangements, whether by institutions or by individuals, but they could be moderated.

What are the possible ways to hold your cash? In banks, they are:

(1) in a non-interest-bearing cheque account;
(2) in a usually low-interest-bearing savings account;
(3) in commercial bank bills, of short duration, usually 30 to 180 days; and
(4) on time deposit, long or short, with the interest rate usually fixed for the period of the deposit.

Only a minimum working balance should be kept in a cheque account. Yielding neither income nor capital gain, it offers only convenience in meeting current expenses. The savings account gives some income, though *at best* little if any more than will maintain its real value in the light of inflation. It has a convenience value in that it allows immediate access to cash, although not usually with the convenience of writing cheques. Short-term commercial bank bills provide liquidity almost as good as cash at the same time as they offer an interest rate close to the overdraft rate. In November 1988, three-month bank bills in Australia yielded over 14 per cent interest compared with a prime overdraft rate of 16 per cent. By May 1989, the three-month bank bill rate had moved up to nearly 18 per cent and the prime bank rate 19 per cent. Time deposits offer few advantages over bank bills except that a relatively high rate of interest might, in the right circumstances, be maintained over a relatively long period, while the bank bill rate fluctuates continuously.

Redistribution: From the Improvident Poor to the Prudent Rich

The use of bank bills leads to some interesting reflections

on the way we can redistribute income from the improvident poor to the prudent rich.

'Course, our society doesn't do that sort of thing, mate,' Charlie reminded me. 'So we think.'

'Even if our society does redistribute income upwards, we can all defend ourselves,' I retorted. 'The means are there.'

'Oh, sure. The means are there. We're not cripples, are we? The average wage-earner, the unemployed, the down-and-out's as free as Alan Bond or Kerry Packer to defend himself against the cruel winds of financial adversity.'

'As free — but he mightn't be able to kick along quite as well?'

'You said it, mate. Kickin' along's not his forte, is it? The wretched poor — or some of them — might cotton on to what to do. You can never tell how smart some of them might be. But how are they going to do it?'

'Defend themselves against financial adversity, you mean?'

'Even mount an attack. It's easy enough to load yourself up with a stack of bank shares — if you've got the hooch. When the Reserve Bank jacks up interest rates, you'd be dead unlucky if dividends didn't lift and the market value of your shares go up. If you've *got* any shares, that is. But there's other ways to wind up richer too.'

'Turn over some bank bills?'

'Right. So interest rates look like going up. Maybe they've even started rising already. You've got some money in the bank. Or maybe you see the rise in interest rates is going to hit the stock and housing markets. You sell off some of your assets before they get hit — or anyway before they're much off their peaks.'

'So you're nicely cashed up as the Reserve Bank moves interest rates up from a modest 8 per cent to 10 and then along the road to 12 or 15.'

'They mightn't do anything dramatic. Sometimes the Reserve — with the Prime Minister and Treasurer denying that they're doing a thing — just nudge the rate up little by little. But after a few months the prime rate might have doubled — 8 to 16 or 10 to 20. Now, if you're cashed up, you could be on clover. You buy some short-term bank bills, turn them over each 30 or 60 or 90 days and you're getting yourself a nice little extra income.'

'Better than at the savings bank.'

'Could be better than anywhere. Of course, there's a problem. Your income's going up. You'll have to pay more income tax...'

'Unless you can offset it against last year's negative gearing...'

'But no chance of unrealised capital gains.'

'You could use some other little trick to get capital gains instead of income when interest rates rise. What about bonds?'

'Dead right. Interest rates go up. What happens to gilts — top-class government securities — and other fixed-interest paper?'

'Their value falls.'

'Like a stone if the interest hike's big. Interest rates double, gilts get cut in two.'

'So you can buy gilts when interest rates peak, then get a capital gain when rates retreat to more normal levels?'

'Or hang on to them. She's the way to get rich, mate. But be sure you've got a steady job, paid off the mortgage and got cash in your pocket before the Reserve Bank kicks rates up. Otherwise, you'll be one of the improvident poor helping along the conspicuous consumption of the deserving rich...'

To sum up, therefore, we need to keep some of our assets in the convenient form of cash or cash equivalent. However, since cash offers no or little income or capital gain and, in an inflationary situation, can lose real value very quickly, cash holdings should be limited to the absolute minimum or be manoeuvred to take advantage of emerging situations, such as interest rate changes. Cash should be held in a form which best combines convenience of access with income. There can be a trade-off between high-yielding 90-day bank bills and nil or low-yielding bank deposits. Convenience of access covers not just getting access to notes and coins to pay for three meals a day but also includes ease and speed of conversion of 'cash' forms into other higher-yielding investments as windows of opportunity open. Take advantage of high interest rates for more income or go for capital gains by buying gilts and other fixed-interest paper when peak interest rates push them down to their lows. But, above all, be careful not to see your hard-won capital erode through putting cash into long-term, low-rate, fixed-interest paper whose value will disappear down the drain even with present-day relatively modest inflation — modest as compared with the 1970s, although those flamboyant days might not be gone for long.

5
Leverage: Options, Futures, Trusts, Financial Muscle

As we followed Charlie along his investment track, we saw him evolve from a man with few economic resources, that is, with few assets and a weekly income just about enough to feed and clothe his wife and kids, into a man of considerable substance. Charlie seemed to lift himself up, as they used to say, by his own bootstraps. But did he? Let's have a closer look at how the bootstraps theory, though not without some moral validity, might be really a bootstraps fallacy.

At any given moment, unless we're utterly destitute, we have a certain amount of money. We have a certain accumulation of assets, albeit small. We can use that cash and asset power directly just as it is or we can reinforce it with what is called 'leverage'. To the uninitiated, that might sound difficult. But it isn't. Despite its technical ring, the concept is simple, something anyone can understand.

The word itself, of course, is one of those admirable expressions that confers status on us, if we use it confidently enough; it sets us nicely apart from our less well-informed fellows, puts us on the clever side of the jargon tracks. So use it freely. Practise it by yourself until you can fling it around with studied negligence whenever you get a chance. You'll find people will sit up and take more notice of you.

What is Leverage?

As it implies, leverage is simply the use of levers. Primitive man could handle only such relatively light weights as his own unaided muscles could lift or shove. Working with his equally primitive fellows, he could lift or shove heavier

133

weights, but still only as much as their combined muscle power could handle. This reliance on muscle power changed only when man came to understand and use tools which could multiply his power, at first modestly and then dramatically. It changed especially when, some way down the track, he learned to use rollers and wheels and ropes and pulleys, in other words, to use levers. Then a weak man could lift or shove many times his own weight: he could build the Pyramids and the Colossus of Rhodes.

When we speak of leverage in the financial and investment sense, we're talking about much the same thing, though of a less directly physical kind. We're talking about expanding our financial muscle power. We're talking about reinforcing our own feeble financial muscle so that we can handle big or at least bigger projects. Leverage of this sort will enable us to control more investment and to play a part in more significant economic activity. Financial leverage puts a few more ropes and pulleys in our hands and enables us, with a pull here or a push there, to accumulate more wealth and play a more active role in economic life.

All of us are aware of some people in the business and financial world who, with varying degrees of skill and power and varying degrees of longevity, control levers in this way. They are like people in a control nodule pulling levers or pressing buttons, so that people work, buildings rise, sheep are shorn, banks lend and ships sail. Some press the right buttons superbly well over a lifetime. These people are usually extremely rich, mostly in Getty's 'can't count' category: men from the past like John D. Rockefeller, John Pierpont Morgan, Henry Ford, Howard Hughes, Aristotle Onassis; and men of the present such as D.K. Ludwig, Goldsmith, Rothschild, perhaps a couple of Australians like Murdoch and Bond.

These are names synonymous not only with great wealth but also with economic and financial power. It's the latter that especially distinguishes them. The net personal wealth of some in this category of powerful men might be no more than some millions of dollars but they might control investment, service and industrial empires worth billions. They hire and fire, buy, merge and sell much as if they alone owned the empire they control. This despite the fact that they are not sole owners. Many other shareholders, some holding almost as many shares in an enterprise as they do, own a large part of their empires. But it's the ancestral line of the John Pierpont Morgans, the Howard Hughes, those who acquire the legal right to govern their vast empires and thus exercise effective control, who have the power. They have the final say. Because they control a crucial percentage of shares and votes, they're able to determine how 'their' financial, industrial or other businesses behave. Left-wing detractors used to deplore that, through a complex web of 'interlocking directorates', a few financial manipulators controlled the world. They never did: they were far too competitive among themselves to combine to 'corner' economic, let alone political, power. But within their own empires, they were indeed powerful; and a web of 'interlocking directorates' and other devices enabled them to apply decisive pressure on economic and financial levers.

That still holds true. Companies are gathered within the fold of a holding/controlling company. Companies independently registered on the stock exchanges are often under the control of one man whose name might not appear even as a non-executive director, although his nominees dominate the board. The webs may now be more complex than in the days of the early buccaneers, but no less effective. For the most part, securities and exchange authorities don't try to limit or regulate this assertion of power unless there is some egregious restraint of trade or exercise of monopoly power.

Movers and Shakers: You Too?

The recent phenomenon has consisted primarily in the exercise of financial power, with the emergence of financial wizards somewhat in the tradition of the mighty John Pierpont Morgan, the most powerful man of finance in the United States in the late nineteenth and early twentieth centuries — though no one of our current financiers has yet exercised J.P. Morgan's immense personal power. Nevertheless, one of these modern successors has said:

We are the gentlemen who finance and create change...When I

read [Alvin] Toffler's *Future Shock* , and he described this vortex of change that whirls around us, and it happens very fast in New York City, and slower in Des Moines, and even slower in the outback of Australia, the thing that was amazing to me was, when I looked at the funnel of that maelstrom, the vortex of that sits right in the middle of my desk. I am the fella who determines what the change will be. If I don't finance it, it ain't gonna happen. I get to decide who's going to get capital, to make the future. Now, I ask you — what's more romantic than that?[1]

We must enter a caveat. Owners, controllers, entrepreneurs are not to be confused with managers and chief executive officers:

the mere fact that a man has a big job and a desk to match does not necessarily mean that he is rich. He is likely to be a manager rather than an owner, a steward for a plurality of economic interests rather than a wealthy entrepreneur. He will, of course, have some of the customary status symbols of the rich — a Cadillac or Rolls Royce, and perhaps even the use of a company plane — and he will usually earn a salary which is large enough to qualify him for most people's definition of 'rich'. But he may well lack the basis of real wealth — capital...The chief executive of a large corporation wields considerable power...but he is ultimately dependent on the people who are the real owners of the business — his financial institutions, wealthy individual shareholders, and so on. He can sign a cheque for a million pounds without giving it more than a passing thought, but it isn't *his* money. If he fails to give satisfaction, the rug may be unceremoniously pulled out from under him[2]

— as, some years ago, Henry Ford II pulled the rug from under Lee Iaccocca.

But we're looking now not so much at the fact of concentration of power in the hands of relatively few men. Rather are we concerned with how they *achieve* their power. The brief answer is that they do it by reinforcing their own financial and other economic muscle: they mobilise and

---

1 Bruck, op. cit., p.246.
2 Davis, op. cit., p.13.

exert 'leverage'. Their talent is to manipulate financial and economic levers so as to exercise control.

You can do it too. You might not *aspire* to be a 'mover and shaker' or a modern capitalist buccaneer; but there's nothing special about those who are. Anyone can be like them. They do nothing that is intellectually, physically, artistically or in any other way beyond the capacities of ordinary people Indeed, they are themselves capable of enormous misjudgements. Some of them preferred to jump out of windows rather than face the consequences of their misjudgements in the aftermath of the Great Crash of 1929. A couple of generations later, the Hunt Brothers, once among the richest men in the world, filed for bankruptcy in 1988 and a fair proportion of financial wizards mislaid their magic wands in and after the stock market crash of October 1987. The magic vanished not only in the major capitalist markets of North America and western Europe but in smaller countries such as Australia and New Zealand too.

Some of the wonder boys broke the law in the games they played with valuable pieces of paper. Insider trading scandals involved those right at the top of the financial pile: Ivan Boesky was convicted and the ace of junk bond traders, Michael Milken,[3] faced racketeering and insider trading charges. Some high-flyers in Australia were investigated and a few seemed to face the prospect of prosecution.

It's not only the private wizards who've been shown to be short on magic. As the Hunts' attempted corner of the silver market fizzled into fiasco, the Federal Reserve Board in the United States was trying to control inflation, with results that bounced the economy up and down like a yo-yo. Paul Volcker, one of the best-qualified Fed Chairmen ever, ended his first year

in embarrassment. He and other governors offered Congress complicated explanations for what had happened, citing all the extraneous factors. They denied that they had lost control. Nevertheless, among themselves, they did not obfuscate. They knew that their management of money in 1980 had accomplished little, except perhaps to deepen skepticism about the Federal Reserve.[4]

---

3 See Connie Bruck's *The Predators' Ball.*
4 Greider, op. cit., p.219.

Public or private the economic celebrities were humbled.

So, if you want to track along with the financial wizards, you're quite capable of doing it; just be careful to keep within the law. If you do go down that track, you'll lose what we might call your amateur status; and we're concerned here primarily with modest and moderate people who want to make enough money to live comfortably as millionaires rather than spend every waking minute building up vast business empires. So what we want to do here is only to identify the various levers, to understand how they work and to help you use them to realise your limited objectives. We don't expect you to use them as much as the mighty financiers but it won't do any harm for you to know as much about the various levers, in their fundamentals, as the giants themselves. It doesn't call for a five-year course in intricate economics. All it requires is that you recall a few things we've already said, adding a small body of knowledge and learning some simple practices and tactics.

First, remember what we said right at the beginning of this book: you've got to get your hands on some money. If you've got your own money to start with, well and good. If you haven't, you'll have to get your hands on someone else's. In either case, further progress — via leverage — will depend on continuing to get access to more financial muscle, that is, more usable funds, than you have yourself.

Let's take a simple example of how this goes. First, you acquire a small stake. This might be no more than a hundred or a few hundred dollars. Let's say it's $200. It might be acquired from family or friends or from hard work and a temporary rejection of self-indulgence. (You might hope that would be the last hard work and renunciation of good times you'll ever know!) You invest the $200 in, say, Golden Nugget N.L., at two cents a share, including broker's commission, just as the gold price is beginning to take off. You're still waiting to receive your certificate for 10,000 shares when the market explodes with spectacular rumours that Golden Nugget has struck a rich lode potentially worth billions of dollars. The price of the shares flashes up to a dollar. You sell while the going's good. Your $200 has become $10,000 overnight.

That's your second starter. You use the $10,000 to make a deposit on an apartment costing $100,000, your mortgage on the apartment being $90,000. The stock exchange boom, originating in the rise in the gold price, has put in investors' pockets a lot of cash which now floods into the property market. Where your apartment is located, prices lift by some 50 per cent in a matter of six months. Your apartment is now worth $150,000. You go to your bank to borrow an extra $15,000 on the increased valuation and use that as a deposit to buy a second apartment for $150,000.

From your original stake of $200 and the $10,000 cash from your stock market coup, you now have assets of $300,000. You've made some capital gains, unrealised except for borrowing money against them. All of the money except your $10,200 has been put up by someone else. Your only other contribution has been your good judgement about what to buy. You're using $225,000 of someone else's money to control assets worth $300,000. You've done it through the use of leverage.

It's as simple as that. If you were to sell your assets when property prices had risen a further modest 10 per cent, you could pay off your two mortgages and have $110,000 in your pocket — or in interest-earning assets while it awaits new investment opportunities. You will have increased your stake of $200 550 times or your coup of $10,000 exactly eleven times. Not at all bad.

High Gearing: Rein in the Risks

Don't overdo it, of course. That $225,000 you borrowed has to be serviced, that is, you have to pay interest on it, along perhaps with periodic repayments of capital. If you fail to meet those payments, the mortgage might be foreclosed and you'll lose control of the mortgaged assets. So you must have a sufficient cash flow to ensure that you can meet mortgage payments. A 'cash flow' simply means revenue or income to meet day-to-day costs and expenses. In the case of an apartment or house — other than the one you occupy yourself — it will usually mean the rent the property brings. So, if you invest in a house or apartment — or, for example, in office or industrial property — you should calculate carefully whether the rent will be sufficient to meet mortgage and other payments. That mightn't leave you with very much net income; indeed, it might result in a net loss of income. In the latter event, you'll need to be sure you have a 'cash flow' from other sources sufficient to make up the loss. (Other sources might mean working overtime or driving a taxi as a second job at night.) You must also beware the possibility that interest rates might rise, so that, if you haven't borrowed at a fixed rate for a fixed term, your mortgage payments might increase, perhaps substantially.

If your cash flow is or becomes insufficient, you can sell your property, pay off the mortgage and realise your capital gains. In other words, if you don't receive a sufficient return on your property investment in terms of rent — current income or cash flow — you have to be sure that you get or will get a sufficient return some other way. There's no point involving yourself in any investment — and facing the burdens of looking after real estate assets — unless you're reasonably sure you'll make worthwhile gains. That means that your expectations of profits either from rents or from capital gains must be pretty rosy.

You could go on from there to the heights. There's no need for you ever to stop. The financial wizards don't: they just keep on doing, on an ever bigger scale, what we've just been describing. You can buy General Motors if you like. Anatole Kaletsky wrote a story about 'The Great American Leverage Game', in which his hero sends a letter to the chairman of General Motors, recounting how he's taken out profitable mortgages on his Bronx condo, so he knows 'a thing or two about leverage and cash flow and all that high finance stuff'.[5] He calculates the stockmarket worth of General Motors — a miserly $24.3 billion — to be way below the value of its assets. On these assets, he reckons he can raise finance to offer $50 billion for the company, GM's splendid cash flow being more than enough comfortably to service the debt. He'll then sell off the various assets to yield a profit of $27 billion, to be divided $13 billion for the chairman of General Motors, $13 billion for himself and 'a billion for a new wing at the Bronx Zoo, just opposite my condo'.[6]

In these days of leveraged takeovers, this little satire isn't so far from reality. The huge RJR/Nabisco takeover in the

5 *Financial Times,* 27 October 1988.
6 Ibid.

United States and the £13 billion ($US21.5 billion) move on BAT Industries in Britain show no company to be immune. One enterprising firm claims to have helped 'over 800 buy-outs' and offers its experience and funds to *you*. They'll send you a video called 'Buy-Out', free for a month, £15 to keep. So if you want to topple your boss, people are there to help.

I'm not prompting you to go down that track; but I am suggesting that there's no need to stop the process of modest, wise leverage until you've built up sufficient assets to keep you in comfort. Just don't get overconfident: remember the process is not always as simple as in Kaletsky's little fable. In the run-up to the October 1987 crash, some operators forgot how important cash flow was to get them through a crisis. The sudden slump in value of their assets left them insufficient funds to service and secure the huge loans they'd taken to finance their acquisitions. So I recommend modest, wise leverage, keeping your eye all the time on adequate cash flow.

As we saw a moment ago, if the market value of residential property goes up, you stand to make a substantial profit — and an even greater profit on the funds you yourself have contributed to the purchase. The bank might have provided most of the funds but you get all the profit. The bank provided $90,000. You tossed in $10,000. The bank will get back only its original $90,000. But you would get back $60,000 if you sold now — six times what you put in.

That means that you'd 'leveraged' yourself into a very profitable transaction. But you won't necessarily put that capital gain cosily into your pocket. You'll do that only if you actually sell the house. Usually, that's not what you'll want to do. For one thing, the profit you make from your sale might attract capital gains tax, perhaps at a high rate.

But, if you don't sell, your capital gain will be on paper only. That has advantages. As we saw, you can increase your borrowings on the security of the increased market value of your property. But there can be dangers too. The huge increases in the market value of residential property in the south of England in recent years and the easy availability of credit — up to 100 per cent of market value; some banks even advertising 110 per cent! — have meant that many people have 'realised' their capital gains by moving up-market for their own accommodation, using increased mortgages to buy other property at inflated prices or, even more dangerously, for consumption.

That might be tolerable so long as the boom in residential property rolls on. But highly leveraged property holdings can become a torment if interest rates rise steeply, as they did in Britain in the latter part of 1988, or if the boom collapses and property values fall dramatically. Either the servicing of mortgages then becomes difficult or, if borrowings have been at or near 100 per cent of the inflated values at the top of the boom, sale proceeds of the mortgaged property won't be sufficient to discharge the mortgage fully. These dangers must be avoided, first, by refusing to buy during the boom and, second, by leaving sufficient margin above borrowings to ensure that, even in a market gone sour, sales will readily discharge mortgages.

Always bear in mind that disposing of real estate is not as easy as withdrawing funds from a savings account or selling shares. Unless you're unlucky enough to be caught in a stock market crash or you're operating in very volatile stocks, you can be fairly sure of selling shares quickly and realising today's prices today or very close to today's prices tomorrow. But residential or other property usually takes weeks or months to sell — and there's not the same clearly identifiable and well-documented market for identical assets as on the stock market. Two shares in General Motors or BHP are exactly the same and will bring the same price on the same day — or very nearly so. No two houses are exactly the same or can be counted on to sell within the same period of time or at the same price, even if they're very nearly identical and are placed on the market simultaneously.

So buy when the market is low and keep within clear safety margins in leveraging your investments. If you think real-estate prices are likely to fall substantially and stay down for a long period, then don't buy and consider carefully whether you should sell. On the other hand, if your best judgement is that the market might dip a little for a short period but will then rebound, you should defer any new purchases but you might be wise to hold on to any property you already have. Does that mean that, even for a short period, you should be content to see your paper profits erode before your eyes?

There can be worse fates. It depends on the circumstances of the slide and how severe it is. Don't be too sensitive about some of your treasured possessions slipping a bit in value from time to time. That's the way most markets are. Indeed, all markets will fluctuate to some extent. But, provided you're confident about recovery and growth as a secular feature, you shouldn't lose too much sleep about it. What you should do is take advantage of peak values. Don't sit passively by while values go up and then, as they inevitably will, plateau out or go into a slide. Take advantage of the peak values. Again, do this by using someone else's money. However, a word of caution flowing from what I said a while ago: don't use other people's money to buy more of the property that's peaking. If you borrow on one type or location of property at its peak, use that money to buy property of another kind or in another location or shares or something else that's in a slump and has a recovery coming up. Never buy anything at its peak; buy as close as you can to the bottom of a slump. When you're leveraging your investments, that's more important than ever. Don't over-extend. Always leave a margin so that you'll easily survive if the market turns unexpectedly sour.

Not *quite* but almost everything of value can be used as security for a loan. Jewellery and some other items can be deposited with a pawnbroker. (But he'll charge you a pretty hefty rate of interest!) Real estate can be used for what most of us regard as more 'respectable' borrowing. The greater the value of a piece of real estate, the more you can borrow against it. If the location is first-class, even though the improvements are modest, it will increase in value over time. Location is always the vital factor in real estate. Most banks and other lenders will require an up-to-date valuation of your property at the time they lend you money on it. That can be to your advantage if you own property whose value, subject to cyclical dips, climbs almost constantly upwards. Bankers know (or *think* they know) what will be a certainty to gain in value and what will almost certainly lag behind. If the market is booming, a current valuation will be to your advantage: you'll be able to borrow more on it as a security for further investments.

That's the simplest form of leveraging. You can borrow against all sorts of assets. In essence, that's what the takeover merchants do: they ask banks and other financial houses to finance their takeover by mortgaging the assets of the company they're acquiring.

There are many other forms of leveraging, some of which might appear to be complex although most are pretty straightforward, for example:

(1)   options; and
(2)   futures:
      (a) currencies
      (b) commodities.

Options

Sometimes a company will issue its shareholders with options to buy shares at a specific future date or during some future period at a certain price, usually a price expected or hoped to be below market at that future date or period. These options, usually allocated according to the number of ordinary shares held, may be issued as a bonus or as a sweetener with a rights issue or at a — usually nominal — price.

Sometimes these options can be taken up profitably. Let's assume that the face value of the company's shares is 50 cents. The options give the holder the right to take up shares at 25 cents in two years' time. During that two years, let's suppose the market value of the shares rises from 50 cents to $3. You are then able to buy shares at a discount of $2.75 or more than 90 per cent of their market value. (If you happen to be a company executive, you might be offered stock options instead of a hike in salary or other benefits. Stock options, as well as being untaxed or taxed at a lower rate than salary, provide an incentive for executives to work to lift the market value of their company's shares, which may then be taken up at a profit. However, holders of stock options need to be careful: if shares from converted stock options are heavily sold, the market might take that as a sign that executives believe the company faces difficulties and send the price sharply down.)

Options to buy (call), sell (put), straddle (call and put), spread (call or put at a spread of prices), strap (two calls and a put) and a strip (a call and two puts) may also be bought on the open market. Options and futures markets, which have expanded throughout the world in recent years, provide plenty of opportunities to invest in any of these varieties of options.

Options are essentially a right to buy or sell in the future. To that extent they belong in the 'futures' markets. They also have elements similar to buying or selling short. However, they do not involve the same outlays or the same extent of risk as shorting. Here's an example.

Instead of buying the shares now and outlaying the full purchase price, you buy a call option, costing let us say 25 cents a share, to buy the shares in six months' time, at a certain price, let us say, $5. If the price of the shares does not reach $5, you will not exercise your option and lose 25 cents per share; but if the share price rises to $6, then you can buy those shares for an outlay of only $5.25. You have made a profit of 75 cents a share.

On the other side of the transaction, you can 'write' or sell an option to sell shares in six months' time at say $5. The sale of the option might bring you 25 cents a share. If the option is exercised by the buyer, he or she must trade at $5. But if the market price stays above this, and the buyer can get more for the shares on the regular market, it makes no sense to exercise the option. Then you pocket the 25 cents per share profit.

Commissions are also payable to the options brokers.

The London Traded Options Market, which claims to lead Europe in the field and to be the 'fastest growing equity derivative products market' outside the United States, regards options as essential to the institutional investor and to enable effective participation in a bull market and hedging against its reversal into a bear sell-out. The claim that earnings can, through traded options, be protected 'even in the severest fall' is largely valid although, as we shall see shortly, options traders still need to show prudence, good sense and realism when the market takes a sudden turn in the other direction. Options on more than 60 leading equities and on the FT-SE 100 index can be traded on the LTOM. It produces *A Guide to Traded Options*, a video and diskette on its operations, and conducts training courses. Options and futures exchanges now operate around the world, in Pacific countries as well as Europe and North America. Early in 1989, Sydney opened a greatly expanded and modernised Futures Exchange, aimed at reinforcing its position as the leading futures and options exchange in the Asia-Pacific region.

In the case of either put or call options, buyer and seller use a kind of leverage. They increase their capacity to trade on a larger scale, that is, in more shares, without making a full immediate outlay of funds. They stand to make proportionately greater profits on their smaller outlays. On the negative or precautionary side, they have also, if you like, hedged their bets, but without this affecting their use of a form of leverage which increases their trading and financial muscle.

Because of the advantages and growing popularity of options trading, you now need to pay close attention to the options market, even if your whole or main concern is with the underlying stocks on the more traditional stock exchange. The futures market now shows a marked tendency to influence, if not yet to rule, the traditional stock exchange indices. The impact on the general index reflects the effect options are having, and will have, on the value of specific shares. Whether this effect is beneficial in terms of a more stable market and gives more weight to the fundamentals of the underlying stocks has yet to be determined. For the most part, the effect — or its scale — will be determined by the professional traders, fund managers and the like; although the individual investor will have a role too. After all, options can be an effective form of leverage for the smaller investor.

But options trading certainly gives more scope to the arbitrageurs, who can play the immediate against the futures market to gather in profits. You can join in that game yourself. But whether this speculation tranquillises and evens out markets or imports further disruption and destabilisation is an argument that has eternally accompanied arbitrage trading. You might have more chances for profits but you might also face more risks in volatile trading.

What we can certainly say is that whether you engage in this form of arbitrage, that is, buying (selling) the security through the lower (higher) price of the option or whether you participate more generally in the worldwide expansion and proliferation of options and futures markets, it will pay you to keep *au fait* with these markets, given their influence on the more traditional markets and the pointers they provide to what, in terms of market thinking, might be coming up. Remember again that, although fundamentals must be closely observed, market sentiment counts especially in the short term. If the chartists think a certain pattern emerging in their charts indicates that the market will move up, then that assessment in itself will be a bull point for the market — although it can be offset or reinforced by more fundamental factors. It's the same with the options/futures market. If sentiment emerging in this market is bullish — or bearish — that's an important indicator to take into account in your dealings on the regular stock market.

Against this background, options have some advantages; but they can also be dangerous. In his book on *Black Monday*,[7] Tim Metz told the story of the patriarch of a Chinese American family he called Yee. In the dead stock market of the late 1970s and early 1980s, financial advisers had encouraged their clients to sell call options, exercisable at prices above the current market. Since the market didn't rise, buyers didn't exercise their options and sellers, usually of stocks they actually held, could collect the price of their call options, perhaps a couple of times a year. When the bull market began in 1982, selling of call options didn't make sense any more, so clients were advised to sell put options. Often they were stock-index options, in which the clients did not hold stock, but essentially made a cash 'bet'. That worked nicely too. Until the crash of 19 October 1987.

Then Mr Yee, who'd been successfully selling put options for years, refused to believe that the bull market and, with it, the wise selling of puts had come to an end. He tried to hold his position while the market collapsed around him. The options he'd sold were swallowing his family fortune. He could hold or close his position. To hold his position, he had to deposit more funds into his account to ensure that he could, on expiration day, meet the exploding market for puts. The deposit required had been $100,000 to cover the

---

7 Metz, *Black Monday*, pp.102–8.

adverse movement on Friday, 16 October, but that swelled to $200,000 early on Black Monday, 19 October.

'"Don't put up the margin, you stubborn old fool! Close out your position [that is, buy offsetting puts] before it's too late!..."', his broker wanted to advise him. But until late in the 19 October session, she couldn't convince him. By then, his losses were 'awesome...it will take $450,000 to settle the bet Mr Yee was paid $40,000 [for the put options] to make...Mr Yee won't be able to pay, but his three grown children will have to reach into their savings and borrow money to bring the Yee accounts up to zero...'[8]

The nineteenth of October 1987 was one of the most traumatic days in stock market history. It doesn't happen often. But always keep in mind that it *can* happen. Don't be like Mr Yee and imagine that a bull market can go on for ever. When the time comes, get out quickly before the roof falls in. The London Traded Options Market might be right that, in some circumstances, options enable you to control your risks. But not always. If you're proud and stubborn, like Mr Yee, they could set you on a course for disaster.

Futures

Most of our investment, in options or whatever other assets, is based on the hope, expectation or conviction that that asset will be worth more (or, if we're selling, will sell for less) in the future. To that extent we're constantly trading in futures. But most futures trading, identified as such, relates to currencies and commodities and sometimes stocks.

Traders in futures

actually are dealing in promises. Not idle promises but contracts. If you give me X dollars on the third Friday of December, I'll give you 30,000 pounds of live hogs that day. For Y dollars on the third Friday of next June, you can have the hogs then. You don't actually have to pay me all the money until the expiration day, and I don't have to give you the hogs until then, either. Meanwhile, we'll both deposit a little earnest money, say 5 per cent or 10 per cent of the price we're agreeing on, with a third party as an added incentive to keep

---

8 Ibid.

our promises to one another. These are futures contracts, literally, contracts to deliver something at a specified time in the future. In addition to hogs, pork bellies, and live cattle, the futures contracts traded [at the Chicago Mercantile Exchange] are based on half a dozen foreign currencies, on such other financial instruments as Eurodollars, Treasury bills, bank CDs. And some futures contracts [at the Exchange] are based on the stock market...related to the level of the Standard & Poor's 500 stock index...Assuming [a] $287 price...in the pit now, this is how the market works: For openers, while $287 may be the quoted 'price' on the December S&P 500 contract, the cost of each contract will be 500 times that, or $143,500. Why? Because the CME says so in its specifications for the contract, which were designed to attract institutional investors and high-rolling individuals. When you agree to purchase a December S&P 500 contract from me, you are promising to pay me the $143,000 on the third Friday of December, the expiration date the CME has specified. (The other three S&P 500 contracts traded here expire on the third Fridays of next March, June and September, respectively.)...You, the buyer, are betting that the stock market will go up. The seller is betting it'll go down. It's like off-track betting except the payoff can be a lot bigger.[9]

Currencies

Trading in currencies offers major opportunities for profit only in situations in which movements of some consequence in currency values are probable and predictable. You buy in the expectation that a currency will rise. You sell in the expectation that its value will fall.

Under a perfect gold standard system, changes in relative values of currencies are nil or few, small and infrequent. The close relationship with gold gives a high degree of external stability. (However, it's not all blessing: a gold standard with external stability almost necessarily implies a relatively high degree of *internal* (domestic) *instability*. A gold standard currency unit contains a fixed amount of gold. A deficit in external payments causes gold to move (not necessarily physically) from one country to another to restore equilibrium. Even under a pure gold standard

9 Ibid., pp.27–8.

system, changes can occur in the value of currencies but with less volatility: changes are likely to take place relatively slowly and infrequently. Much the same applies under a gold-exchange standard, where gold does not constitute the actual currency but stands behind the note issue which can, at least in theory, be exchanged into gold on demand.

A high degree of stability among world currencies was maintained by the International Monetary Fund during the period from 1945 to 1971. The lynchpin of the system was the United States dollar linked to gold at $35 an ounce. Values of other currencies were related to the dollar and its guaranteed gold link. This established a stable relationship among world currencies which could be changed only in conformity with certain rules set down within the IMF's Articles of Agreement. These rules were sometimes broken. For example, a government sometimes devalued its currency by more than 10 per cent without first seeking the Fund's approval. But governments did so infrequently and the international legal, financial and practical suasions to abide by the rules were significant.

In the circumstances of a gold or gold-exchange standard or effective management by such an institution as the International Monetary Fund, the scope for speculation in currencies is limited, though not entirely absent. In most ways — and in all the more sober ways in which we envisage the major economies developing for the benefit of those who participate in them — currency stability is highly desirable for the conduct both of domestic business and, most demonstrably, of that crossing national frontiers. Rates of payment are reliably fixed and the prospect of financial speculation dominating the real economy reduced. Terms of competition won't be sharply altered by abrupt shifts in relative currency values and interest rate movements will be associated less with currency changes and speculation.

> Speculators may do no harm as bubbles on a steady stream of enterprise. But the position is serious when enterprise becomes the bubble on a whirlpool of speculation. When the capital development of a country becomes a by-product of the activities of a casino, the job is likely to be ill-done.[10]

---

10 Keynes, *The General Theory of Employment, Interest and Money,* p.159.

Speculators have been more than a bubble on a steady stream of enterprise in two particular periods during this century: in the inter-war years from 1918 to 1939; and after the breakdown of the IMF, often referred to as the Bretton Woods system, since 1971.

We have already noted John Maynard Keynes' speculation against the German mark in 1920 and 1921. At that time, although the mark was especially volatile, other currencies also fluctuated substantially in the aftermath of war, including the American dollar, sterling, the French franc and other European currencies. Sterling rose against the American dollar largely through differences in central bank policies; and, at much the same time for reasons far from clear, the German mark gathered unexpected strength. This was between the European spring of 1920 and the summer of 1921, just at the time that Keynes, operating on margin, had decided to speculate against the mark. As a result, Keynes found himself in desperate trouble. He

...could not wait for three months [until the mark resumed its collapse]. As the later days of May [1921] ebbed away, it became clear that he was ruined. Between the beginning of April and the end of May he had lost £13,125. A small syndicate, for part of the resources of which he was morally responsible, also lost £8498. Previous gains were wiped out, and his small cover. Sales had to be effected. His firm asked him to pay in £7000 to keep his account open. They gave him favourable treatment, which helped to carry him through...It would indeed have been a disaster if the man who had so recently set world opinion agog by claiming to know better than the mighty of the land had himself become involved in bankruptcy. One can imagine the banner headlines. He was never really near such complete disaster...[His publishers] Macmillans...promptly sent him a cheque for £1500. Did he finger it lovingly?...There was the £1500 lying on his desk. It was a just reward. But it was no longer his. It would be paid into his bank and at once paid out again, to swell the balances of those sagacious persons who thought that the mark had a rosy future and the dollar a poor one.[11]

---

11 Harrod, *The Life of John Maynard Keynes*, pp.296–7.

Keynes' assessment of the future of the mark was correct. As he believed, the mark did indeed slither down a precipice. But only after a delay. By 1923, a barrowload of mark notes was needed to buy a loaf of bread. The dollar came to be worth a million marks and resumed its march along a road that would make it the world's dominant currency. Keynes, who 'was temperamentally daring and confident of his own reasoning', 'went deeply in' again and 'by the end of 1924 he reckoned that the value of his assets...was £57,797'.[12] He had been correct. Only his timing had been off. But that initially poor timing could have meant his ruin just as surely as if he'd been totally wrong.

The Keynes experience is instructive in that it demonstrates that huge profits can be made out of currency speculation when rates are volatile — but that the risk of ruinous losses, even for the skilled and well-informed, is real. Not only judgement but also timing must be right. Keynes was a man who could assess a financial and economic situation better than any man alive; but he sometimes thought his judgement would be vindicated next week or next month. When it wasn't proved right for several months, even he faced personal ruin.

The opportunities for currency speculation have grown massively since 1971 and have been internationalised by improved communications enabling huge amounts of money to be instantly traded anywhere. Variations in value can consequently be large and sudden. Will the United States dollar be worth more than 1 Deutschmark 85 next week or next month? Will it slump below DM1.60? Or will it rise above DM2.10? Speculators might see a long-term trend for or against the dollar but they will find it harder to pick short-term fluctuations; and the short-term trends could kill them well before their long-term analysis proves correct.

For example, in the middle of January 1989, the United States current account deficit blew out by a couple of billion dollars compared with the previous month, a result much worse than majority expectations. But what happened? Did the dollar fall, as might have been expected from the weak American payments situation? Not at all. *It rose!* Why? Because the Federal Reserve Board was expected to react to

---

12 Ibid.

the poor current account result by tightening money and pushing interest rates up. Investors would consequently be more eager to buy higher-yielding dollar securities. Through most of January and February and on to April and May, the dollar continued to strengthen and consolidate, forcing periodic central bank intervention by the major economies, selling dollars to hold its value down.

This illustrates the dangers of currency speculation. Should you, therefore, try to pick trends and benefit from fluctuations in currencies? If you have a magic touch — and few of us have! — or like risk, yes. If you have funds you can genuinely spare for what is little more than a gamble, again perhaps yes. But don't risk anything you can't easily afford and think twice before risking what you *can* afford: look around for a more secure investment on which your good judgement can pay better dividends. This applies especially if you're disposed to back your analysis of short-term trends. In the long-term, you might be right, but, as Keynes himself is reported to have said, 'In the long-term, we're all dead.'

There are other ways in which you can speculate on movements in currencies. Deregulation in most Western economies has meant greater freedom for everyone to borrow, lend and spend in other countries. Suppose you want to raise a loan for investment in your own country.

You need, let's say, $100,000. You can borrow that in Dutch guilders or Swiss francs at, say, 7 per cent. If you borrow in Australia (in May 1989), you have to pay between 17 and 20 per cent, depending on the source and purpose of your loan and the security you can offer. Let's say, in any event, that the interest rate in Australia is twice that in Switzerland. Wouldn't you be foolish not to take the loan in Swiss francs? Maybe the answer is yes. But you should consider several factors.

The big consideration is that you'll have to pay interest and repay the loan in Swiss francs. Will the Australian dollar fall in relation to the Swiss franc and, if so, by how much? Over a period of years in the mid-1980s, the Australian dollar lost about half its value *vis á vis* some strong currencies. (So did the United States dollar, with rather different timing.) That meant a loan of $100,000 denominated in Swiss francs became a repayment burden of $200,000. Moreover, interest payments doubled in terms of Australian dollars. The $100,000 loan at 7 per cent became a $200,000 burden, with an effective rate of interest of something like 14 per cent.

Of course, the trend might be in the other direction. Suppose you took out a loan in French francs in early 1988 and repaid it in early 1989. One million French francs was about $250,000 at the earlier date but only about $180,000 at the later date. An interest charge of 10 per cent (FRF100,000) was reduced from $25,000 to about $18,000. So the borrowers got a good deal. But was it a deal that could be relied upon? Or was it just a lucky break?

Some transactions are more complicated. For example, some international bonds in the Australian sector of the Eurobond market have been structured so that they can be redeemed in Australian or United States dollars at the option of the borrower. Interest rates have been generous — in the region of 20 per cent. If the Australian dollar remains steady in relation to the American dollar, lenders get that generous return; if it falls, they do even better; but, if the Australian dollar appreciates against the American dollar, lenders gets a lesser return than 20 per cent — much less than the interest rate for a straight Australian dollar bond if the appreciation is substantial. For lenders, for example, in German marks or Swiss francs or Japanese yen, there is a further exchange risk arising from fluctuations not only between the Australian and American dollars but also between those currencies and the mark, franc or yen. So the less sophisticated investor — the classic 'widow' — could, at least partly from ignorance, run risks with such instruments arising from a possible appreciation of the Australian *vis à vis* the American dollar — and wider fluctuations which might reduce her return in her own non-dollar currency.

What you should aim for in dealing in other currencies and backing your judgement about fluctuations in their value is to operate within large margins for error. You should calculate that, even in the worst scenario, you would still come out on the right side if you borrowed a specific currency at a specific rate for a specific term. If your margins for error are large, you could make a profit, *almost* — but not certainly — no matter what. But if your profit depends on currencies moving only fractionally and relative interest rates similarly moving only inside tight margins, you'd be best advised to restrict your liabilities to those currencies in which you have your assets and cash flow. In recent years, some currencies such as the Australian and the American dollar have been valued not according to the fundamentals of their payments position but according to interest rate margins offering on their domestic and Eurobond financial markets, compared with those of fundamentally sturdier currencies. If the market were to revise its attitudes, giving a heavier weight to fundamentals and a lesser weight to interest rate differentials, the value of what might be called the highly leveraged currencies could fall sharply. That's not a wild, outside chance: markets have shown themselves capable of changing their sentiments dramatically, without much warning and without much regard for what might normally be regarded as sane and relevant economic criteria — or their former irrationality.

As part of this approach but going beyond it, you will always be wise not to borrow in other currencies when your own currency has peaked, especially if its strength depends on high interest rates rather than trade-and-payments fundamentals. If you borrow in other currencies, it will be best to do so when your currency is at its low and fundamentals are likely to cause it to rise in the course of the loan. Again, margins, cycle settings and timing are crucial.

If you develop into a really smart currency operator, you might decide to surrender your amateur status and become a professional currency adviser. Perhaps you could set yourself up in an elegant pad in Paddo, with a view of Sydney Harbour, or in a homestead near Yass from which you can watch your Merinos graze — you don't have to be in a big city — and advise your clients how they should take payment for their exports or pay for their imports. You won't need any grand or expensively equipped office: an ordinary telephone, a fax machine, a personal computer and a steady flow of financial information on to your screen from one of the reliable world-wide agencies will see you through nicely. You can of course deal in currencies on your own or others' behalf, if you want to, but you don't have to; all you need do is advise, let's say, an Australian wine-exporter how to get the best foreign-currency return on his sales. In Europe, should he deal solely in national currencies or have a fling with European Currency Units?

Should he shift his money into yen or marks or American dollars or bring it home pronto? These advisory services are not yet everywhere in demand as much as in Europe and the United States; but the trend is clear so long as currencies remain volatile.

So, if you want a comfortable, interesting and financially rewarding business, that might be the niche for you. There is a possible snag: if governments ever get clever enough to adopt and coordinate their economic policies so that currency fluctuations ameliorate and something of the stability of the period from 1945 to 1971 is restored, most currency advisers will have the rug pulled out from under much of their business.

Commodities

Markets for raw materials — commodities — have always been volatile. Australian wool-growers were enriched by a strong wool market in the late 1830s; but high prices collapsed to throw many into bankruptcy in the early 1840s. Flocks that had represented great wealth suddenly were only worth boiling down for tallow. Cotton boomed during the American Civil War in the 1860s and slumped when the war was over. 'Price levels for basic commodities fell steadily for more than thirty years [after 1866] — the era known as the Great Deflation.'[13] Wheat had been $2.06 a bushel in 1866; it fell as low as 35 cents in the 1890s. Tungsten became a glamour metal when the main source of supply in China was closed off by the success of the communist revolution in 1949; but the boom was brief. Wool sold for £1 a pound during the Korean War in the early 1950s and many other commodities leapt in price; only to decline sharply afterwards.

This volatility makes life hard for producers, though it offers prospects of huge gains to speculators. Many attempts have been made to stabilise commodity prices, mainly through international producer or producer/consumer agreements. One of the most successful of these, the International Tin Agreement, operated by maintaining a buffer stock during the 1960s and 1970s but collapsed in

---

13   Greider, op. cit., p.245.

the 1980s when buffer stock funds were exhausted, causing the price of tin to plunge. The International Natural Rubber Organisation, which, in March 1989, inaugurated its second International Rubber Agreement, is at present robustly healthy; but a series of International Wheat Agreements, which earlier had some success, couldn't survive huge farm supports and subsidies, especially of the European Economic Community after 1963. OPEC (Organisation of Petroleum Exporting Countries) started uncertainly but then controlled production and lifted prices to unprecedented levels in 1973–4 and, after a split in 1976, to much higher levels still in 1979. However, the Organisation's production controls failed and prices slumped from above $30 to below $10 in 1985, recovered to about $18, sank again to about $13 and, in 1989, surged from about $16 to $20 a barrel. The dollar price concealed even greater movements in other currencies, against which the dollar fluctuated wildly between 1979 and 1989. In terms of German marks or Japanese yen, a price of $16 had lost value to be worth only about eight 1985 dollars in early 1989; the price of oil, in marks or yen, was probably lower than at the bottom of the trough in 1985. But then (up to May 1989) the dollar began to surge upwards again.

It is this highly unstable market that provides opportunities for huge profits — and huge losses. You can buy many things from wool to fat lambs, government bonds and turkeys. You can buy around the world, day and night, in London and Chicago and on the Sydney Futures Exchange. Keynes speculated in commodities as well as currencies:

> Towards the end of 1920 he began to take an interest in cotton, and at the beginning of 1921 he opened an account in this commodity and dealt heavily. Then his interests broadened, and we find him trading in lead, tin, copper, spelter, rubber, wheat, sugar, linseed oil and jute. All this dealing was based on a close study of general influences affecting the world markets in each of the commodities. He maintained this active interest until 1937, when he fell ill and decided to abandon it; it was one of the few sacrifices which he made to the clear need for conserving his energies.[14]

---

14 Harrod, op. cit., p.299.

The most spectacular commodity operation in recent years was the attempt by the Hunt brothers to corner the market in silver.

Nelson Bunker Hunt...went after [oil] concessions in Libya; one of the concessions, in which he had a half share, turned out to be a winner...Bunker bought real estate, horse farms, cattle stations, and oil leases in Canada, the US and the North Sea. But he was still left with a great deal of cash, and a New York commodities broker persuaded him to try the silver market. Inflation, he said, was bound to grow worse and this, combined with the unsettled outlook for the world in general, was sure to boost the price of silver. Bunker's brother Herbert agreed to join him in the venture and they began to buy. They did quite well at first, and it encouraged them to step up their purchases.

Meanwhile,...Colonel Ghadaffi, the country's young revolutionary leader, was threatening to nationalise the oilfields, and by May 1973 Bunker had lost the principal source of his wealth. He decided to plunge more deeply into silver. During the next few years the brothers built up by far the largest private hoard in the world. They failed in a bid to acquire a silver mine, but managed to convince a group of rich Arabs that they would stand to gain considerably by joining them in a silver-buying partnership. The price went up and up, and in January 1980 it hit an all-time peak of $50 an ounce. Bunker's judgment appeared to have been triumphantly vindicated. But profits remain paper profits until one sells — and the brothers did not sell. On the contrary, they went on buying. Silver started to fall, partly because so many people were selling their family silverware for scrap and partly because other speculators were getting out. By mid-March the price was down to $21 an ounce. The brothers were still showing a handsome profit on their earlier purchases, but they had taken a beating in the futures market and on the silver they had bought when prices were much higher.

Playing with futures — the buying and selling of commodities to be delivered in the future — has been compared to 'climbing aboard a big dipper which has no brakes and no seat belts'. You put down 10 or 15 per cent with your order, and hope for the best. If it comes off, the rewards are impressive, but if it doesn't, losses can mount rapidly. You also face further cash calls, to keep the 'margin' at the same percentage. The brothers were getting margin calls for millions of dollars a day and they did not have the necessary cash. When the news leaked out, the silver price dropped still further, to just over $10 an ounce. The Hunts were bailed out by a consortium of banks, who put together a massive loan, but they had to mortgage most of their possessions, including their homes, cars, horses and paintings. And they were forced to appear before congressional committees to answer the charge that they had attempted to 'corner, squeeze, or manipulate the silver market'. The media, not surprisingly, gave them a rough ride...[15]

Operations on a Hunt brothers' scale can threaten damage to the banking and financial system even of an economy as huge and fundamentally sound as that of the United States. On 26 March 1980, a representative of Bache Halsey, the second largest brokerage house in the United States, called the Chairman of the Federal Reserve Board, Paul Volcker, out of a meeting of the Board of Governors to plead for his intervention: the Hunts couldn't meet margin calls and, 'if something didn't happen', 'Bache would be wiped out'. The next day, known as 'silver Thursday',[16] the price of silver plunged from $15.80 to $10.80 an ounce. Some people feared a major financial panic. If the price fell below $7, the Hunts' collateral would be worth less than the hundreds of millions of dollars banks had lent them for their speculation. On Friday, 28 March, a temporary price resurgence saved Bache and some others but a new crisis loomed:

...the Hunts had bought futures contracts for silver totaling 19 million ounces from Engelhard, the giant international minerals firm. Futures were normally used as a hedge against sudden price changes, an agreement to pay a certain price six or nine months later when the commodities were delivered. But futures could also be a high-risk gamble — betting that the

---

15 Davis, op. cit., pp.31–2.
16 Greider, *Secrets of the Temple*, pp.145.

price would be higher in the future. The Hunts lost their bet. Delivery was due on Monday, March 31, and Engelhard was demanding cash for its silver — $665 million.[17]

If the Hunts defaulted, the price of silver would crash and outstanding bank loans with it.

While the bank loans to the Hunts were huge — $800 million in total — they were not in themselves enough to threaten the banking structure. But, if the Hunts defaulted to Engelhard, the consequent repercussions might 'set off a general panic among investors, pulling their huge deposits out of the exposed banks like First Chicago and threatening their liquidity'.[18] On Sunday evening, 30 March,

> the bankers held an all-night bargaining session with the Hunts and Engelhard representatives. The negotiations led ultimately to the terms for a private bail-out — a new loan of $1.1 billion from thirteen banks which would extinguish the Hunts' old debts, give them the means to settle with Engelhard and stretch out their obligations over ten years. Paul Volcker was down the hall in another hotel room...In the end, with certain provisos, he blessed the transaction...[19]

Keynes' successes and the Hunts' spectacular failure spanned an era during which commodity trading became a major activity in exchanges around the world, particularly in Britain and North America. In 1988, the worst drought in North America since the 1930s pushed the trading volume at Chicago's MidAmerica Commodity Exchange up nearly half as much again as in the previous year, setting an all-time record with nearly three and a half million contracts. Similar expansion marked other exchanges; and a general resurgence of commodity prices that was already under way before the drought of 1988 reinvigorated trading everywhere. So commodities are a field for you to know and perhaps to cultivate.

But the Hunt brothers' experience demonstrated dramatically that, although the opportunities are tempting

---

17 Ibid., p. 190–1
18 Ibid., p. 190–1
19 Ibid., p. 190–1

and volumes can be huge, commodity trading carries risks of severe losses, even when the downside potential seems small. The essence of commodity trading is that there should be such risks: the commodities are those most widely traded with highly fluctuating prices. Some commodities, those most frequently traded in the largest volumes, have their special exchanges: Chicago for grains, cattle, pork-bellies and a wide range of farm products; the London Metal Exchange for non-precious metals; the London Commodity Exchange for cocoa, coffee, spices, vegetable oils, sugar and jute; London and Manchester for wool; London for tea and rubber (Plantation House), diamonds (Hatton Gardens), furs (Beaver House), and grains (the Baltic Exchange).

Commodity futures may be traded like shares, through a broker, such as Merrill Lynch, the large American broking firm with branch offices throughout the world. Those who deal in futures are producers and users of particular commodities, looking for greater security, and speculators in those commodities, looking for gains but also providing what can reasonably be seen as a useful service. By providing a link between producers and users, speculators can be seen as a kind of insurer. They absorb the risk associated with price fluctuations and take the profit if their judgement is vindicated by the future movement of prices.

The mechanism of futures trading can be described fairly simply. Each commodity has a specific trading unit which represents the quantity of the commodity covered by one futures contract. It is unwise to trade in fractions of a contract, because of the difficulty in disposing of extra fractions, which makes for higher prices for what is actually bought. (It is the same with the barter contracts used by Comecon countries to avoid paying out hard currency. They have to rely on experts to dispose of the unwanted fractions.) The orders to buy or sell futures contracts may be placed with any member of the various commodity exchanges in Britain or North America...Attention should also be paid to reports in *The Wall Street Journal* or the *Financial Times*. The section on British commodity prices in the latter journal is...particularly good...because it provides not only prices but also specific amounts traded, from one ounce to ten tonnes, depending on the commodity. American prices are also given on the same page.[20]

But don't imagine commodity trading is easy. Keynes knew it wasn't; the Hunts learned it wasn't — the hard way. This was confirmed in the middle of 1984, when an Australian investment advisory service put forward a 'Sugar Commodity Trading Plan' to its clients, prefacing its proposals with an appraisal of 'Risks and Rewards':

> All investors and market traders have heard of the potential fortunes to be made out of commodity trading. The financial press abounds with advertisements promising glittering riches and quite unbelievable returns on investment funds by a vast range of complex commodity trading schemes.
>
> What is not so often pointed out is that statistically about 85 per cent of investors who trade the commodity markets lose money.
>
> Commodity trading is probably the most speculative investment medium available and for most but the absolute professionals is a sure-fire way of losing money.
>
> You must therefore understand that the very nature of the investment which involves a small deposit on a Commodity contract with large borrowings (high gearing), whilst offering high rewards, carries high risk. So before you invest money in any commodity trading system you must accept the high risk of losing all the money you invest.
>
> With this understanding, we draw your attention to a situation in the Sugar market that appears unique and where a profit potential for a minimum outlay looks most appealing.
>
> We have designed a Commodity Trading Plan incorporating Sugar that limits investors' risk to $1050, or any multiple of this figure you can afford to speculate.[21]

This was as maturely honest an introduction to the plan as anyone could have wished. The main premises of the plan were that (1) the price of sugar had fallen to a twelve-year low; (2) the contract had been divided into tenths so that the risk could be limited to about $1000, thus bringing

---

20 Purcell, *Private Investment,* pp.73–4.

21 'The Sugar Commodity Trading Plan', A Commodity Research Project by Paul Terry Commodities Pty Ltd, June 1984.

it within the scope of many more small investors; and (3) the October 1985 contract would be bought, anticipating a price of 8.4 cents a pound US sixteen months ahead. Over a two-year period, a price of about 10 cents a pound was needed for the investor 'to break even'.[22]

Let's take a look at some of the commentary. The authors of the Plan argued that the price of sugar in *real terms* was at an all-time low, 5.5 cents a pound US compared with 3.5 cents in the depths of the Great Depression in the 1930s. This price, below cost of production, had already forced closure of some mills in Puerto Rico, Jamaica and the Philippines. Use of sugar as 'a viable alternative energy source', especially in Brazil, would lift demand. So 'the downside risk is probably about as small as one could hope any risk to be' and 'the upside potential should be rewarding'. Sugar had reached a high of 66 cents a pound US in 1974 and 45.5 cents in 1980. If it reached 66 cents again, a $1000 investment would grow to $7000.

The authors of the Plan were honest and perceptive. But the sugar price didn't go up; it went down — to 3 cents, in real or nominal terms the lowest ever. Later it rose, but didn't reach 10 cents a pound US until 1988 and in early 1989 dipped below 10 cents before rising shakily above 14 cents. Even so, allowing for inflation and the decline in the value of the United States dollar, it was probably selling in 1989 for as little as in 1984.

So what if you had invested in 'The Sugar Commodity Trading Plan'? When your contract terminated in October 1985 you wouldn't have lost all your money but you probably would have lost half of it and, if you'd continued to roll over your investment, you'd have found it hard to make any money in the five years until 1989, if then. You would have done much better to put your money elsewhere. There was one saving grace: unlike the Hunt brothers, investors under the Sugar Commodity Trading Plan did *not* buy their futures on margin. They paid the full price for their contracts at the outset; that, according to the Plan, 'is the limit of your liability; there will be no margin calls'.

The sugar debacle is a cautionary tale, though not the whole commodity story. A closer analysis needs to be made

---

22 Ibid.

of what might be possible by following commodities carefully and engaging in knowledgeable, disciplined trading. The *Wall Street Journal* and the *Financial Times* contain excellent daily reports on commodity markets. (So do the *Australian Financial Review* and a few other top-flight financial and economic newspapers around the world.) The *Financial Times* gives a summary report daily on commodity markets in London and New York. The London report has a rundown of prices on the London Metal Exchange (LME), as well as on markets for 'softs'. The US report covers much the same range, although perhaps with more emphasis on grains, beef, pork and oil markets.

You can mine a rich lode of statistical information on the daily commodity page of the *Wall Street Journal,* which gives cash or spot prices applying to sales for immediate delivery, as well as futures prices, over a wide range of commodities, under such headings as grains and oilseeds, livestock and meat, food and fiber, metals and petroleum, wood and precious metals. Reports cover the American markets — Chicago Board of Trade, Chicago Mercantile Exchange, Commodity Exchange New York, New York Cotton Exchange, New York Mercantile Exchange and so on — as well as London, Liverpool, Winnipeg, Sydney, Paris and other markets. Like the *Financial Times*, the *Wall Street Journal* publishes commodity indexes — Dow Jones Futures, Dow Jones Spot, Reuter United Kingdom and CRB Futures — which show broad trends in commodity prices over time.

Commodity markets are subject to a range of influences. Agricultural and pastoral commodities are affected by weather, especially in the major producing areas. A severe and persistent drought in the inland areas of Australia will have a major impact on merino flocks and thus on the supply and ultimately the price of fine wools. Long spells of dry, hot weather at crucial times in the great grain belt of North America will affect wheat, maize and soybean prices and these will carry over to affect beef prices, perhaps lowering them in the short-term as cattle are brought to market prematurely and then raising them sharply as cattle numbers fall for subsequent selling seasons. A strike in Canada might affect nickel prices; political instability in Chile or Zimbabwe might threaten copper supplies; or a sudden surge in demand for stainless steel might dramatically lift the markets for its basic materials.

In July 1989, the Chicago Board of Trade took action to frustrate what it thought was an attempt to corner the market in soybeans. As a result, on 19 July, the *Wall Street Journal* reported that 'fallout spread from the squeeze scare in the soybean pit' to other grain markets. This is the sort of tersely colourful language often employed with quaint directness in commodity markets. What are 'softs'? 'Short covering in the cattle'? 'Cash premium over three-month metal'? 'Taken off LME warrant'? Or 'arbitrage selling'? They are just market jargon, none of which is difficult. 'Softs' (food items) are distinguished from the metals. 'Short covering in the cattle' means that some traders bought for delivery in the near future to ensure against loss from (that is, to hedge against) possible movements in cattle prices. A 'cash premium over three-month metal' means that the market required buyers for immediate delivery to pay more than for metal three months ahead when prices were expected to be lower. But, the report said, this premium was diminishing; the present and future markets were evening out. 'Taken off LME warrant' means that some nickel had not been reported to the London Metal Exchange, in an attempt to mislead the market that stocks had fallen. The market wasn't fooled and wrote prices down. 'Arbitrage selling' means that sellers took advantage of differing prices on a couple of markets, perhaps buying low in London to sell at a higher price in New York. The effect of arbitrage trading is to eliminate a price differential and establish equilibrium. A new breed of 'arbitrageurs' have emerged in recent years, more aggressive and playing for higher stakes than those in the older tradition.

> The arbs are descendants of the classic traders who have taken advantage of price discrepancies in different markets as long as there have been markets. If apples sold for 15 cents apiece in New York and 12 cents in Connecticut, why not go into the apple business, buy in Connecticut, sell in New York, and pocket the 3-cent difference? If you did, you were an arbitrageur, an arb.
> The game sweeping Wall Street [in the 1980s], 'risk arbitrage', involves the stocks of companies targeted for

acquisition. The stock market is one of the two markets for these stocks, and the takeover offer price is the other. Buy on the stock market now, sell to the acquirer at a higher price under his offer, which expires a month or so hence, and pocket the difference.

The 'risk' in risk arbitrage is that the acquirer might decide (or be compelled legally) not to consummate the deal. That risk is why the market price of a takeover target's stock is lower than the acquirer's offer price. Once the news of the impending takeover has been reflected on the stock market, the difference usually is only 5 per cent or so. However, nowadays, would-be acquirers are commonly setting their prices as much as 50 per cent or more above the target's preannouncement price in the market. So, risk arbitrageurs getting wind of an impending deal ahead of the announcement can make a killing.[23]

Some of the commodity trade jargon is amusing. What is 'stale bull liquidation'? Those dispirited bulls had been buying for a rise; but they've become bored with waiting. They've gone 'stale' and decided to 'liquidate' — to sell off their holdings.

How can we sum up commodity markets? There's money to be made out of them — quite a lot. One analyst concluded that:

The best year-on-year [investment] results [in 1987–8] would have been achieved by buying commodities...a US sugar contract or a soybean contract...would have doubled the original $A investment. It was very much a case of buy the commodity, not the stock: CSR's share rose only a modest 15 per cent in 1987–88...Anyone who picked the boom in aluminium would similarly have done better investing in a New York contract (which gained two-thirds in $A terms) rather than in Comalco shares, which rose 27.5 per cent.[24]

But all that was in hindsight.

Losses can be made, too — very big ones. So go easy. Don't emulate the Hunt brothers. If you think you have the

23 Metz, op. cit., p.16.
24 *Australian Financial Review,* Sydney, 1 July 1988.

talent, try to emulate John Maynard Keynes. But remember even he sometimes boobed. So you'll win some; and you'll lose some too. Even your 'certainties' — *vide* the Sugar Commodity Trading Plan — can bomb out. So don't put too many eggs in any one commodity basket. Study the markets as Keynes did: he took a good look at cotton in 1920 before acting in 1921; and, as he entered other markets, he knew what they were all about. That didn't mean he always won; but he minimised his chances that error would be the product of ignorance.

> The true speculator [said Bernard Baruch], 'is one who observes the future and acts before it occurs. Like a surgeon, he must be able to search through a mass of complex and contradictory details to the significant facts. Then, still like a surgeon, he must be able to operate coldly, clearly and skilfully on the basis of the facts before him.[25]

However, while you're gathering the facts, always remember that, in commodity markets, as with stocks and currencies, the fundamentals are not always decisive, especially in the short-term. Much more important will be your capacity to read the minds of those who operate in the markets: their penchant for Micawberism or blind pessimistic panic, their phlegmatic shrugging off the bad news or their disbelief about the good, in other words, their almost invincible irrationality about almost anything. You often need to be a market psychologist rather than a rationalist.

However great your talent as a psychologist or clairvoyant, you can't keep track of the whole range of traded commodities all the time. You'll have to choose a few that appeal to you — especially those that titillate your instincts for profit. Let's take a couple of examples. At the beginning of 1989, palladium looked like a metal with a future. Ford were talking of using it in their new catalysators instead of platinum. A remarkable experiment was reported to have achieved cold nuclear fusion, using heavy water and palladium. Already demand for the metal had pushed prices up, fairly dramatically. Both the Ford and the cold-

---

25 Davis, op. cit., p.222.

fusion prospects contained a lot of blue sky, especially the cold-fusion 'breakthrough' whose practical application must, at best, be years away and for which some better or cheaper substitute for palladium might be found. So, despite these promising speculative elements, and although fundamentals seem good, you'd be wise to study the market and carefully assess the blue sky and market responses to it before rushing too heavily into palladium.

What about gold? In calendar year 1988, a troy ounce of gold lost 2.3 per cent of its value compared with the previous year. Not much — and far better than the slump in gold shares after the October 1987 crash. Gold fundamentals remained good. But the Metals and Minerals Research Services consultancy group estimated that gold output in 1993 would be 1,780 tons, 60 per cent up on 1983. Not all sources would contribute to that increased output: the huge increase in Australian production in the last few years 'could halve in the next five years. By 1993 over half the mines operating today may be closed. Only a handful will be producing into the next century'.[26] To offset that, however, United States, Canadian and other mines will probably expand production, lifting world output by 4.5 per cent a year up to 1993. Does that herald a spectacular fall in the gold price between now and 1993? Perhaps. But not necessarily. By the middle of 1989, gold had slipped $20 to $40 below $US400 and no guarantees could be given that it wouldn't slide lower or quickly again break above $400.

Another authority, the Gold Institute, which has an interest in identifying a strong gold market, concluded that, although gold output increased by 9 per cent from 1,298 tonnes in 1987 to 1,415 tonnes in 1988, there was no over-supply. More than 1,200 tonnes was absorbed in the Indian sub-continent, south-east Asia and Japan. Industrial demand for gold remained steady at about 1,589 tonnes, supply from scrap fell and so did supplies from communist countries.

What then does the future really hold? The gold price will depend on several factors: discovery of new mines, supply from all mines taking account of new processes for recovery of the metal, industrial demand, use of gold as a

---

26 *World Gold Supply over the Next Five Years and Beyond,* by MMRS, London.

store of value whether for personal security or for national reserves and backing for the currency, trends in inflation which will turn people towards gold or, if prices fall and currencies strengthen, reduce incentives to hold gold. You'll need to weigh all these factors carefully if you decide to play the gold commodity market, to buy low and hold for a rise or sell forward hoping for a fall. Should you buy gold in ingot or other metal form or gold shares? Past experience suggests that a sharp lift in the gold price pushes gold shares up even further; when the gold price falls, gold shares fall faster and deeper than the metal. So you'll need to make judgements both about trends in the gold price and whether shares are a better bet than bullion.

When you've selected your favourite commodities, spread your risks over them and over time. Never have so much running on anything that you could be badly hurt if your judgement proves wrong. And don't take your eye off the ball. Read the commodity reports and keep 'full bottle' on the broad economic environment. The hog cycle might be a cycle in its own right but it operates within or alongside broader economic cycles. The supply of hogs might rise and fall but the hog market can be affected too from the demand side, for example, if fashions move from pork to beef to chickens and back again or if, though traditional consumers move away from pork to beef, large populations in, say, former developing countries, change their eating habits to buy more meat, including pork. Keep your eye too on those strikes in Peru — but don't get carried away by them. Strikes have a habit of being settled and the impact on supplies and prices is often less dramatic than the market's fantasies. Get out before the market, on sudden good news, leaves you holding an armful of copper you can dispose of only at bargain prices.

Some commentators suggest that commodity trading is the best way to get rich quickly. Perhaps it is. But you need to be lucky, often in a million-dollar lottery way. Commodity trading is not as totally dependent on luck as a lottery. You *can* apply knowledge and judgement. But you must acquire knowledge and get used to exercising judgement. Even then, as we've already shown, the most formidable traders slip. Recently, China, so new to capitalist ways, established Sinochem to trade in oil futures. This round-the-clock operation by the Chinese to make money on trends in oil prices lacks enough qualified traders and is desperately short on experience. They could, one commentator suggests, 'be chopped off at the knees' as market movements prove too much for them. What could happen to Beijing's government traders could happen to you: China could be you writ large a billion times.

So treat any commodity trading as only one of a cluster of investment vehicles available to you. Keep a wise balance among your various investment operations, shifting the balance from time to time among shares, property, commodities, currencies and the rest as you see changes emerging in specific circumstances, as well as in political, economic and social trends, at home and overseas, which could affect fundamentals or fashions in demand and supply.

Leverage and Delegated Investment

Some investment procedures may appeal because they seem to add to the leverage of the small operator — to increase your muscle power, particularly in handling investment spreads — but, in reality, they delegate investment decisions to others. They enable small investors to abdicate most of their responsibility. They're for the fearful and defensive: 'Why stick your neck out?' one property trust asks.

That doesn't mean these investment procedures cannot have value. Millions of investors participate in at least some of them. But investors who want to make the most of their opportunities — that's you — should examine them carefully before committing any substantial part of their resources to them. Remember you aim to be a millionaire, a part-time but independently thoughtful quasi-entrepreneur, not a mealy-spirited drudge slavishly following the judgement of others.

What are the main examples of delegated responsibility?

Mutual Funds: Unit Trusts

Mutual funds, called unit trusts in some countries, are a device through which small investors can get a stake in a spread of companies and, if desired, in a spread of countries or regions. The essence of the system is that the managers sell units in the fund, and the proceeds are used to buy shares in companies the managers favour. The fund might be $1 million. With that million dollars, the managers buy shares in, say fifty companies. Some governments require that managers put no more than, say, 5 per cent of the fund into any one stock, so that the risk is spread. Managers might select domestic shares or, for example, spread purchases over Western Europe or Asia or North America, identifying the fund accordingly. You can have a Select Japan, Select US or Select Europe Fund, a First America, First Japan or First Europe Fund, a Japan Growth Trust, a Japan and Pacific Fund, a choice of seventeen offshore investment funds or even a choice of 'tracker' funds, which buy into such a range of stocks that they become virtually stock exchange index funds. Such funds 'track' the index — the local, the national or, for example, a world index. Some of the trusts publish a 'Guide for the Investor' giving an account of a wide range of unit, mortgage, share and 'planned income' investments.

An essential feature of all the plans is that some 'expert' takes responsibility for managing others' investments. Another essential feature, implied in what has just been said, is that fund managers have the authority to buy and sell shares according to their own, largely unfettered judgement of market trends. A conference on superannuation funds in Sydney in May 1989 suggested that trustees had unloaded too much of their responsibility on to fund managers and had done too little in formulating investment strategies.

Some funds run ambiguous advertisements, for example, 'You have a portfolio of £10,000 or more. How much interest do you expect?' The interest turns out not to be interest payments to the investor but interest taken by the fund in the investor's affairs. The claim is that the smaller investor will not get red-carpet treatment from a stockbroker but that 'the individual' will get 'a high level of service and attention' from the fund. What does that mean? Nothing is spelt out. In fact, the fund managers decide what shares to buy without consulting the unit-holders and vary the portfolio according to their own judgement. When the time comes for the unit-holder to sell, the only 'interest' you can expect is to be asked how many units you want to dispose of and to be told the bid price and, if relevant, the cancellation price for your units. Do unit-fund managers show more 'interest' than a stockbroker in framing a portfolio to suit an individual unit-holder's needs? Each investor must form his own judgement. But, on the face of it, it seems unlikely.

Having bought, let's say, a million dollars worth of shares, the fund is divided into units to be purchased by investors who thus become unit-holders. You might note that, without implying that the arrangement won't benefit the unit-holder, it certainly stands to benefit the fund organisers. One financial adviser, writing in support of unit trusts, says:

> Imagine that you were a bright entrepreneur and you were making heaps of money buying shares or properties and reselling them at a profit. After a time you decide you could make a lot more money with extra capital so you ask some friends if they would like to contribute to a common fund which you would manage on their behalf. Profits would be retained in the fund to make it grow faster and for your time and expertise you would expect the fund to pay you a management fee.[27]

The question is whether you want to be 'a bright entrepreneur' and make 'heaps of money' — which could lose you your amateur status — or whether you want to hand over your money to 'a bright entrepreneur' so that he can make 'a lot more money'. Of course, as the financial adviser goes on to say, 'everybody', including those who hand their money over to the 'bright entrepreneur' might, 'do very well' — or 'everybody could lose their money'. A great deal depends on keeping your fingers crossed and hoping the 'bright entrepreneur' is bright *in the way that you want him to be.*

Each unit-holder who buys into a trust will, in effect, have a share in twenty or fifty or whatever number of domestic and/or overseas companies. Your risk is spread and your investment will be managed by self-styled 'experts' — the 'bright entrepreneur' or, if that man of talent is or becomes

---

27 Whittaker, *Making Money Made Simple,* p.216.

an organiser or trustee rather than a manager, then by a manager whom he and perhaps his colleagues appoint. Some financial advisers accord these managers — faceless men, for the most part — something like superhuman powers, far beyond the capacities of the 'average', individual investor. But the managers are not necessarily as experienced and gifted as the unit-holders are led to imagine, although competition among mutual funds should lift the level of competence. The unit-holder has an asset which can be sold at any time and thus retains relatively high liquidity. The market establishes an offer price for the units — the price at which units may be bought; a bid price — the price at which units may be sold; and a cancellation price — the price, usually below the bid price, which is the minimum permissible price to be paid for units offered to the fund for sale by holders.

The principal disadvantages of mutual funds/unit trusts are that as a unit-holder you put yourself entirely in the hands of the fund managers. You can sell your units but, if the managers perform badly or the market turns down, you could lose heavily. (Some Australian trusts, listed and unlisted, have not performed well and have suffered heavy losses. They should not necessarily be taken as typical but their performance should be kept in mind as examples of what might happen.) Some contend that mutual funds have the virtue that, although they perform more modestly than leaders in a bull market, they fall less sharply when the bears arrive. This was not borne out in the October 1987 crash. Keep in mind too that, though fund managers are not infallible, they are more assured of income from fund earnings than you are and their rewards are usually considerable. It follows that the fees you must pay to the fund are often high, although these should be set against commissions you would have to pay in independently conducted share and property transactions.

Unit trusts are a creation to make investment easy for the small investor who wants to abdicate responsibility but they also provide a lucrative living and considerable financial power for those who control and manage the trusts. As I've said, costs can be high. Most trusts are widely advertised in the financial press. Glossy prospectuses are the norm. In the end, the unit-holders must bear all these costs: there is no other source of funds. The earnings of the trust are therefore watered down, while, at the same time, the balance of soundness against risk might remain much the same as if you had formed your own investment judgements and made your outlays directly on your own behalf. The unit-trust managers tend to choose the less speculative stocks, the market leaders for which conservative critics would find it more difficult to belabour their judgement. However, market leaders often are low-income, low-growth stocks, but subject to market fluctuations as much as newcomer high-income and/or high-growth stocks. Unit managers tend to wind their investments down to lowest-common-denominator 'safe' stocks in a way that almost guarantees that unit-holders will benefit poorly from their investment. Where they have been more venturesome, as with some Australian property trusts, their adventures have tended to turn out badly.

Finally, we might note the harsh but not unfair judgement of some detached observers that the competence of most professional fund managers and investors is modest and that many indeed do more harm than good. One experienced commentator goes so far as to say that the clients of most would have done better 'by appointing a monkey to select a broad portfolio of shares at random'.[28] That might be a libellous judgement but it might balance any tendency to regard fund managers as superhuman — or for the client to think that a fair average competence in making his own investments is beyond him.

Investment Trusts

Much the same applies to investment trusts, which differ from mutual funds/unit trusts in that the funds contributed by small investors do not have to be spread so widely, for example, with a maximum of 5 per cent for any one share, and can be invested not only on the stock market but also in real estate and other markets. Investment trusts are also normally permitted to indulge themselves in extensive leverage: that is, unlike mutual funds, managers of investment trusts are permitted to borrow funds to enlarge

---

28 *Financial Times*, 14 January 1989.

the scale and scope of investments. This leverage offers potential for much higher returns but also entails greater risk if the managers are less competent or the markets in which they have invested turn down.

So huge is the actual and potential demand that mutual funds/unit and investment trusts are the subject of much hard-sell advertising. That in itself should be enough to make you cautious, if not cynical: advertisers must think there's a good deal in it for them. The trusts or funds vary quite widely in composition, although the fundamentals are much the same. In Australia, Westpac Banking Corporation has a Mortgage Trust and, for rolling over lump-sum superannuation payments, an Approved Deposit Fund. Perpetual Trustees have four 'Common Funds' — a Mortgage Fund, a Group Property Fund, an At Call Common Fund and a High Income Approved Deposit Fund, all of which are 'like unit trusts in that your money is pooled and invested by Perpetual on your behalf'. Equitilink has a Growthlink Trust and a Worldlink Trust. There are many, many more. Nowadays, a useful portion of media revenue must come from financial institutions promoting a multitude of investment vehicles. These are largely for the uninitiated. The 'little fellow' who's never really had much money and is open-mouthed in amazement, for example, at the size of his superannuation payout, must be overwhelmed by it all. He thinks he can't possibly handle his financial affairs and he's terrified by what he often rightly conceives to be his tenuous hold on financial security. That promises a bonanza for the financial institutions, most of them eminently respectable, but some of them of doubtful competence.

Claims are often sweeping and tendentious, suggesting for example, that the small investor, with something like $50 a month, can take on and give a licking to the stockmarket. You'll have a stake, they say, in great multinational Japanese, American, British and French companies — but you won't have to do any 'hard work'. All the decision-making on what shares to buy and when will be done by the fund managers — without worrying you. Charges made by the funds are compared favourably with those made by stockbrokers. Past performance is highlighted, although a sometimes compulsory disclaimer can be made to the effect that the past is no necessary guide to the future and values can go down as well as up.

All of this is valid enough, although it gives a glossy picture of the investment status of and opportunities for the contributor. The impression is sometimes given that he will become something of a big-time operator, that he can fundamentally change his financial status with small outlays at small cost. This isn't really true. The little fellow who puts his money into these funds remains a little fellow — indeed without even the clout of the small shareholder who buys directly.

Advertisements properly emphasise the advantages to many investors, for example, of delegating investment decisions to fund managers. Some advertisements acknowledge that their competence is vital: the 'experience and the stock-picking expertise of our fund managers will be crucial to catch the early gains in the run up to [the single European market in] 1992'. But the wording is careful: it *implies* that its fund managers are brilliant but makes no explicit claims. Other claims, for example, that 'many investment professionals have been known to choose [the particular plan] for themselves', nicely fuzz anything too specific.

Sometimes, the managers ignore both those opportunities which are too exciting and those which are too dull. Over the calendar year 1988, many fund managers kept away from and others bought only sparingly into the Japanese share market because they were afraid, looking at high price-earnings ratios and low dividend yields, that they might be caught in an abrupt market correction. They both cut their participation and, when they bought at all, selected 'safe' stocks. Both approaches caused their funds to underperform. Fund managers in Britain also ignored property which, early in the 1980s had languished, but which, after 1985, boomed. Boredom with a flat property market in the past thus carried over into an unboring market in the present. Again, this caused their units to underperform. Admittedly, fund managers should not too readily be drawn into exciting or overheated situations nor should they too readily allow themselves to be sucked into a property boom which, in the nature of things, cannot last forever. But the underperformance of funds in relation to

Japanese shares and British property underlines the caution which is characteristic of fund managers and their inflexibility in moving investments around to take advantage of profitable situations. Individuals with a modicum of common sense, energy and flair are likely to perform much better in pursuit of their own interests.

Most advertisements emphasise the advantages of 'expert' delegated investment, while glossing over costs. Avoidance of brokers' commissions is not clearly set against costs of fund management, which are usually described as 'low'. However, initial and continuing management costs can be high, without that being immediately evident to the investor. So you need to read the fine print carefully before buying units.

Some funds tend to polish up their past performance by choosing a statistically favourable time-range. The claim might be made that the fund increased by more than 100 per cent over, let's say, a five-year period from the beginning of 1984 to the end of 1988. But many stockmarkets were subdued in early 1984 and had made a substantial recovery from the October 1987 crash by the end of 1988. The picture would not have been so rosy for the period from the beginning of 1987 to the end of 1988. We all know how politicians, public servants and others in the business of tranquillising the public mind, select statistics sensitively to advance a particular cause or demolish the opposition. Perfectly respectable people do it. So avoid being too easily gulled by statistical claims of fund managers and others in the financial services field.

Incidentally, if instead of putting your money into the fund above which doubled over five years, you had put your money on deposit with a bank, compound interest would have taken $100 to $161 at 10 per cent and nearly $200 at 15 per cent over the five years. So the fund's performance, though not too bad, was far from brilliant; and simple deposit with a bank would have been relatively risk-free.

In the six months following the October 1987 crash, confidence in unit trusts declined sharply. In Britain, funds were reduced by more than a fifth. Losses and consequent loss of expectations might take the funds years to recover. As a consequence, early in 1989, a prominent multinational insurance group launched an equity fund which *guaranteed* investors against loss. This warranty seemed to be iron-clad. And so in a sense it was. But the guarantee had to be paid for. There was no annual management charge as such; but, as well as an initial charge of 5 per cent, the promoters kept all the income from the fund. Just how much this would be would depend on how well funds were invested but could reasonably be expected to average around 5 per cent a year — and the promoters might have been tempted into high-income rather than high-growth stocks.

Whether or not they were, a further question was whether you — the unit-buyer — would get some bonus by way of capital gains or whether you could look forward to no more than the guaranteed return of your original outlay — reduced in real terms by inflation as the years passed. Again, the result would depend on how well funds were invested — and prevailing market conditions. However, if the stockmarket were in a bull phase, you would be likely to do better by buying equities directly yourself, rather than rely on the choices of the fund managers, who would in addition take all the income from their choices. In a falling market, you'd do better to have your money somewhere else, even deposited passively at a good rate of interest in a bank. So guarantees might settle your nerves but somewhere down the road you might find that you would have done much better, with little if any more nervous tension, by declining their dubious solace — as well as the equally dubious solace of having fund managers make your choices for you.

Regulatory authorities in some countries require fund advertisers to include warnings of the 'Smoking can be a health hazard' kind. These sometimes simply acknowledge that 'the past is no guide to the future and shares can go down as well as up'. In Britain, such fine-print warnings are mandatory and are frequently expanded to: 'the price of units and the income from them may go down as well as up and is not guaranteed. You should regard your investment as long-term'. Some explicitly declare their advertisement to have been 'approved by an authorised person under the Financial Services Act 1986'. Others are still more detailed, especially where the 'scheme' might have special characteristics, for example:

There is no recognised market for shares subscribed for under the Scheme. Both property values and the rental income from property may fluctuate. Prospective investors will be advised to consult their professional advisers prior to investment in the Scheme...

Mutual funds/unit trusts and investment, including cash management trusts, will appeal most to those wanting to abdicate responsibility for their own investment. Even they — the ones who feel they can't cope — might do better simply to deposit their money with a bank in a way that gives them a clear and assured margin above current inflation. (The Bank of New Zealand claims unequivocally that its 'Smarter Cheque Account pays higher interest than cash management trusts'.) So if you aim to maximise growth and income you should think carefully before you put your money into managed trusts. Unless you are already so rich that your aspirations to join or advance within the ranks of the millionaires have already been satisfied, you are likely to do much better by accepting responsibility for your own investments.[29]

Investment Clubs

One form of leverage which is also, in part, an abdication of responsibility, is the investment club. As discussed earlier, association with small or large investors of like interest can be valuable. For the most part, these will be informal associations, of value largely for an easygoing exchange of information. On no account should the exchanges be limited; on the contrary, they should be enlarged as you gather confidence and understanding and as you can make more of communicating with all sorts of people. The maturity you gain as an investor should help you place sounder valuations on specific exchanges, so that you will act on or give weight to some and discard other information

---

29 In general, my advice to investors is not to hand over responsibility for the management of their money to any persons or groups unless they can see special advantages in doing so, or unless they have insufficient time to devote to such management themselves. Modern computer techniques permit small groups, and even individuals, to operate as efficiently, or more efficiently, than much larger entities, and this fact should not be forgotten (Hugh Dominic Purcell, *Private Investment: Microeconomics at the Personal Level*, p.12).

as worthless. That is an essential part of the process of successful investment. However, investment clubs normally purport to do more than this.

Investment clubs may be formed which take on more the character and form of an amateur mutual fund. Under such an arrangement, a small number of club members, say, up to ten or twelve, might meet regularly to discuss and decide which shares to buy. They can buy stock in larger volume, so perhaps reducing brokers' commissions. They are also able to spread their risks. However, investment clubs suffer from the problems of all committees: uneven competence and wide variations in the active interest of members, impatience by some and undue caution by others and a tendency, through lack of information or discipline, to pay insufficient attention to fundamentals. It has been suggested that investment clubs can be successful if they follow some general rules:

1. There should be a concentration on convertible bonds, and once bought, these should never be sold unless their capital value makes conversion of the bonds worthwhile.

2. No stock should ever be bought on a 'hot tip'.

3. No stock should ever be bought which has a high price-earnings ratio.

4. No penny stocks, especially in exploration companies.

5. No open-ended investment trust shares, only closed-ended ones (that is, the number of shares issued should be restricted).

6. No shares in shaky currencies.

7. No stock to be sold merely because it has not risen in price.

8. Concentration on high yield rather than capital appreciation.

9. No government bonds while inflation remains high, unless there are real indications of a downturn in inflation.

10. No restriction of investment to the stock market. The commodity markets, for instance, are worth investigating.

11. Never, never sell short, and never buy options (warrants and rights being much better and cheaper); also, never buy on margin.[30]

---

30 Ibid., pp.7–8. Note that a 'warrant' (a term not used in some countries) is a right to buy a specified share at a set price at a certain time or times in the future. It is sometimes called an option, for example, in Australia, and can be traded on the stock market separately from the underlying share.

Although these rules will have their strong protagonists, each will be strongly contested. Existing investment clubs might well debate them — and the discussion could be pretty lively, though probably inconclusive. That illustrates the difficulty of forming and maintaining an investment club that will yield profits and satisfy the aspirations of all its members. The drones will lean on more active and imaginative members and detract from their performance. If you belong to the active and imaginative, you will do much better to operate independently on your own account.

Your chances of becoming a millionaire through membership of an investment club are remote. For you, any advantages of membership are likely to come only from the exchange of information it provides. Even in that, you will probably be best fitted to analyse the information you get — and you will certainly want to add data from non-club sources that could be much more productive. Diversify your sources and be your own analyst are good rules to live by.

Films

'What about films?' I asked Charlie.

'Wouldn't have minded being in on *Crocodile Dundee*.'

'Why weren't you?'

He grinned. 'No bugger asked me. But a few years ago, I saw this ad. Some jokers were making five films: *The Great Bookie Robbery, Tracy, The Body Business, Petrov* — those were telemovies — and *The Trailblazer*, a feature film. Budgets between $2.9 and $4.5 million, not real big stuff and they had the right underwriters — headed by Rothschilds — and fund managers J.C. Williamson.'

'So you gave it a burl?'

'Chucked me two bob in. But you got to remember promoters don't let you in on a deal unless the risk's too big for them to handle, so they spread it to 'investors' — that's soft touches like you and me. In other words, it's not a handout on a sure thing — not a retrospective offer to take a slice of a goldmine like *Crocodile*. It's a high-risk enterprise. But the fiscal come-ons were good. The investments ended up being 133 per cent deductible.'

'And there were non-tangibles?'

Charlie laughed. 'Smack on, mate. Saw meself as a Cecil B. de Mille. Rubbin' shoulders with a bevy of beauteous babes. Hikin' off to the Cannes Film Festival. Boastin' to me mates. All that stuff. They didn't have too much trouble getting jokers in.'

'You made money out of it?'

'Made a bit. Got me tax down. Coupla the films did well. Nothin' real grand. But, all over, I didn't lose.'

The Sport of Kings

'Better than the horses?'

Charlie looked at me quizzically. 'Depends what you mean by that, mate.'

He dug silently into the alluvia of his memory. 'You know, I had this job once, off-siding to one of our pollies. Got to be a Cabinet Minister. Nice joker. Labor. We were having talks with this Brit — Conservative, real establishment chappie. Afterwards, we had a feed together, and the Pom bloke, thinkin' conversation was draggin' a bit, tried to brighten it up with some light sportin' stuff.

'"Believe you're interested in racing?" he says to my Labor bloke.

'My feller perks up. His eyes shine. "You *could* say that," he confesses.

'"Well, so am I, actually. I have a little proposition you or your friends might fancy," he says cheerfully. Real friendly chap, he was. Smile full of white teeth. You know the Brits turnin' on the charm.

'Now, my bloke's the sort of racin' man who puts a couple of dollars both ways on somethin' he's heard about in the pub and goes to the trots with Mum for a night orf. So he pricks up his ears, thinkin' he's going to get somethin' real hot for the Derby or some other flash race.'

'And did he?'

'Did he! "We have a breeding programme," the Pom says. "Just bought a new sire actually, fine bloodline, won a million pounds. He'll be standing this season, covering a strictly limited number. Forty thousand pounds a time. If you have some brood mares..." '

'Quite a conversation stopper.'

'My bloke choked on his horse-radish.'

'So you can be into racing in different ways?'

'Look, mate, the racing industry's a lot of things. You can keep right out. Maybe that's the wisest thing. Or you can take your few bob each Saturday to the TAB. Or buy a ticket each November in a Melbourne Cup sweep. That way, you won't win much but you won't do much cold either. Almost any other way you're a dead cert to lose.'

'Almost?'

'Betting's a dead loss. No system works. The bookies and the tote, they do all right, although the on-course bookies aren't having it as good as they did.'

'What about owning your own horse?'

'Ah, now, that's the great draw. Real status thing. "I got a colt half-brother to Bonecrusher," you tell your mates. Shuts up the other big-talkers.'

'But does it pay?'

'Hardly ever. Own your own horse, hundred per cent, it costs you thousands a year to keep and train, cart to the races, pay the fees, all that. You get a Phar Lap, you make money. But how many Phar Laps are there? So you can form a syndicate or a company.'

'That spreads the cost burdens.'

'Right. Cuts the cost of your entertainment. 'Cause that's what it really is. Cuts the cost of any winnings too but since you're lucky if one horse in ten wins in any one year, the big thing is that the company or syndicate cuts your losses a lot more than your winnings.'

'You said you're *almost* a dead cert to lose on racing. What's the exception?'

'Breedin', mate. You get a few good thoroughbreds — they're not cheap — breed from 'em, hire the stallions to cover mares at thousands of dollars a time and you can be in the money. But you've got to do it full time — or have enough money so you can put in a few million and wait your time to get more millions back. Like that pools bloke — what's his name?'

'Sangster?'

'That's the joker. Makes a lot of money out of breedin', they say. Won a few races too. But he had to make his pile first — out of somethin' else.'

'So it's not something for the battler or the entrepreneur?'

'Wouldn't say that absolutely. But you've got to be lucky. Take Sir Tristram.'

'Who's he? Another Pom?'

'A horse Pom. Bought in 1976 and taken to New Zealand. He'd had a few races but he was bought for stud. Syndicated into 40 shares at $3,000 each. Since then, he's sired a couple of Melbourne Cup winners. Some of his yearlings've sold for more than a million dollars each. Ten this year for more than $4 million. An American offered $26 million for him in 1982 but the syndicate wouldn't sell. Now the shares are worth $350,000 each — that's $14 million. But there aren't too many Sir Tristrams around.'

'You've been doing your homework, Charlie.'

'You're no good without it, mate. Either you do your homework or you do your coin. It's as simple as that.'

'Any of these breeding operations on the stock market?'

'Not many. But a few. Blandford Park, for example. When the price of their yearlings leap at auction, their share price goes into a canter on the stock market.'

'But there's still no profit in owning horses — to race, I mean?'

Charlie grinned. He saw the disappointment in my eye. 'Sorry, mate.'

'Then why do so many people do it?'

'Just to enjoy themselves.' He grinned. 'Like one of the Brits who's in the game put it, "It's all to do with fun. When God invented sex, I'm sure he didn't think it would catch on the way it did".'[31]

Insurance

With films and racing, you put your faith in the movie mogul and the horse. In a way, that's delegating your responsibility too. But the ultimate in delegated responsibility, as well as the most widespread and aggressively marketed, is life insurance (or assurance). Two aspects need to be separated. The first and basic form of life insurance protects against injury or death. This is a service for which risk can be actuarially assessed. The insurer guarantees compensation and, for payment of a premium,

---

31 *Financial Times*, 25 March 1989, WEEKEND V.

the insured knows that, if things go wrong in agreed ways, he'll receive agreed compensation for himself or his family — subject to careful reading of the small print.

However, the second form of life insurance is quite different. 'Endowment' and like insurance is in the nature of an investment. Savings are made and 'invested' so as to provide for payment of a certain amount of money after a certain fixed period, whether the insured is then dead, injured or fit and well.

Traditionally, life insurance policies, of the 'endowment' type, have been a widely recommended favourite of the tribal elders. To ensure that policies were adequate and paid up to date was part of wise family management. Much of this has now been vastly expanded and institutionalised into superannuation and pension-fund schemes embracing a large percentage of the total population in the wealthier countries.

In mid-1989, a prominent and reputable Australian insurance company was advertising investment in a superannuation fund. The plan called for contributions of, say, $3,000 a year for 20 years. 'After 20 years of building up at, say, 16 per cent p.a., your fund would be worth over $250,000 — even after allowing for superannuation tax.' That sounds splendid. Twenty years payments at $3,000 a year, totalling $60,000, would balloon to over $250,000 at the end.

But what will $250,000 be worth in the year 2009? If the inflation rate averages about 7 per cent, the real value of the dollar will be halved every ten years. So, in 2009, $250,000 will be worth only about $62,500 in 1989 dollars — just about what the investor paid in, although most contributions would have been in dollars declining in real value at an average annual rate of 7 per cent. But even that $62,500 is uncertain. Inflation might average 10, 15, even 20 per cent. And the $250,000 payout is based on the fund 'building up at, say, 16 per cent p.a.'. That 16 per cent isn't guaranteed and might turn out to be exceptional. The average build-up for the fund might be no more than 10 per cent a year, perhaps much less. In that event, the payout in nominal dollars might be only $200,000 or $150,000 or less, in other words, it might be worth only $50,000 or $40,000 or less in real terms of 1989 dollars. Not a great result.

But this is one of those situations where you need to look closely at the tax implications. As the insurance company pointed out, 'If you're on $40,000 now, with no super and want to retire in 20 years, you're currently entitled to put in $3,000 each year and claim a tax deduction for it. Because you're on 50.25 cents in the dollar, that same $3,000 is only costing you $1,493 in real terms.' In these circumstances, your payments, net of tax, might amount to only $30,000 over the twenty years — which relates much better to the $40,000 to $60,000 you're likely to get back. Of course, if you're not on the maximum income-tax rate, your net payout would be commensurately greater: in effect, the government would be 'paying' you less, through a tax allowance, because, with your relatively low taxable income, it assumes it will have to pay you more in social security benefits later, when you retire. However it goes and whatever your gross or net-of-tax contribution, you're not likely to make any great fortune out of your superannuation 'investment'.

Nevertheless, the advertisement claims that its plan offers the contributor 'somewhere safe from the plundering of inflation and [Treasurer] Mr Keating's best efforts'. But does it? Certainly the insurance company will do well out of it: it will have use of contributors' money over a long period to invest as it wishes and it will not have to repay, almost certainly in depreciated dollars, until way down the track. But, even allowing for tax benefits, you might well get back in real terms less than you contributed and any thought that you are securing your financial future could be an illusion.

Generally, these insurance, pension and superannuation schemes need careful assessment. So do the tax advantages that go with them. These can be very considerable; but you'll need to assure yourself that they're big enough to offset any catches in the schemes. The cynic might say that tax advantages get themselves pretty fully discounted in the packages the promoters offer, so that the government, through the taxpayer who's also the policyholder, carries the can rather than the insurance company. You should be aware too that tax provisions are complex and change frequently; so you should consult an accountant or superannuation expert on the more technical, detailed aspects of your particular situation.

However, up to certain amounts — the formula for calculating them is complex — superannuation payments in Australia normally pay a maximum of 15 per cent tax, some of which may be deferred and, if the superannuation payout is rolled over on retirement in approved ways, the tax liability might again be eliminated on the rolled-over funds and reduced on future earnings of those funds. In mid-1989, the AMP was promoting a rollover paying 14.25 per cent *'current average crediting rate per annum'*, with a 'guarantee' (of nominal capital) and 'no up front fee' (although there were other 'charges'). No tax would be paid on the rollover itself, 15 per cent would be paid by the fund on its earnings and no tax would be paid by the contributor on the earnings until all or part of the money was withdrawn. Money remaining in the fund at death would be tax-free to the contributor's heirs. These benefits are largely a saving of tax on income already earned. But they are still important. A tax dollar saved is as good as an income dollar made. But bear in mind that there are other ways of enhancing income, perhaps very substantially, and there are other ways too of minimising tax in legal and acceptable ways.

Like other insurance companies and societies, the AMP Society tends to parade its benefits flamboyantly. For example, in May 1989, it claimed that its annual report 'reveals how you can own more shares and more property than anyone else in Australia'. The smaller print said that this could be achieved by 'being an AMP policyholder', adding that 'AMP is a mutual Society, owned entirely by our two million policyholders'. All of this, though true enough, rather exaggerated the effective ownership and control enjoyed by the individual policyholder.

That doesn't mean that you should shove superannuation and like schemes to one side. You should consider them carefully to see how they fit your personal situation. They can be part of your total wealth and financial security. For example, although Charlie has some harsh things to say about 'insurance' as broadly defined, his public service job has required him to contribute to Commonwealth superannuation over many years. When he retires, he'll get an inflation-proofed pension and a lump sum payout that he can convert into more pension or roll over into an approved deposit fund or a deferred annuity, with tax advantages, or simply take in his hand and invest as he wants, without any tax benefits. But Charlie's is a special case. Not many superannuation schemes have the built-in safeguards of the Commonwealth Superannuation Fund.

Nevertheless, superannuation as an investment is highly regarded by many distinguished observers. 'Superannuation retains its place as the premier investment...Superannuation is such a great investment that the [Australian] Government has placed a limit on the amount that can be contributed in any one year...Superannuation is the *essential* investment for everybody...'[32] These assessments should be given due weight. However, don't be overwhelmed by them. Do your own thinking and make your own assessments. One thing seems certain: even if superannuation, pension and like plans offer a degree of future protection against some of the sharper slings and arrows of outrageous financial fortune, they're unlikely to make you a millionaire except in dramatically depreciated dollars twenty to forty years down the track.

'My Mum had me insured the day I was born. Thought it was her duty,' Charlie confided to me. 'Remember how all those hard-sell salesmen used to come round, door to door, flogging the bargain scale of the century?'

'They didn't make much.'

'The salesmen? Arthur Miller had a play about the death of one, didn't he? No, you're right, they didn't make much. But my Mum fell for their line. Fat lot of good it did us. By the time I collected it was worth more than a starling's fart but it didn't last much longer — in real terms, it was nothing like what she'd paid. All those years she'd struggled to find the premiums when money was real hard cash — you could keep yourself on a coupla quid a week — then when I collected, money wasn't the real McCoy any more...'

'But you got bonuses?'

'Sure. How did they call it? "An endowment policy with full bonuses". The policy was for £500 and we got £100 bonuses — or $1,200 total — they'd changed over to dollars by then. How does that work out? Twenty-one years the

---

32 Whittaker, op. cit., pp.135–43.

insurance company had had the use of Mum's money. Five per cent a year on £500 for twenty-one years would have brought in more than £500. Simple interest. Compound, God knows where you'd finish...'

'But she didn't pay £500 from the start. In the first year, she'd have paid only a few pounds, second year a few more, and her last premiums weren't real money either...'

'That's right. Some of hers was depreciated but all of theirs. And they always had the comeback that if I got knocked over by a bus, Mum stood to collect prematurely. She'd have loved that, wouldn't she? They scared a lot of people with worst-case scenarios. But the fact of the matter is my Mum paid in mostly good money for twenty one years and the insurance company used it all that time to make themselves rich and paid us back in depreciated currency. They called the £100 a 'bonus', as though we were doing real well — they were doing us a favour. They did the same with Dad...'

'How was that?'

'He insured himself soon's he married Mum. Same as mine — endowment with bonuses — but more. £2,000. Big time for those days. Thought he was doin' the right thing by Mum and me. Then before he was fifty, he pegged out — suddenly. By that time, the worst of the inflation had got going. When the old man took out the policy in the 1940s, two thousand quid was about ten years' average wages — eight anyway. By the time Mum collected, how much was it? $4,000 — lucky to be eight months, let alone eight years.'

'But at least your mother got something when he died.'

'Oh, sure, and she needed it. But she didn't need to pay all that money to insure against premature death. For that, she should have paid only a few dollars a year — not the stiff premiums she had to come up with each week. It was supposed to be endowment, wasn't it? Who'd it endow? The insurance company, maybe, not Mum. With bonuses! In real terms, she'd be lucky if she got back a tenth of what she'd paid in.'

'But, Charlie, isn't that being a bit wise after the event? There had been inflation, after all. There could have been deflation?'

'Could have been, yes. First thing I'd say on that is, if there *had* been deflation, Dad would have been dead lucky to have had a job most of the time and Mum couldn't have paid the premiums anyway. That wouldn't have helped a whole lot, would it? But you're quite right. If she'd taken out the policy at the beginning of the Great Deflation in the 1860s and been able to pay all the premiums, she might have got more back in real terms in the 1890s. The bonuses would have been a bit light on, because the insurance company wouldn't have done much good business — and there's not much pressure on them to be generous. It's their ball-game, not the little guy's who's paying the premiums.'

'What about the Great Depression?'

'Same thing. Anyone who collected on his endowment insurance in the 1930s might have come out a bit ahead in real terms. He wouldn't have made any fortune. Again, the bonuses would have been light on; but he'd have been able to buy more with his £500 in 1933, say, than in 1928.'

'So isn't it all just a matter of luck?'

'You'd need to have been real lucky to collect your insurance during the Great Deflation or the Great Depression — if you hadn't been forced to surrender them long before they matured. But there've been a lot of years in between and after — times when what you've been paying in has been losing value right from the minute the premium leaves your fingers. No, mate, I've been poor and I tell you, the odds are stacked against the bloke who hasn't got much. I've got nothing against insurance companies. It was an insurance company that lent me $10,000 to get going properly on the stock exchange twenty years ago. Remember?'

'So what's the gripe?'

'No gripe, mate. Just that insurance companies act like anyone else aiming for the big time. They collect other people's money and proceed to make millions out of it — billions these days. Now just look at this advertisement.'

He unfolded a full-page-spread advertisement from the *Financial Times* of 7 March 1989.

'It's the AMP — the Australian Mutual Provident — they're still a "Society", aren't they — working for their policyholders?'

'So their slogan says: "Australians sharing Australia" — although policyholders don't seem likely to get to share it real soon. They tell me the Society salts away about a quarter of its assets in reserves, so Granny's not likely to get a lick at today's bonanza.'

'Nor her great-grandsons on past performance. Anyway, you know the AMP?'

'Who doesn't? My Mum took out a policy for me with the AMP just as your Mum did for you with her insurance company. Solid institution — good image — better than the pretty lousy image of the insurance industry as a whole.'

'O.K. Well, this advertisement says the AMP had its first office in London a year before Blériot flew the Channel in 1909. Started in Australia sixty years before that. Now it claims it writes "nearly a third of all Australian life insurance and retirement fund business".'

'Could be right.'

'I'm not queryin' the claim, mate. But what else does it say? They got assets of "over £12 billion". That's about 25 billion Australian dollars, give or take a fiver or two.'

'Doesn't surprise me.'

'Nor me. But listen to this: "AMP continues to spread its investments broadly, over shares, government and fixed-interest securities, property, energy and natural resources, and at the same time to seize growth opportunities when they occur".'

'What's wrong with that?'

'Nothin', mate. But where'd those assets come from?'

'My Mum and other people's Mums?'

'You're dead right, mate. I don't know how your Mum's placed but I know where my Mum was when Dad died — frantic poor. This ad says, "we" — that's the AMP — "mean to continue our profitable growth...to give our policyholders the security that only financial strength can provide". My Mum'd like to read that. She'd be real fascinated to know how wrong she must have been about all the security she thought she didn't have.'

'So what do we do about it? About the insurance companies? Abolish them?'

'No, mate, just try to understand what they do. As I said, they're no worse — they're no better either — than anyone else who goes round tryin' to get their hands on your money. They've all got to offer something, so — in the case of the insurance companies — they offer you financial security. Up to a point, they do: straight insurance against accident and death; third-party on your car; flood, fire and earthquake on your property. These might be all right — though you'd better read the fine print before you break any windows. They appoint the loss-assessors too; and you don't have much comeback on that. But that's not really what I'm getting at.'

'It's more the practice of using other people's money?'

'You put your finger right on it, mate. Now those "shares, government and fixed-interest securities, property, energy and natural resources", where did they come from — all $25 billion of them? Originally, from all the little people like your Mum who paid their weekly few dollars and cents...'

'That's mobilisation of capital...'

Charlie laughed. 'Sure is. No one does it better. All those insurance salesmen collecting the pennies and farthings — and after a while it adds up to $25 billion. That's mobilisin', all right, mate. That's mobilisin' real good.'

'It's made our economy strong.'

'Right again. I'm not arguin' about that. But, if the little fellers ever got much out of it, it's never been real obvious to me. So what you've got to do...'

'Is get your hands on someone else's money yourself?'

'Exactly. My Mum had no idea of economics and finance. None at all. She thought she was doing the right thing taking out insurance. My Dad didn't have too many clues in that area either. And, of course, when I started off, I didn't have any more than they did — less if anything. One generation passes its ignorance on to the next. Its fears too. But I was damned sure I wasn't going to go through what they did. Never two bob to call my own. So I said to hell with the AMP — and the National Mutual and the Prudential and all the rest. But I didn't stop there. That'd be too negative. I went a step further. I reckoned I'd be my own AMP. I'd insure myself. I didn't hand my money over to the AMP to do my investing for me and make another $25 billion for themselves. I scrounged around for some money and did my own investing...'

'You didn't make $25 billion.'

Charlie grinned. 'You're smack on there, mate. Not yet anyway. Just give me time. But I've made enough. I've got more "security" than poor old Mum and Dad ever got out of the insurance companies.'

'But of course you're talking about times past. Insurance is more sophisticated now — more pension plans and that sort of thing. They take more account of inflation.'

'They'd need to — and you pay for that. You don't get anything for free.'

'What about insurance bonds?'

'Lots of people've bought 'em. Billions of dollars worth. Lots of people were disappointed too when they lost value in the October '87 crash. Capital-guaranteed, they're not much protection against inflation. Get your depreciated money back, though. Unit-linked they could be better — depends on how well the funds are managed. There are some tax advantages — not as good as superannuation funds...'

'Then why not just buy super funds?'

'Government won't let you have the tax perks past a certain amount. So then you're left with insurance bonds. Look, mate, they're essentially the old life insurance but you pay just one premium and your bonus is what the company says the fund's earned. Much like a unit trust but with some tax breaks. No age limit either for insurance bonds and no health bar.'

'So insurance bonds aren't a bad investment?'

'I'm not sure I see it that way, mate. But I'm looking for more than just a meagre pension at the end of all this struggle and strife. Some financial advisers swear by insurance bonds. Others avoid them. Truth's somewhere in between. And what I do know is there's lots of people who want assured pensions — or as assured as they can afford. They want peace of mind for their retirement. They don't want to be bothered looking after their own investment. And they're scared. Dead scared by the "mysteries" of all this investment hokey-pokey. They want others to do it for them. OK, I'm not saying anything against them or their approach or the service the insurance companies provide in giving them what they want or think they want or what the insurance companies and social-security-minded politicians and governments tell them they want. That's all right with me.'

He pulled out a newspaper clipping. 'You said insurance is more sophisticated. OK, it is. But that doesn't mean it's any better — that is, for today's version of your Mum and mine. Now here's a bit out of the *Financial Times*.[33] The British have always been smart insurance operators.'

'Smarter than the Australians?'

'We learned our best tricks from them, mate. They set up their companies all round the Empire. Now this report's about pension plans. Says Fidelity's the best. It's an investment arrangement. Take out your policy and choose the unit trust or "Fidelity's Managed Portfolio" to invest the proceeds in. You can have a trust with one fund manager or a committee of managers — but you depend on their managers, however you choose. Fidelity's got a good investment record and its charges are standard: initial charge of 5.25 per cent plus 1.5 per cent on the first lump sum or twelve regular payments. Annual management fee of 1.5 per cent. Norwich Union's Plan looks cheaper with an annual policy fee of £20 and annual management charge of 0.75 per cent but they apply only about 70 per cent of your contributions to buying units; the rest goes in commission and administration expenses. Course, these are for relatively well-off jokers. The Fidelty won't handle contributions of less than £2,000. But what I'm getting at is this...'

'There's a bit more transparency?'

'Right. You can see a bit better what they're up to. But the pension plans are much the same as the old insurance policies. They take your money and invest it as they like — although you can choose your 'investment vehicle', as they say. At the end of the time, you get a bonus — your units will be worth more — if they've invested well. If they haven't, you'll end up a bit light on. And who knows how much your good money's going to be worth when it's all over? Not many of the insurance companies are going to dip out but — like my Mum — quite a few of the little people who take out pension plans aren't going to make a killing out of it. Straight insurance or unit-linked, you don't get all that brilliant a deal.'

Charlie gazed out the window — not a window of opportunity, which he so liked to talk about, but this time a window of reflection. 'There's just a couple of things I'd add,' he finally said.

---

33 4 March 1989, WEEKEND III.

'I think I know the second. What's the first?'

'The AMP and the rest of the pension and other fund people, they're really in the big time now. The institutional investors — using our money, mate — dominate the share markets, go in big and get out big. They even take some of our God-given privileges away. The new issues that used to have to go to all shareholders — the little ones as well as the biggies — they're going increasingly now just to the big boys — the institutional investors. Big placements and the rest instead of spreading the honey round to the little bloke who holds a hundred shares and could do with a bit of sugar. So the little bloke gives his money away to a pension fund and then he's finding it harder and harder to get some of it back by operating on the stock market himself. That brings me to the second thing. Which is...'

'Never delegate responsibility for your investment to others?'

'Absolutely. Unless you have to. Look at Lear..'.

'He who made the Lear Jet?'

He looked at me scathingly. '*King* Lear. He gave everything away to his daughters. And what happened? They used it in *their* interests, not his...'

'Cordelia didn't.'

'And look where she ended up. No, it's not a matter just of insurance companies. Never abdicate your responsibility for your own investment to anyone — unless you're cornered. And I mean really cornered, by sickness or some other incapacity you can't do anything about. If you do abdicate responsibility, don't start blaming other people if they let you down.'

'What about if they *take* you down?'

'That's different. You'd better watch for that too. But I'm not talking about criminal acts here. I'm talking about honest, decent, reasonably competent people to whom you might — one way or another — entrust your financial future. They might spend the odd minute or two thinking about your interests but they'll spend all the rest thinking about their own. Some American economists have been doing some work on what they call, in their high-falutin' way, "agency theory". What it amounts to is what we all know: ask someone — pay someone — to act for you and, unless you keep an eye on them the whole time, they'll go at their own pace, feather their own nests, even occasionally take you down but certainly not grab opportunities as you'd like 'em to when they come up...'

'And there'll be a whole team of salesmen, analysts, managers, directors waiting to suck up *your* honey all along the line?'

'Just what they say here, mate. So, if you've got any sense, you'll leave them to it — with someone else's dough — and get on with making your own fortune by your own efforts, without them.'

'Self-reliance, eh?'

'There's no substitute, mate. Never abdicate responsibility for your own future. I never have. I'd rather collect stamps — and make a fortune out of it — than let someone else pick and choose what might be good for me.'

6
Manna for Magpies: Collectors and Collectables

Charlie rarely regarded his stamp-collecting as a fit and proper subject for public confession. But he'd been an addict since his father had presented him, as a small boy, with some exotic specimens collected during wartime service. I suspect Charlie's collection is now worth more than the entire fortune of most of us ordinary mortals.

An Addiction, Mostly Male

In his addiction, Charlie was of course just behaving like the rest of us. Almost everyone collects something some time. Men tend to be addicted more than women. Some collect anything and everything: they can't bring themselves to throw away even the most obvious rubbish. Their houses, garages, offices, cars — everything capable of storing anything — get filled with junk. They collect paper — for their memoirs, the novel of the century, an academic treatise — as well as more solid junk. When they die, their executors find among their papers the certificates of sucker shares bought in the course of a long lifetime: shares in companies that never found gold, never cured baldness and never made the promised excursions to Mars. The companies went bung but the magpie-shareholder never parted with his certificates. If these avid collectors buy a skungy house no one wants to live in, they can't bring themselves to get rid of it. If they've bought a stake in Sturt's Stony Desert or some bleak rocks in the Outer Hebrides, they hang on to those too. They just collect — until they die.

Women are less romantic. They rarely collect for

collecting's sake. They'll assemble a vivid array of jewellery; but because it's beautiful and they enjoy wearing it. Among the many values a wife may have is her capacity to get rid of her husband's old golf shoes or — more practically — have him sell some useless bit of land on which he's been paying rates, so that she can use the money to buy some uncut diamonds she's hankering after. These male and female differences highlight some considerations central to sound collecting practice.

The first is that a collector needs discipline. Indeed, we need some measure of discipline to do anything well: to manage our activities efficiently and organise use of our time. Well-organised, well-managed, disciplined investors will make the most of their talents and perhaps profit even from their addictions. Some addictions are so debilitating that they simply must be got rid of; but some need only to be wisely channelled in profitable directions. Collecting is one of those fortunate addictions that can be wisely and profitably channelled. The addiction isn't cured but adapted so that the right things are collected in the right ways.

Rules for Collecting

What are the basic rules for wise and profitable collecting?

The first and overriding rule is that there must be a market for what you collect. Let's take some examples.

Stamps look like having a good market for a long time to come. But what about other things? Such as Judy Garland's shoes? The shoes Judy wore in *The Wizard of Oz* were sold in June 1988 for $US200,000. A rewarding experience for whoever had acquired and held the shoes for the auction. But will the June 1988 buyer get his money back when he sells in, say, June 1998? How long will Judy's memory be part of the folklore of the entertainment world? How long will her shoes continue to ignite a fierce will for acquisition — or even sound a note of nostalgia — sufficient to hold the price up and — more important — increase it so as to make it profitable, in real terms, to hold a non-earning $US200,000 asset for a number of years? To get back $US200,000 in depreciated currency in 1998 won't be enough. Taking account of inflation, and earnings foregone on the 1988 outlay, over half a million and up to 1 million dollars will be needed for the 1988 buyer just to break even. The gradual erosion of the sentimental attachment to Judy Garland's memory might make the realisation of such a price more and more unlikely. So, as a great fan of Judy Garland, by all means sentimentalise about her shoes but ponder how much you are willing to pay for that and, concurrently, calculate coldly how much you can afford to pay if it's to be a wise long-term investment. If you're willing to pay a lot for sentiment, that's one thing. But if you're looking for profit, that's quite another.

Judy Garland's shoes just *might* have a long-term market. So might Ned Kelly's hat or armour. But, as a kid, you adored Joe Bloggs, didn't you? He was a great man in your run-down street way back in the tough times of the thirties. Kept the little suburb's spirits up when the downtrodden community was about to fall to pieces. Fair enough. But who — apart from you and a few other local historians — remembers him now? How many people will treasure his shoes or hat or the lining from his threadbare overcoat? Not too many. So, if you want to have something of Joe's you can touch, that's fine; but don't expect to make a profit out of it.

Stamps

Other things mightn't jerk the tears as Joe Bloggs' mementos do, but they can make you money. Stamps, for example. They have a big market, throughout the world. Almost everyone has a fling at philately at some time. That's a big plus. With collectables, you need a large, everyday market. You need to be able to buy and sell easily. The tens of millions — hundreds of millions? — who collect stamps belong to all age groups. Some of them — Queen Elizabeth is an example — are very rich. Many are very poor. Some are ready and able to outlay thousands of dollars on a 'penny black' or the like. Some can scarcely afford but will dearly want to acquire some pretty stamp from the Antarctica or Rwanda worth no more than a few cents. So the market is huge and varied enough to accommodate any buyer or seller.

The collecting itself is easy. Many, having started in

childhood by soaking stamps off the family mail and swapping with other kids at school, continue right through life. Sometimes, collecting consists of throwing into a convenient box or drawer stamps which arrive fortuitously. At other times, the collector acts with more deliberation, to gather series depicting birds or art or sport or history or — if you're a hard-headed realist — stamps that pander to your unqualified lust for profit. If you're clever, you'll run pleasure and profit together.

In looking for profit, the ultimate criterion is scarcity: supply related to demand. Sooner or later, a gathering crowd of collectors seeking a small, finite number of genuine examples of a particular stamp will force its price up. By this criterion, the earliest stamps, produced in small numbers and long ago salted away in well-kept collections, have become highly valued. But scarcity isn't always easy to forecast. Some collectors imagined that stamps issued during the brief reign of King Edward VIII would quickly acquire value. They didn't. Too many millions were issued. They were standard issues, carrying the king's head, used for most letters posted in Britain and the Empire. If they'd been commemoratives, issued briefly in small numbers, they would have acquired more value. Much later, envelopes 'carried to the Moon' by the first lunar-landers seemed likely to become rare collectors' items. They didn't either. So many people had believed they would and so had got in on the act that few collectors were left to sell the specially stamped envelopes to. The bonanza never came. It's like a goldfield: if you're the only one who knows the nuggets are there — or will be — you could become a Monte Cristo; but if the whole world knows there's gold in them there hills, you might be lucky to get a 10 per cent return on your miner's pick.

Mostly it's the unexpected — the issue that no one thought would become a rarity — that bounds up in value.

So be doubtful when everyone and his mate talk about a collector's sure thing. The publicity will almost certainly kill it stone dead. The true bonanza is more likely to sneak up on you unheralded. Some years ago, Charlie picked up some British stamps embodying a new printing technique. No one guessed at the time that the stamps would acquire any special value, since it was assumed that the technique would continue to be used indefinitely. It was not. So they became quite valuable — not 'penny blacks' but worth many times what Charlie had paid for them, with the price still going up.

Scarcity is decisive. If as many copies are issued as any conceivable number of collectors are ever likely to want, then the price of that issue will stay drowned below sea level for ever. How then does scarcity appear and how can you identify it? Scarcity can derive from an issue being limited, often in the smaller issuing countries or in unnoticed commemoratives in big and small countries; or it can occur through printing and design errors. If only a few stamps have the errors and you can buy them at issue price, then you have a potential fortune in your hands. But some errors occur in millions of sheets and the sheets are not quickly withdrawn and destroyed. The value of those won't be greatly enhanced.

Some issues have an inherent limitation of supply. For example, first-day covers, as their name implies, are supposed to be issued and stamped only on the day the stamps first appear. Supply might be further limited by being issued at only one spot: for example, at Edinburgh to commemorate the Festival or Cape Canaveral to commemorate the launching of a rocket or shuttle. Since no more first-day covers can be produced once post offices close on that day, supply is finite and value should, in theory, increase considerably over time. Always bear in mind that scarcity must be related to demand: for the price to rise people must want more than there are. If there are only half a dozen examples but no one wants to buy them, their value will be nil, despite their 'scarcity'.

Therefore, you have to postulate a large body of first-day-cover enthusiasts and a comparatively small issue of covers. If the first-day issue is preceded by massive publicity, the issue can be huge even though limited to one day and one place. However, if the issue is small, a later interest in a particular cover — or a surge in the fashion for collecting first-day covers — can dramatically increase the price. That's the sort of situation for which you should be on the look-out.

You should also be aware how that situation can change. In recent years, some postal authorities have taken to selling first-day covers long after the first day. Like stale sandwiches in a railway buffet, they remain on sale for months, stamped for the day of issue. The size of the issue is thus much less limited. A countervailing factor is that the greater ease of acquisition might lift the fashion for collecting first-day covers. Again, scarcity in relation to collectors' fervour will be decisive.

The evidence is that you can make money, sometimes a great deal, out of stamp-collecting. Over the five-year period from June 1976 to June 1981, the compound annual rate of return on stamps bought and sold in the United States was almost 33 per cent — better than the return on any other investment. However, those who did not take their profits during that period found that values *fell* by 6 per cent between June 1982 and June 1983. From being the best investment, stamp-collecting for a while became the worst. Later its performance improved, although not to the top of the collectables.

Markets: Stamps and Coins

That raises two important questions. Collectables call for active participation by the collector, usually driven by an obsessive passion. Owners have been known to weep openly when they've had to sell, even at huge mark-ups. So — can you easily get out of collectables when you need to or when you see the market turning? And will you want to surrender your collectables when the market tells you you should?

The market for some collectables, such as stamps and coins, is reasonably well organised. The stamp market, in particular, has become highly organised at the retail, commercial and auction level in many countries. Stanley Gibbons is an old and widely respected name but there are many other dealers. At any time, a host of buyers is seeking deals with a host of sellers; but a couple of points should be borne in mind.

First, the stamp — and more so the coin — market is not as well and carefully regulated as the stock exchange or the real estate market. Safeguards are fewer and less stringent for the ignorant and unwary. Market trends are difficult to identify in advance. There is little focus of public attention or publication of indices, broken up in the case of the stock exchange into such categories as industrials, resources, futures; and, in the case of real estate, into sales, rentals and price categories; trends in capital cities and regional centres; and rural, commercial, industrial and residential property. These guides are lacking, at least to the ordinary collector, so that you'll have to identify signals for market advances and retreats yourself or rely on the advice of self-interested professionals or possibly ungifted amateurs.

Second, when you buy and sell shares, you pay a commission usually according to a scale fixed by the local exchange. Except for large off-market deals, the big buyer or seller trading each day, including the multimillion-dollar investment houses, get the same price and pay fees according to the same scale as the little investor occasionally buying a handful of shares. With stamps and coins, trading is less predictable. The margin between what you paid for an item and what you get back when you sell has to support a multitude of small traders who never come together in a formal exchange to provide the 'pure competition' between buyers and sellers that the stock exchanges aspire to. Auctions might provide a more 'perfect' market; but is an auction likely to to be the right vehicle for your periodic transactions?

Third, the commodity is not uniform. Any hundred ordinary shares in Broken Hill Proprietary Limited or General Motors or British Petroleum are the same as any other hundred ordinary shares; you sell precisely what you bought, without having anyone examine the share certificate to assess its physical condition. Not so with stamps. One example of a stamp may differ from another because one is new the other used, because one has a heavy or badly placed postmark, because its corners are folded, because the watermark is imperfect or because of a wide variety of other small differences which will graduate quality from excellent to poor. For example, the 1946 Renner set of four mini-sheets from postwar Austria would sell at $1,500 to $2,000 but they need to be in mint condition and offered at auction. You might have bought without knowing that certain saleable qualities were lacking or that some minor damage would bring your selling price down. Of course, you might have been lucky — you might have bought an upside-down watermark without the seller noticing; so that now you can reap a windfall reward. But you will need to keep your stamps in good condition. If you allow them to deteriorate, their market value will be much less than you paid for them.

So the markets for stamps and coins, two of the most popular collectables, are established, widespread and fairly well organised; but they're not as well regulated and predictable as the stock exchanges or the property markets. The well-known investment firm of Salomon Brothers in New York estimated that coins had risen in value by 14 per cent from July 1987 to June 1988. But how is this gain to be realised? Is it a gain to be made by professional dealers in coins more than by the hopeful amateur? Always, you need to look, in a practical way, at the prospect of actually realising gains, as distinct from reading about what you've made on paper. In general, you need to be knowledgeable and to exercise care, especially if you collect stamps and coins for profit instead of or as well as for pleasure.

The pleasure aspect raises that other question: will you want to dispose of all or part of your collection when the market dictates you should? Sound money-making requires well-timed decisions on when to sell just as much as well-timed decisions on when to buy. When there is no longer any financial advantage for holding on, you should get out. Will you do this? Or will you fall in love with your collection so that you won't have the heart to let it go? Will you hang on to it until the end — and pass it on to your heirs? Of course, if you bought well in the first place and regard your collection as a long-term investment, holding on can have value; but you should be sure that's not just a rationalisation. If you let the pleasure of collecting rule you, then your collection is less a form of investment and more a personal indulgence — a luxury consumption outlay.

Jewellery — 'Fall in Love Quickly!'

This applies with even more force to such collectables as jewellery and commemorative pieces. Diamonds are a girl's best friend, and jewellery made from intrinsically precious stones and metals are an easily transportable and widely convertible form of wealth. Some of the rich fleeing the Russian Revolution after 1917 could take part of their fortunes with them. Not their palaces or dachas. Furniture and paintings they had to leave behind. But jewellery and gold they could carry. Some Europeans speak of a 'family rule' always to keep some gold, precious stones or jewellery available to meet a possible emergency. There's much to be said for these precautions; and, in more settled times and tranquil environments, profits can also be made.

Between mid 1976 and mid 1981, the compound annual rate of return on diamonds in the United States was nearly 17 per cent, a fairly high ranking on the scale of profitable investments during the period. But alert investors should then have got out, because up to mid 1983 the return was zero and later still was negative. Towards the end of 1979, quick and lively investors might have put the proceeds of sale of their diamonds into silver which, under the Hunts' attempt to corner the market, rose five times in value from August 1979 to peak at more than $52 in January 1980. But they should have abandoned silver quickly before the Hunt corner failed and the price of silver collapsed. In 1986 or 1987, they could have profitably returned to the diamond market to buy at depressed prices for the substantial recovery in 1988. Salomon Brothers estimated that diamonds advanced 24.9 per cent between July 1987 and June 1988. Since then demand has remained strong, especially in Japan, other Pacific rim countries and Europe. The De Beers' Central Selling Organisation sold $US4.2 billion worth of rough diamonds in 1988 compared with $US3.07 billion in 1987. Experts deduce that the supply of gem diamonds is significantly below demand. ('Supply' is a term I must qualify in the case of diamonds because De Beers are in a position to exercise significant control of gem diamonds coming on to the market.)

The tightness of the market, admittedly under this monopolistic control, was borne out by De Beers increasing their prices by 13.5 per cent in May 1988 and a further 15.5 per cent from March 1989. Auction sales of diamonds from the Aredor mine in the West African Republic of Guinea confirmed the buoyant market, especially for gems of outstanding size and quality. On the second of March 1989, the Australian company Bridge Oil, which operates and owns 40 per cent of the mine, auctioned its largest find, a high-quality stone of 255.61 carats, for $US10,036,000 —

the highest price ever paid for an uncut diamond. The stone was reported to be 4 centimetres in length, 3.1 centimetres high and 2.2 centimetres thick. It weighed 51.12 grams. Earlier, Bridge had found a 100.2-carat stone in 1986, a 142.96-carat stone in 1987 and a 181.77-carat diamond, auctioned in November 1988 for $US8,620,000.

Is it then better to invest in such a company as Bridge rather than in diamonds themselves? The stock market reaction to Bridge's record-breaking sales was not encouraging: the price of Bridge shares on Australian markets scarcely stirred — then sank back into a heavy torpor again. Indeed, near the end of May 1989, Bridge shares had fallen 15 per cent, despite a substantial rebound in the general market. Should you then invest in diamonds at all? The sellers who dominate the diamond market know where their demand comes from: their advertisements 'emphasise that diamonds are not so much an investment as a gift of love'. Maybe. But one hard-nosed diamond expert in New York responded to the De Beers advertisement by urging diamond buyers to 'Fall in love, very quickly'.[1]

Successful investors, whether in diamonds, other gems, precious metals and jewellery, just like investors in shares and property, will need to follow the market so as to buy in a slump — about 1983–4 for diamonds — and sell in a boom. Like other investors, they must be prepared to take their profits when the market beckons. But matters are not always so simple. Emotional factors often predominate.

> What makes one rich woman really different from another (or so they tend to think) is the quantity and quality of their jewels...The ideal is a flawless gem which is big enough to draw envious glances...An engagement ring is generally reckoned to be the first rung of the ladder, but many attractive women start a good deal earlier than that. A rich man is expected to hand out baubles from the moment he makes an advance. A pair of diamond ear-rings can do a lot for his cause. A mistress will try to persuade him to add other gifts as the affair progresses; a wife will insist on it. Expensive jewellery can compensate for a great many things, including neglect ('You are always working') and sexual inadequacy ('You are always tired').

---

1 The *Australian Financial Review*, Sydney, 1 July 1988.

Quarrels, birthdays and Christmas provide suitable excuses for the formal handing over of diamond bracelets, emerald necklaces and other trinkets. Designers are constantly encouraged to explore fresh and exotic avenues, but true snobs hanker after jewellery with an interesting history: a necklace which belonged to Marie-Antoinette makes a better conversation piece than one which has just emerged from the workshop.[2]

So any idea that a million-dollar diamond is just another investment of no more sentimental value than a scrunched-up share certificate has to go out the window. Women especially become attached to and hold on determinedly to their trinkets. As an investment, that is like living in your own house but without the bonus that you can mortgage your house for more profitable investment as its value increases. From diamonds and jewellery, you get no income and paper gains in value are unrealisable, except by actual sale. (Some gold-miners have sold at a high price for future delivery, in order to raise funds; but that is a special and limited case. Your pawnbroker is always available too!)

There are some costs in holding jewellery. Insurance is one. Another is income foregone; jewellery earns no interest, rent or dividends. The market is volatile and hard to predict; and valuation can present a problem when you decide to realise your capital gains — or cut your losses. Whose valuation do you accept — or indeed seek? Can any given valuation be put to practical use?

I vividly remember the day a lady rang me to say she had $70,000 worth of opals and she wanted to use them to buy a house. She said that a dealer/valuer had given her a written valuation at $70,000 but she would let them go for $35,000 as a part deposit on a house. Knowing that sellers of properties are extremely wary of taking anything but cash I suggested that she sell them to the dealer for $35,000 and thus be in a much stronger position to make an offer on a property. Her reply staggered me: 'I have already tried that, but all he will offer is $8000'.[3]

---

2 Davis, op. cit., pp. 139–40.
3 Whittaker, op. cit., p.249.

So you'll need a sound, reliable valuer — and a willing purchaser within the terms of that fair valuation — when the time comes to realise on your beloved jewellery. That might well be a time of personal energency, when your strong-box of jewellery and your drawerful of loose diamonds are all you have to guarantee you bed and board or enable you to retain your old-fashioned but still precious mink. If that emergency never comes, your heirs might gasp at the sparkle of your gems but might be more willing than you to dispose of them, perhaps to a trader who will tell them they're all fakes anyway — a slander they might be naive enough to believe.

And while you can trade gold freely, gems are different. 'Diamonds', reported the *Wall Street Journal* on 14–15 April 1989, 'aren't going to be a futures trader's best friend after all'. The New York Commodities Exchange — Comex — had done a year of research into creating the world's only diamond-futures contract, to be traded along with pork bellies, bonds and beef. But De Beers and diamond dealers called the tune — as they had when an earlier attempt briefly succeeded in the 1970s. Those who control the market now don't want to lose their power to set prices; so any idea that you might be able to trade your diamonds on an open market, where masses of buyers and sellers come together to set prices, look like being well down the track. In the meantime, you'll have to put up with the fluctuations of a monopolistically controlled, very imperfect market that, in effect, throws you back on to valuers and dealers — or, if you've got a really big one like the Aredor Mine monsters or a splendid one like a Duchess of Windsor, on to the auction market.

Old Masters and Other Delights for Hard Heads

If women are more disposed to collect jewellery, men are more disposed to collect Old Masters — or art works generally and antiques and first editions. They're also addicted to vintage cars: Ford Roadsters, Bentleys, Rolls Royces, Volkswagen convertibles, Mini-Mokes, all of which can be pleasurable and sometimes sound investments. From cars to Old Masters, all can be worthwhile collectables, giving joy and offering some prospect of gain, especially in an affluent society which now reaches far across national boundaries and in which insatiable consumers are always looking for distinctive items with which to indulge anything from a genuine cultural passion to a crude pretension. But Old Masters and the like have much the same drawbacks as jewellery. When you buy a Rembrandt, you tie up a million dollars — or, these days, tens of millions; you get no income — or cash flow, to use the more commercial jargon; you have to insure it; and you can't be sure how much you'll get when the time comes to sell. Even in the finest of the world's galleries, brilliant fakes have been discovered. So you'll need to exercise care when you buy if you're to avoid a damaging loss when you sell. You'll also run a risk of becoming too devoted to your paintings or antiques or first editions so that their role as an investment diminishes and their status as a very expensive, though durable, consumable is enhanced.

Let's consider some of these points in a little more detail. Gems, jewellery, precious and semi-precious stones *can* increase in value, especially during a period of inflation when, by definition, money loses value in relation to real goods.

'I'm paying 120 percent more for my diamonds than I did last year, my labor is up 35 to 40 percent. My product gets marked up again and again. Rings that sold for $170 four years ago are $350, maybe $400. I can sell all I can make.'[4]

That was an earlier diamond boom. In 1989 came another. And not only diamonds but also quite humble minerals can constitute a fortune in collectables. In July 1988, Arthur Chapman sold his collection of metals, minerals and gemstones, including such items as silver azurite and copper carbonate, to the Sydney City Mining Museum for one million dollars. 'Some [items] are quite priceless,' Chapman said. 'I've been offered phenomenal prices for some of them.' The cost? Not much in terms of cash outlays: he said the collection 'cost a lot of hard work' over the greater part of a lifetime.

---

4 Greider, op. cit., p.16.

But we need to be careful about conversion of our assets into collectables. Arthur Chapman was on a winner; but many others collect things of slight interest to others or items of little commercial value. Genuine first-editions of famous literary works can be extremely valuable — and continue to gather value over time. But a morocco-bound first edition of *A Short History of Bandywallop* might not turn a market frantic. Nor will collections of old newspapers or magazines, sporting records and the like, except in rare circumstances. (A photograph of Don Bradman batting as a small boy in a school match in Bowral might be an exception; though even that would be unlikely to sell for a fortune.) But hard-headed realism has never deterred millions of people from putting such items aside in the belief that 'they'll be worth a fortune later on'. On the other hand, they'll throw away children's toys, for which a collector's market has recently emerged. But these are 'quality' toys of worldwide repute which will have value, not if they've been tossed around, as they should have been, by the kids at Christmas, but only if they're in virtually mint condition, just about as good as the day they left the factory.

We need always to keep in mind the distinction between the stern virtues of investment and the looser joys of consumption. If by good fortune the two can be combined, that's fine. Some people get a genuine joy out of buying houses. It gives them as much pleasure as loving well or dining at gourmet restaurants or spending a night at the Opera Ball. That there is joy in the enterprise doesn't necessarily diminish the value of the investment; indeed the incentive of pleasure will enhance the search for and could help ensure the value of the investment. Certainly if you enjoy what you're doing you're likely to give more of your energy and talent to the enterprise than if you're dragooned into it. But you must be careful that you don't cross a line that divides the joy of sound investment from the pleasure of having something you love, no matter what the cost. If you enjoy consuming something — for example, by wearing jewellery — that will not necessarily mean that what you've bought is a secure investment offering worthwhile returns, especially compared with alternative investments. It might be; but it needs a close, hard-headed look.

We can take one specific example. Charlie travels a lot these days. Let's tune in when he and his wife stop off for a few days in *Hong Kong*. In the shops offering sparkling jewellery, his wife's eye lights on a necklace of several strands of pearls with diamond clasps.

'Eighty-four thousand dollars!' Charlie exclaims.

'Hong Kong dollars,' his wife reminds him.

'They'd better be!'

'But what an investment,' his wife responds.

'An investment? At *that* price?'

'We'll get twice as much for it back home.'

'We'll need to — and we'll need to sell it as soon as we get off the aircraft.'

'Nonsense, darling, it'll be just like money in the bank...'

Is she — the eager consumer cum investor — right? Or is Charlie — the cautious investor, reluctant to allow himself to be deceived about prospective returns — right to hold back, unless he yields to the temptation to splurge on a well-deserved gift for a loved and loving wife?

For the moment, let's put to one side the generous-gift impulse and consider the transaction as an investment only. The jeweller is asking $84,000. It wouldn't be surprising if his mark-up were some 40 per cent. So the value of the necklace when it came to him was perhaps about $64,000. That included a reward for the designer and the skilled work in fashioning the design. 'Fashion' is a well-chosen word. Whether it is fashionable is relevant to its value now and *might* be significant to its future market value. If it is a fundamentally well-designed piece, it might gain in value. If it is little more than a 'fashion-name' piece, its future value might lie almost entirely in the materials from which it is made. So you'll have to make a judgement whether the piece will gain in value over time or in other environments.

This investment element might apply with greater certainty to antique jewellery of a design that has commended itself to many buyers over generations than to a modern piece still to be tested over time. The Marie-Antoinette example quoted above would have the commendation of history. So would jewellery formerly belonging to, let's say, the Duchess of Windsor. But then you'd be paying a great deal more for them than for a modern Hong Kong piece; and you'd have much more powerful built-in guarantees of their market value — and accretions in value.

So we might need to reduce the $60,000 to, say, $40,000 or less, to arrive at a value for the pearls and diamonds, plus a little bit of gold that constitute the intrinsic worth of the choker. But would $40,000 be right? Or would it be much less? How do you check the 'intrinsic value'?

For the average buyer, it's pretty difficult. Charlie's wife makes a practice of carrying a small, very professional-looking magnifying glass of the kind jewellers use to scrutinise precious stones. When you screw such a glass knowledgeably into your eye, you might give the Hong Kong jeweller some pause, however honest he may be. If your act is convincing, he might be fooled into believing you're about to catch him out, if he's overcharging; so the magnifying-glass ploy might not be entirely worthless. But you'll need some training if your act is intended not only to impress but also realistically to separate the good from the fake. You might uncover the more obvious deceptions but you'll need to be well trained to put an accurate value on gems of varying quality.

So what about that pearl-and-diamond collar as an investment? Will it accumulate value in the years ahead and always be available for some ultimate financial emergency? Most of us like to have fall-back positions. I like to have a series of financial defences in depth: a certain amount of cash — not too much because it costs too much to hold — and resources promptly convertible into cash, for example, in a savings or other interest-bearing account. A little further down the convertibility track are interest-bearing deposits, on fixed but shortish terms, with a bank or similar reliable institution. Even more readily negotiable than the fixed-term deposits are shares in public companies. If I have to sell in an emergency I might have to forego some prospective profits or even take a loss, but my stockbroker can sell those shares and get cash for me at short notice. So we go down the convertibility track until we get to such things as stamps, coins and jewellery.

Let me be clear that these items are not to be despised in economic and financial terms. Over a lifetime of care but not necessarily the single-minded dedication of the true philatelist, a collector can have stamps worth tens of thousands, hundreds of thousands or even millions of dollars. But there's a psychological as well as a convertibility hurdle to be jumped before most collectors can bring themselves to throw their collection on the market. That psychological hurdle will be there even in an acute financial emergency.

Much the same applies to jewellery — perhaps with even greater force. You can slip along, heavily disguised, to a pawnbroker or you might even ring Christie's to find out when they're holding their next auction. But at what point will you bring yourself to part, temporarily or permanently, with the treasured mementos of family and romance?

The answer for most of us is that we'll probably do it only in that ultimate emergency when the invader is already at the gate, when we desperately need resources for food and shelter, when the crisis has become pretty much a matter of personal or family survival. Short of that, we'll probably hang on to our personal treasures, so that, effectively, they become inconvertible into liquid resources for everyday purposes. They'll still be an investment; they'll still be part of our financial defences in depth; but, if we place too great a reliance on them — if they constitute too large a proportion of our total investments — they'll tip us into the ranks of the conspicuous consumer rather than those of the hard-headed investor.

Of course, even if you never realise on your 'investments' in jewellery, they will eventually be part of the heritage you pass on. Most of us will have a number of purposes in accumulating wealth in various forms and these purposes will vary over time. Sometimes, we will need more income to meet daily living expenses, care for a growing family, provide for our children's education and so on. At a later stage, with the children grown up and independent, current income might be less important and the accumulation of capital, especially if it's untaxed, might have more attractions. Then a time might come when we start thinking about what we can pass on to those we love: income-producing assets and assets gaining in value, together perhaps with some 'cultural' treasures.

'Old Masters', Impressionist and other paintings and antiques could be among those treasures. As investments on which capital gains might be made, they can have more value than modern jewellery. (*Antique* jewellery falls more into the category of the 'Old Masters' and other antiques.) A well-organised market exists for them. Auction houses exemplified by Christie's and Sotheby's sell them in a large and active market or they can be sold more privately.

Many successful financiers, industrialists and entrepreneurs amass formidable art collections partly as an investment but, more obviously, to express a cultivated lifestyle. John Pierpont Morgan, assisted by such buyers as the Czar of Russia, pushed pre-World-War-I prices to levels comparable, in deflated dollars, with today's. J.P. Morgan's collection was fabulous; and the collections of some others were modest only by the standards he set. Several galleries and museums in the United States such as the Frick and the Getty have had their origins in private collections of the super-rich.

> New York's Museum of Modern Art was started by a Rockefeller, and museums like the Guggenheim would not exist if it were not for the enthusiasm and generosity of the families whose names they bear. Some second- and third-generation heirs have devoted their whole lives to patronage of the arts. Paul Mellon, whose father founded the National Gallery in Washington (it houses his art collection), is a prominent example...He once told an interviewer that he had taken as his life's work the goal of 'spending my fortune sensibly'. [5]

In Australia, the earliest successful settlers had hanging on their walls valuable paintings brought from Europe together with the less-esteemed products of local artists. For the wealthy of the 1980s, part of the 'fashion' — the way rich people behave — is still to collect 'art' and this creates a market in which the wealthy compete to acquire the most sought-after pieces.

'Old Masters' have tended to bring the highest prices and to be the most secure investments; but the Impressionists have provided stiff competition in recent years. To such an extent that at least one wealthy collector, Jaime Ortiz-Patino, is reported to have been selling some of his

---

5 Davis, op. cit., p.124.

Impressionist masterpieces — for more than $US50 million — and to be looking around in other less costly areas where it is possible to build up a splendid collection. In July 1988, one Monet sold for $US8.3 million and another for $US31 million; $US15.5 million was paid for a Van Gogh; $US3.5 million for a Chagall; and $US2.6 million for a Manet. A world market is now well established, prices — up to the time of the last auction — are well known and publicised. The tendency, though not invariable, is for Rembrandts or Van Goghs or Picassos or Cézannes to bring ever higher prices at each successive auction. A painting worth millions of dollars which earns no income can, in these circumstances, be profitably held — and enjoyed — for several years, purely as an investment.

Australians have participated in the soaring art stakes. Alan Bond bought Van Gogh's *Irises* at Sotheby's in New York in November 1987 — just after the stock market crash.

Irises is not an overly large painting [Adam Smith wrote.] 'It is twenty-eight inches by thirty-six inches. It had been on display for a week. Van Gogh had painted it in 1889 in the garden of the insane asylum at Saint-Paul-de-Mausole, where he was a patient. Joan Payson Whitney, old Standard Oil money, had bought it for $84,000 in 1947.

'What shall we say to start?' said [Sotheby's auctioneer] Marion. 'Shall we say fifteen million?' The audience murmured.

'I have fifteen million,' he said. 'Fifteen five, sixteen. Over here, seventeen, eighteen, nineteen, twenty on my left, twenty-one, the phone in front.'

Several of the Sotheby's staff, in black tie, were on the phones to bidders.

'Twenty-one in the center, twenty-two, twenty-four, twenty-eight by the two of you, twenty-nine on the far phone.'

When the bidding went through $40 million, the crowd applauded. At $42 million, there were gasps.

'Forty-eight million.'

'Oooooh, eoowwww,' said the crowd.

'Against you, in the back. Shall we say fifty million? Forty-nine million, on the far phone.'

There was a pause.

'Forty-nine million,' said Marion. 'Fair warning. Sold for

forty-nine million.' Marion banged his hammer. The crowd applauded. The auction took less than four minutes. [6]

With commission, *Irises* was said to have cost Bond $US53.9 million. He had paid that huge sum, it was said, not to 'fill a cultural void in his own life' but as 'a gold-plated investment'. [7]

But the market can be tricky. In July 1987, during a boom in Rupert Bunny paintings, one sold for the then record price of $462,000. That same year, the Queensland Art Gallery bought Bunny's *The Bathers* privately for $1.25 million. That was matched at an auction in November 1988 for *Une Nuit de Canicule.* However, the market was irregular. If you had the right Bunny, fine; but you had to pick what was right. *The Card Trick,* expected to bring $350,000, was passed in at $275,000, while a smaller, less fancied painting thought to be worth $70,000 sold for $220,000, and *Portrait of the Artist's Wife on a Balcony,* valued at $US150,000, brought $US220,000 in New York.

If the artist is well known and has a secure reputaion, values are likely to mount over the decades. George Washington Lambert has been recognised for generations as one of Australia's finest painters. His painting, *The Blue Hat,* sold at auction in 1973 for $22,000 and in 1981 for $67,000. In 1988, it sold first for an unknown six-figure sum and then, in November of the same year, for $600,000.

Even allowing for inflation and income foregone, these are considerable gains. But the works of renowned artists are priced so high that, for the most part, only institutions or those who are already rich can afford them; and even the rich must be discriminating in what they buy or their investments will turn sour. Therefore, we might have to wait until we're already millionaires before indulging our acquisitive urges, remembering that, to be profitable, our acquisitions should gather value night and day as they hang quietly on our walls.

Some paintings can still be bought by millionaires-to-be. For example, some Aboriginal art offers a low entry price, with a prospect of large capital gains. Works of a small

---

6 Smith, *The Roaring '80s,* pp.15–16.
7 The *Australian* Magazine, 22 April 1989.

group of artists in traditional Western Australian sand paintings are reported to have lifted in value by 500 per cent over a short period and some to have shown a 1000 per cent gain in two years. But a perspective of ten years might be needed to be sure that gains will hold. Paintings can be the flavour of the month or the year. So quality is the key. If you enter this field, buy paintings that will have an appeal and a market overseas — and buy the best.

What we mustn't do is indulge any propensity flowing from the 'I don't know anything about art but I know what I like' syndrome. (But equally we should resist any propensity to refuse to buy a 'goldmine' painting or to sell it too soon merely because we hate it.) When you're investing, you might not know anything about art but you'll need to know plenty about the art market. If you don't, beware! You'd be well advised to stick to collecting outdated share certificates or used match-boxes. And if you go out and buy just any original painting because it's cheap enough for you to afford, you'll fill a blank space on a wall; but you're unlikely to make a wise investment.

On the other hand, you can be lucky. At least one Australian was discerning enough to collect Sydney Nolans when that now most successful of Australian artists was unknown. He never sold them — fortunately, he never needed to — and so had a treasure-trove to pass on to his heirs. That was more good judgement than luck; but you can sometimes be lucky too.

Some years ago, a friend of mine was rummaging through junk at a weekend street market in Brussels. Her eye lighted on a small watercolour. She thought it 'very nice'; and somehow it 'reminded' her of another painting. So she bought it for a couple of hundred Belgian francs, the equivalent of five dollars or so. When she next went to London, she consulted an expert. He took a little time but made no bones about his judgement: it was a Turner. Its value? Several thousand dollars then, certainly a great deal more now. One of Turner's greatest works, *Seascape: Folkestone*, sold for £7,350,000 in 1984 and was believed five years later to be worth about £20 million ($A40 million). To pick up a Turner in a flea-market was just luck, of course, much in the category of winning a lottery or stumbling over a gold nugget along the Ballarat or Bendigo road. But the experience also shows that it can be very profitable indeed to recognise valuable pieces of art. If you 'find' them or can buy them at a good price, you can make a small or perhaps even a large fortune.

Commemoratives, 'Heirlooms', 'Collectors' Items'

Don't confuse genuine art works with popular products despite their decorative appeal and their possible link with commemoration of some historical or other event. Beware especially the frequent hype about commemoratives. Australia's bicentenary was an unmatched occasion to sell 'collectors' items'. Just as one example, 'The Australian Collectors Treasury 1988' issued several items privately to collectors. The 'Treasury' identified itself as a division of Bond International Pty Ltd and was thus perhaps a subsidiary of the well-known public company. Any affiliation with any Government body or authority was explicitly denied.

Among the host of advertisements, by a wide variety of companies, for items connected in some way with the bicentenary were two from the 'Treasury' which were comprehensive and informative, detailing for the customer the product he was being asked to buy. One was a 'Commemorative Pocket Watch' which, by all accounts, was a first-class, accurate timepiece made by well-qualified tradesmen. The watch's case was finely sculptured, the principal motif being ships of the First Fleet sailing into Botany Bay. There were other features typically Australian: the Southern Cross formed part of the design. The words of the Australian National Anthem, *Advance Australia Fair,* were inscribed on the other side of the watch-case. The second item was a bicentennial tankard. Again, this was a finely-finished piece of work, attractively presented and potentially appealing to quite a large market — especially in the bicentenary context.

As we've noted before, the market value of an item depends on its scarcity, that is, its supply in relation to its demand. The advertising for the watch and tankard seemed to guarantee that the supply would be limited. For example, each of the watches was to be individually numbered; rather like a limited print of a distinguished painting by, let us say, Toulouse Lautrec or Hans Heysen. In the case of the tankard, only 5000 would be made, after which the moulds for their making would be destroyed. So the requirements for scarcity would seem to be satisfied from the supply side. Demand would then need to stand up no more than modestly to allow a reasonable expectation that those acquiring either watch or tankard might turn a useful profit — apart from the pleasure of owning something exclusive.

The watch, tankard and similar items may be perfectly legitimate items, offered for sale at reasonable prices. But the tankard and watch were explicitly claimed to be a 'Collector's Pocket Watch', a 'cherished heirloom' or a 'true heirloom', the implication being that they will gather appeal and value over time. Would such claims prove to be valid, at least in the longer term? Each buyer would need to form his own judgement; but he should not too readily assume that he is making an investment on which he will be able to realise substantial capital gains. Little demand might exist for souvenirs of a bicentenary or the like once the year is over. Consequently, any accompanying proofs of value, such as a certificate of authenticity or guarantees of 'limited availability' might have little relevance to a market which is indifferent to the extent of the supply or the authenticity of the items.

Some other advertisements are less explicit in marketing collectors' items but are implicitly in that category. In November 1988, Westpac Banking Corporation invited its customers to 'acquire [a] genuine Miner's Lamp, to enrich your home with its beauty, craftsmanship and fascinating history'. Why would anyone want a miner's lamp? Each lamp was claimed to be 'rarely, if ever, seen outside museums', to bear 'the original insignia of the maker and [to be] individually numbered. A Certificate of Origin, attesting to its authenticity and an interesting booklet providing historical information are included'. A miner's lamp might have been the last thing the potential buyer wanted; but who could resist such a huckstering advertisement?

Even governments engage in this trade in collectors' items, often at great profit to themselves though of dubious advantage to 'investors' at the demand end of the trade. On

6 November 1988, the Perth Mint advertised a 'Holey Dollar' containing one ounce and a 'Dump' of one-quarter of an ounce of fine silver at $45 a set! The contained silver, at current market prices, was worth about $10.

On the same date, the Reserve Bank of Australia advertised a 'Commemorative $10 Note' in a 'souvenir folder', at $14 each, plus $4.25 for postage and handling. In other words, collectors were being asked to outlay $18.25 to get a note in general circulation worth $10 — a rake-off of 82.5 per cent!

But this was generous compared with an offer by an organisation called the 'Brisbane Coin Gallery' which offered a 'great Xmas present' of a pre-decimal coin set, to a face value of three shillings and tenpence half-penny (about forty-six cents), for $19.95. Birthday year sets — only seven years were available — were offered at $24.95 each. If you bought two birthday sets — at a total cost of nearly $50 for 92 cents worth of coins — you would receive a 'Brand New $1 note'. If you bought three sets — worth nearly $75 — you would receive 'a Circulated Australian $1 note'. You would need to be buying rare coins indeed to justify this mark-up and very rare coins to offer any prospect of profit however long you held them.

Much more appealing was the offer of the Koala, Australia's first platinum coin, produced in four denominations by the Perth Mint and marketed by the government-owned Goldcorp Australia, at a wholesale price between 3 per cent and 9 per cent above the ruling market price for platinum. The Koala offered reasonable prospects of gain to those who were bullish about the market for platinum. Investors would nevertheless need to weigh the advantages of hoarding Koalas against the alternative benefits of, for example, buying shares in platinum-miners. Unfortunately, platinum miners in Australia are few and investors might need to look to South Africa to get a slice of the highly concentrated action.

What these offers indicate is that there are plenty of collectors among us and that all sorts of authorities, companies and individuals are ready and waiting — lying in ambush — to pander to and sometimes take advantage of our bowerbird instinct. If you enjoy gathering all sorts of things and are prepared to spend a lot of money on this harmless recreation, then by all means go ahead and fill your home with whatever canny traders are eager to supply. But do it with your eyes open. Do it in the knowledge that much of it is junk and most, though not without value, offers no capital gain. Beware of being too ready to accept something as a 'valuable collector's item' on the say-so of the seller. Don't buy a 'valuable collector's item' just because a reputable company or a government authority is flogging it. They will be willing to make a dollar at your expense, if you're foolish enough to let them! So be hard-headed. By all means indulge your weakness for collecting. But be realistic in assessing whether it represents an investment — even a poor one — or simply a form of consumption like playing the horses or guzzling cake.

'I've got a mug commemorating the Duke of York's visit to Australia in 1927,' Charlie told me.

'You must treasure it.'

'You're dead right, mate. The Duke opened the first Parliament in Canberra. Later became King — called himself George the Sixth.'

'That must've added to its value.'

'So everybody said. Dad'd been using it to fill the water bowls for his canaries. He was just a kid then. When King Teddy abdicated to marry Mrs Simpson, he got one of the few brilliant flashes he'd ever had about "investment potential". Poor old Dad, he wouldn't have known a good investment if it had stood up and whacked him on the snozzle. But this time he thought he was on to something. You know what he did?'

'Raffled it at two deeners a time?'

'He'd've done better if he had. No, he bought a glass device to funnel the water to his canaries — cost him two bob, more than the mug — and he stuffed the mug carefully into a cardboard box and hid it under his bed.'

'Where is it now?'

'Under *my* bed — in a manner of speaking. Dad didn't leave much but I got his mug.'

'How much'd it be worth?'

'As a memento of the Roaring Twenties? Art nouveau? Commemoration of a great historic occasion? Relic of a beloved monarch? Who knows, mate? But I wouldn't part with it for less than five dollars.'

I couldn't help laughing. 'I'll give you ten.'

'No, you won't. I won't sell. Not for a hundred. I don't think I'd sell even for a thousand - if anyone was stupid enough to offer me that much. No, mate, I'll keep that old mug till the day I die — in memory of dear old Dad and his canaries.'

7
Conclusions

None of us, as individuals, has much alternative but to accept the world as it is. We can exercise our democratic rights but change, if it comes where we want it, might come slowly. Whether as citizens or investors, in awaiting a more perfect society and economy, we must live and act within the existing environment, making the best of circumstances to win profits or cut losses. Opportunities for dramatic gains are more apparent in periods of rapid economic change and turmoil; but drama and turmoil add to risks. Investment always calls for care but the imperatives are greater when instability is high.

What can we look forward to? What are the prospects for a more stable evolution of the world economy in, say, the last decade of the century? To answer that question, we need to dig back a little into the past.

The Rise and Fall of Keynesianism

The period between the two world wars was one of economic disruption and turmoil, not because of any failure of resources or scientific and technological progress but because of poor political direction and economic management. Just as economic analysis failed, so well-based macroeconomic policies were lacking. Indeed, until the 1930s, economics was heavily oriented towards microeconomic analysis of the firm, of 'pure competition' and 'perfect/imperfect' markets. Little attention was given to what we now know as macroeconomics: the 'science' of reaching and keeping equilibrium or stability in the national and world economy.

John Maynard Keynes changed all that. The revolution, based on his analysis, which effectively began after the Second World War, gave us, between 1945 and 1970, a quarter of a century of unprecedented growth and stability. Employment and investment were high, idle resources and inflation low. World trade boomed, not without discrimination but with more regard to most-favoured-nation principles than before. Levels of living rose, in the poor countries as well as the rich. Science, technology and a better-educated and skilled labour force, as well as high levels of investment, brought massive increases in productivity. Man went far towards conquering disease and improving the environment. He began to invade space. The first men walked on the moon. In that quarter-century almost everything seemed possible. By 1970, the Keynesian revolution had created a vastly different economy and, with it, had transformed political attitudes within transformed societies.

And then it all fell apart. Why? We must resist the temptation, on the one hand, to enmesh ourselves in a complexity of detailed causes or, on the other, to be too simplistic. But a significant element was that Keynesian macroeconomic policies no longer worked; and, as always happens, when the economy became disordered much of the rest of the political and social environment became disordered too.

Why did our macroeconomic policies, which had worked so splendidly for a full quarter-century, quite suddenly work no longer? Why had Keynesian policies, which had seemed so well adapted to a stable domestic and world economy, suddenly become of no use to us, indeed a drag on the stability they had previously conferred?

The answer lies not in failure but in the success of Keynes' macroeconomic policies and the way they changed human societies, as well as the economy. Those policies made many things possible: from the walk on the moon to decolonisation, the sexual revolution, the liberation of women, the creation or at least a more convincing promise of a world market. The Keynesian revolution alone didn't achieve these things; but it made them achievable. Without it, they would have been much longer coming and some might never have come at all.

So much were the economy and society changed by Keynesian policies that those policies became the instrument of their own obsolescence. The problems of the 1930s, for which they were devised, faded into history, by the 1970s becoming only a distant memory for older generations. But economists continued to think in Keynesian terms and politicians to apply Keynesian remedies even when the circumstances for which they had been devised had gone.

What crucial changes made Keynesian policies inoperative? Let us be clear that, if a non-caring society re-establishes a buccaneering economy reminiscent of the nineteenth and early twentieth centuries, the essence of Keynesian policies will again become relevant. In other words, they are still the remedy for the turmoil of the 1930s, if those days of deep and persistent depression ever return again.

But the problems of the late 1960s were not those of the demand-shortage 1930s; they were supply-shortage problems of an economy trying to do too much with too little, exactly the opposite of the complex of problems on which Keynes' genius had been focused.

Even so, why didn't a Keynesian system still work? That system said that if aggregate demand is deficient, you move it up through government stimulation of investment and consumption until demand and supply come into equilibrium at the point of full employment of labour and other factors of production. If then aggregate *supply* becomes deficient — or, put another way, if aggregate demand overshoots — you apply governmental policies to turn investment and consumption down so as to restore equilibrium at the level of supply for full employment of labour and other factors. There might be some stickiness but Keynesian macroeconomic policies should correct an excess quite as well as a deficiency of aggregate demand.

Why then didn't they? The reason is more social and political — more human — than economic. Economic policies deal with people and people change, their social and political attitudes evolve. But, to use economic jargon, the reason that Keynesian policies no longer worked when demand was excessive was that by about 1970, too many inbuilt stabilisers had been established to keep aggregate demand up. Many of these stabilisers were social services — involving income transfers from the rich to the poor (and some of them not so poor). These had become, almost, 'the untouchables', except for being pushed upwards. And there were many other stabilisers besides. Government participation in the economy had enlarged vastly between 1945 and 1970. In the last few years before the breakdown, real expenditures on such things as education, roads and transport, medical services, as well as income transfers, doubled and promptly began to double again. That was in real terms — before substantial inflation got under way. Most of those expenditures were inflexible too, except upwards. The society had undergone a dramatic change, a fundamental change in character. Social welfare once provided could not be taken away; nor could education, health and other services. Some expenditures were more flexible: defence could be pushed down in some countries in real terms; expenditures on roads and other infrastructure could be reduced or delayed. But, by and large, these were *investment* expenditures by government. (Even much of defence had a flow-on civilian investment character.) If the infrastructure were allowed to run down, then production and productivity would suffer — and it did. Consumption expenditure by governments stayed up or increased; only investment expenditure could be reduced.

The Breakdown, Stagflation, Making Things Worse

The breakdown was precipitated in July 1969 when, after the most dramatic decade of public spending ever, President Nixon's Administration or, more correctly, the Federal Reserve Board acting independently, tried to fight what was, in retrospect, a modest inflation, by raising interest rates and tightening credit. Not only had the Americans joined the Keynesian club as full members during the preceding decade but also they had put a man on the moon and fought an expensive war in Indo-China. The Fed's measures turned employment and production down and hit investment and productivity, but consumer demand stayed up and, with it, inflation. After a lag, the

United States exported its inflation to the rest of the world, which then followed the same policies to halt its own inflation, only to turn the inflationary disease into an epidemic and, as it proved, make it endemic. By the beginning of the 1970s, the trauma of inflation and unemployment was well and truly established. 'Stagflation' — as the jargon named the new virus — infected the body economic and quickly spread. The oil shocks of 1973 and 1979 made it worse.

The crucial feature of stagflation was that governments trying to battle inflation by 'damping down the economy' succeeded only or mostly in cutting back investment (including public infrastructure investment), productivity and production. Supply and the future efficiency of supply were diminished; they were diminished in an inflationary situation in which, if consumer demand stayed high, more goods and services had to be produced to bring supply and demand into equilibrium. And demand, especially consumer demand, did stay high; the inbuilt Keynesian welfare stabilisers, which could be cut very little if at all, saw to that. Political — and social — attitudes were decisive: 'in American politics, the Keynesian idea seemed to work fine on the upside, but it wouldn't work at all on the downside'.[1] And not only in America, but also throughout the non-socialist world. So the strong tendency was for consumption to stay up (a fact that the statistics of the past twenty years in most of the developed countries confirm) while supply was pushed down. Inflation, instead of being reduced, was intensified.

'Those policies never had a chance,' Charlie said. 'They just couldn't work, not *against* inflation and not *for* anything else worth wanting. Look, we had inflation, right? That meant we had too much demand and not enough supply. So to get back on an even keel, we had to get demand down or supply up. No two ways about it, mate. One or the other. And what did we do?'

'We slowed down the economy.'

'And what did that mean?'

'We had less supply.'

---

1 Greider, op. cit., p.333.

'And what about demand?'

'Depends which part of demand you mean. Investment got hit. Consumption stayed up.'

'You're dead right. During the 1970s and into the 1980s, consumption in Australia kept going up all the time. *All the time.* It never stopped. They're not my statistics. They're the Government's...'

'They can be wrong too.'

'Ten years later they damned well *ought* to be right. Anyway, consumption stayed up...'

'Did *all* consumption stay up?'

'No, mate, the restrictive policies - high interest rates and all that — moved the components round — quite a bit, in fact. From time to time, people could buy fewer houses, fewer cars and washing-machines. But the demand shifted to rents, food, clothes, entertainment and other non-credit items — among the poorer people. The cost of those items went up faster than ever.'

'The tough policies must have redistributed income among consumers a bit too.'

'Two things about that: the government spent billions on the unemployed, the needy, the sick — welfare of all kinds. That kept consumption up. Reduced suffering. I admit that. But the little bloke still got hit.'

'He lost his job or his wife gave up looking and his real wages dropped.'

Sacrificial Victims: The Poor

'Not only that, mate. In the United States, in the recessions of the early 1980s induced deliberately by the Fed, labour copped nearly 60 per cent of the loss in income — nearly three-fifths. Farmers and small business lost 20 to 25 per cent. Corporate business which could afford it best bore less than a quarter of the income loss.'

'Was it the same here — in Australia — in the same circumstances?'

'Pretty much. Details vary, but the broad picture remains the same. And there's a lot more to it than that.'

'The banks did well?'

'Dead right, mate. The recession of 1981–2 in the United States — caused by Fed policies, mind you — was pretty fierce. Some sectors had nearly 30 per cent unemployment. Total of 12 million out of work — only a third drawing unemployed benefits. About 5 million others forced to withdraw from the work force. More bankrupt firms than at any time since 1933 and you know what happens?'

'Income goes up?'

'*Real* per capita *income increased.* The real economy was on its knees but finance flourished. When interest rates went up to stop inflation, personal income from interest rose by 67 per cent — two-thirds as much again. By damping down the economy, the Fed succeeded in redistributing income on a vast scale *from the poor* — that's right, from the poor — to the rich. All the welfare payments by the United States Government in 1982 — to unemployed, veterans, the lot — came to $374 billion. But the rich collected nearly as much, $366 billion, from the increase in interest rates. So, despite all the welfare, tens of millions of Americans were a lot poorer. Nearly 5 million were forced to live below a pretty tough poverty line. But the top 10 per cent of Americans holding about 90 per cent[2] of the country's financial assets were richer than ever. "Damping down the economy" meant they had a ball.'

'So if you want to be among the winners, you've got to own financial assets?'

'My oath, mate. You stick to working forty hours a week and paying for your pension, you're going to get clobbered. What's more, you're going to get clobbered by governments, treasurers, central banks, all that lot who say they're doing it for your own good. If you don't take a walloping now, they'll tell you, it'll be worse for you a bit down the road. Sure enough, they're right in this sense: whichever way it goes, it'll be worse for you now or later — if you're the little bloke who only works for his living. So, to stop getting clobbered time and time again — to beat the system and make it work for you, instead of against you — you've got to get yourself some financial assets. You've got

---

2 This and preceding figures are taken from Greider, op. cit., pp.455–7, who added, 'People could sense easily enough that there was something wrong about a system that, in effect, selected certain victims to serve as the scapegoats for everyone else's benefit. The moral problem became even more obvious when the sacrificial victims were largely chosen from among the weak and powerless' (p.469).

to get out of that fixed working-for-wages pattern and get your nose into the investment/finance feedbag. Call it the capitalist feedbag, if you like — and I'm not using that word pejoratively. Capitalism's all right. I've done OK out of it. But you've got to be in it. Not just working for it. You've got to make it work for you. You've got to make the breakthrough. Do it completely is one way — be a full-time buccaneer. Boost your working wages with investment income is another. But one or the other. Nothin' else for it, mate.'

'Getting back to that 1981–2 recession in the States, although real *per capita* income went up, are you saying, Charlie, that production went down?'

'Sure. It had to, hadn't it? The real economy slumped. Industrial production was down about 12 per cent. It happens everywhere — in Australia or anywhere else. If the government slows down the economy, it's always the real economy that slows down first. Factories shut, mines cut back, builders stop building. Workers stop working. They stop being paid by their bosses and get paid instead by the government — for doing nothing. But it's not only current production that gets cut. It's investment — and, down the line, that's got to mean productivity. So the rundown in investment means supply is less likely to catch up with demand in the *future* as well as right now.'

'So they were wrong to apply Keynesian policies?'

'I'd put it another way, mate. Keynesian policies had changed things so much that policies to cut back economic growth — real economic growth — just wouldn't work. It didn't matter whether the cut-back policies were Keynesian or something else. They tried price and income policies. Then they got hooked on monetarism. That was even worse than an outdated Keynesianism. I'm not arguing for one against the other. In what I'm talking about, they were both wrong — dead wrong. Monetarism tried to cure inflation by cutting the money supply — which meant cutting real growth, even throwing the economy into recession. Then you keep paying all the unemployment benefits and pensions, building the roads and schools, slicing infrastructure a bit but holding most unproductive spending up or even increasing it. And of course you give the banks and the rich the biggest bonanza of all time. If you're an investor and already rich or clever enough to be able to snake-charm the financial markets, monetarism was great — it's still great. But for the rest, monetarism's been a bigger disaster than an unreconstructed Keynesianism — but it's taken us all those years to realise it.'

'Have we realised it yet?'

'I doubt it, mate, I really doubt it. Sometimes I think we've got ourselves dried out; then off we go on the monetarist plonk again. Talking about MO's and raising interest rates. How stupid can you get? After all these years. Like in the 1930s, most of the things we did then only made things worse; most of the things we've done since 1970 have only made things worse too.'

'We had Roosevelt's New Deal in the 1930s.'

'We've had nothing equivalent since 1970. A wishy-washy, half-baked, unconvincing "supply-side economics", that's all. And we've had no Keynes.'

'So whatever we tried, instead of getting better, inflation got worse?'

Shifts in Economic Power: Trade Flows

'That was the first phase, mate. If you've got less of something and the same amount of money chasing it, then prices have nowhere to go but up. You don't have to be a genius to work that out. But there was a second phase.'

'Imports?'

'Right. If you cut supply at home and plenty's available overseas, then you import it. Of course, the overseas suppliers might take a while to catch up with demand. But they did — Japan and Taiwan, South Korea, Singapore, Hong Kong, a bit later Malaysia, Thailand, Indonesia, the Philippines and, of course, in the last few years, China. We shut everything down here, they opened everything up there. We handed the Australian market to them on a platter.'

'And turned ourselves back into a farm-and-mine economy?'

'Ruined our balance of payments, blew out our overseas debt and became a heavily weighted commodity exporter again, with all the anxieties that go with it.'

He let his thoughts run. 'You know, twenty years ago, we were exporting Holden cars, men's clothing, biro pens...'

'Where to?'

'Quite a few places. Even as far away as West Africa. West Africa! What do we send there today? Nothing. But Holdens were one of the most popular cars there then. And we threw it all away.'

'Because we tried to fight inflation the wrong way?'

'We didn't *think*, mate, we didn't *think*. And we're still not — we're still pushing interest rates up to "damp down the economy". After twenty years, mate, after twenty years...' He threw his hands up in despair. 'We still haven't learnt.'

He paused, then went on. 'The Treasurer's still talking about the economy "running too hot". "The fast lane", he calls it this time. Fast for whom? Not the little fellow. 'Course, he's not alone. The Chairman of the Fed says the American economy's growing too fast. "Unsustainable", he tells us. The Chancellor of the Exchequer says the same thing about the British economy. "Get growth down to sustainable levels" or something of the sort. So what do they do? They start "pulling the string", as Ronald Reagan used to call it, to throttle back the economy. Slow growth down, even reverse it into recession.'

'What else can they do with growth that's unsustainable?'

'But is it "unsustainable"? That's the whole point. I'd say growth — good sturdy growth — isn't "unsustainable", it's *essential* if we're to get back to stability — back to equilibrium domestically and internationally. Look, mate, if the growth's just coming from runaway consumption, especially based on wild credit, you've got to get that consumption down or hold it steady. But don't push real growth down — growth in production and productivity — because that's where your equilibrium's got to come from.'

'Like Japan and the east Asian dynamos?'

'Exactly. They don't worry about the economy running too hot or being in the fast lane or growth being unsustainable. Because it's not — even when growth's over 10 per cent a year. If you've got the right growth, with supply attuned to consumption and the factors of production, including labour and investment funds, fully employed, you're not going to be in much trouble. If you are, it's the sort of trouble I'd like us to be in for a change.

How'd it be to see Australia running hot, neck and neck with Japan? Boy, I'd cheerfully give my old man's canary mug away to get an eyeful of that...'

As Charlie said, some countries seemed immune from the mainstream Western disease. Japan suffered relatively little inflation or unemployment. Investment continued at high levels; so did exports. Productivity and production surged almost continuously upward. The oil shocks caused a temporary dip in Japanese perfection. They also hit Germany, the nearest European equivalent to Japan. Germany, Japan and Switzerland maintained investment, productivity and production, with low rates of inflation and strong payments balances. As the years passed, they were joined by newly industrialising countries which also seemed immune from the preponderant Western disease.

The Process of Self-destruction

Why was this? They weren't superhuman. They just applied the right policies. Essentially, they applied positive policies encouraging investment, production and productivity. Savings were encouraged, interest rates low, funds directed to real investment. Currencies were undervalued or at least not overvalued; and they weren't periodically pushed up to artificial levels to 'fight inflation'. These positive policies produced a supply and concurrently a financial surplus to meet and finance deficits of those mainstream Western countries applying anti-inflationary policies which restricted investment, productivity and production.

How had such destructive policies come about? When the mainstream Western economies became disenchanted with Keynesian policies, the policies they put in their place, especially monetarism, were equally destructive, with the same damaging effect on investment, production and productivity; and, ironically, they gave the same upward thrust to inflation until surplus countries such as Japan, West Germany and, increasingly, the newly industrialising countries of east Asia made good the supply shortfalls.

The problem was then converted into one of financing the external deficits, most dramatically that of the United States. The deficits of those countries with supply shortages could only be met by countries with surpluses. During the

1970s, the oil-rich countries provided much of the finance. In the 1980s, Japan, Germany and the east Asian countries provided it, either by direct lending and investment or through unrealistically low exchange rates and accumulation of gold and foreign currency reserves.

If this held inflation back, it created massive financial and currency problems, leading to financial situations that, in the longer term — and perhaps in a shorter term — really are unsustainable. But, as individual investors, we have to live with these situations and try to make money out of them. The imbalances, the massive financing to meet them, the fluctuations in exchange rates, especially of the American dollar but also of the currencies of other major and middle economies, have caused a huge, unprecedented surge in international finance and speculation. This has created and will continue to offer opportunities for gain but the risks can be intimidating.

The Prospects for Stability

So, with that as background, what do we have to look forward to in the 1990s? If mainstream Western governments can adopt policies to stimulate investment, productivity and production, policies that will stimulate real growth to keep pace with consumption as well as with private and public investment, then we can look forward to stability of the kind we enjoyed during the period from 1945 to 1970.

These mainstream governments will need to take a leaf out of their own book of forty years ago:

> as [wartime] controls were gradually lifted, the predictable postwar price inflation did occur — 8.5 percent in 1946, 14.4 percent the next year. Yet, despite the huge swell in government debt, the inflation after World War II was notably less intense than the price spirals that had followed other major wars. A substantial share of the government debt, vast as it was, had been spent on real capital formation — investment in new factories and new technologies that raised the productivity of the nation in real terms. If real production increased more or less in step with the expansion of money, it would not be inflationary. [3]

Much the same sort of leaf can be taken out of the books of Japan and the newly industrialising, east Asian countries, which have stimulated investment, productivity and production and consequently been able to maintain high growth, low unemployment, high and improving living levels and a strong external payments position. Indeed, they have been the true 'mainstream' countries of the past twenty years.

Comforting as it might be to imagine that, after twenty years of instability, the United States and most Western governments will now take the right leaves out of the right books, any such expectation could be illusory. There is still a heavy dependence on interest rate hikes and other monetary and fiscal devices to curb growth of the economy — not only growth of consumption but more importantly growth of investment; and it is growth of investment, leading to improved productivity and enhanced production, that is the best counter to inflationary pressures. In other words, governments still seek to lick inflation by curbing the very things whose healthy expansion will put an end to it.

The prospect for the 1990s is, therefore, that instabilities will continue and could get worse. More ministers and officials now speak approvingly of supply-side measures; but their primitive supply-side, mainly tax-cut policies, together with such buzz-word expedients as deregulation, privatisation and restructuring, are unlikely to be enough. Any adequate theoretical framework is still lacking and integrated policies to stimulate investment, productivity and production have yet to emerge.

Therefore, the prospects are that you, the investor, must envisage much the same environment persisting as in recent years, with the possibility, on the one hand, of grave worldwide crises as disequilibria and distortions intensify or, on the other, of a gradual alleviation of conditions as governments fumble their way towards saner policies. The speed of any gradual alleviation will depend on how soon governments can embrace and coordinate sensible macroeconomic approaches; and acceleration might come

---

3 Greider, op. cit., p.325.

only from a crisis or collapse of a magnitude even more serious than any we have experienced so far.

'Whichever way it goes, there's going to be a lot of volatility,' Charlie said. 'Suppose governments really do get their act together at last, there's going to be a great mess to clear up. The financial débris can be handled — so can the pretty massive redirection of trade that'll be needed — but they'll both call for a lot of careful thinking, as well as goodwill and cooperation. We'll need something of the kind we had after the Second World War when we were clearing up the mess both of the war and the 1930s.'

'Suppose they don't get their act together?'

'Mind you, I think they will. I reckon it's a matter of when rather than whether. I liked the way they handled things after the October '87 crash. Showed they'd been reading their history — and learned something from it. Not a lot, but something. So they might muddle through. But if they don't, if things just go on getting more and more out of kilter, credit gone mad at the personal, corporate and government level — wild flows across the international exchanges — then I don't like to think where it'll end. Look at our plastic card credit. Massive. In Australia — and most other developed countries. Not Japan though, although they tell me they're catching on. But we can't even control consumption in that area — our credit cards. If we can't manage that, what can we manage? That's what worries me. If we keep on letting things get more and more wacky — more distorted in terms of consumption and production, more distorted as among major world economies — the results won't be just economic, mate, and the social and political fall-out'll be damned hard to predict.'

'What about the communist countries? What's going to happen there?'

'Too hard for me, mate. I'll tell you this, though: what's been started's going to be real tough to put into reverse.'

'They could get rid of Gorbachev.'

'And Deng. He can't have too much time left anyway. But what'd it change? Can you see a Stalin or a Brezhnev in Moscow again or a Mao Tse Tung in Beijing? And what about the Eastern Europeans?'

'Independent? Taking on a new political system?'

'A new *economic* system too, mate. Not exactly capitalist

— not right away — but clearly moving away from socialism, some countries faster than others.'

'A sort of neo-capitalism?'

'You could call it that. A mixed economy — the mix getting less state-regulated all the time.'

'So, what'll be the effect of neo-capitalist economies in Eastern Europe, China, perhaps even the Soviet Union itself?'

'It won't happen overnight. There'd be chaos if it did. As I see it, there's bound to be turmoil anyway. But, with luck, it can be contained — and imagine hundreds of millions of Europeans — and a billion in China — making a bolt for a better life — more real investment, more for consumers, more international trade...'

'It's trying to happen already.'

'Wait till it builds up a real head of steam — if it does. Then it's got to affect the whole world economy. Not just peripherally, mate, but fundamentally.'

'And that's going to affect amateur investors the world over?'

'Amateurs, professionals, farmers and manufacturers, financiers — the whole box and dice. What'll be the effect on commodity markets — metals, grains, sugar, meat? What about capital flows? Real investment. Demand for capital equipment and new technology. So how about trade? The so-called removal of barriers within the European Community from 1992 could be dwarfed by changes in trade between Eastern and Western Europe.'

'What about Pacific rim trade?'

'Hard to see the limits, mate, if China wakes up — without a nightmare. We might have to revise our ideas about a lot of demand and supply magnitudes. Bound to affect Australia — our farm and mine economy, of course, but it'll issue a new challenge to diversify. It's hard to see all the details but I tell you, mate, the decade to the end of the century's goin' to move real fast. We'll only see how much the world's been changed when we get a chance to look back. I wouldn't like to try to predict more than that, but the investor's going to have to keep on his toes.'

'But he could make a lot of money on any one of a lot of things in tumult?'

'Or lose it.'

The Impact on Investment

How will these prospects affect real investment on the one
hand and what Keynes called the 'bubble of speculation' on
the other? How true is it that 'what is happening in the
financial markets today bears the same relationship to what
happened in the "go-go years" of the 1960s as Caesar's
Palace bears to the local church bingo game' and that 'we
are turning the financial markets into a huge casino'?[4]
What windows of opportunity will open, with what risks for
you, the amateur investor, wanting to get your limited
resources working to greatest advantage at minimum risk?

There'll be some specific situations to watch. For
example:

> It is the Australian market's sharp swings of sentiment that
> appeal to many adventurous foreign investors: it acts like an
> option on the rest of the world. Accounting for a little over 1
> per cent of the world's stockmarket capitalisation, Australia can
> be counted on to fall further than other markets when troubles
> mount for the world economy; yet when those troubles fade it
> soars the swiftest. Overseas (mainly British) investors were big
> buyers of Australian shares in the first nine months of [1988],
> but have sold many since. As soon as interest rates appear to
> have peaked (next summer [1989] at the earliest), expect
> foreigners to return in force. [5]

But the implications go far beyond such specific
situations. Perceptive investors will need to keep an eye on
the evolution of broad policies for the domestic and world
economy and act within the economic environment they
set. That sounds like a pretty tough order; but we can hope
that perceptions honed over recent years will manage to
cope with the complexities ahead.

Apart from the evolution of macroeconomic policies,
there are other unknowns. The socialist tide has ebbed.
Deregulation, privatisation, policies so far crudely perceived

---

4 Brooks, *The Takeover Game*, p.32. Brooks was quoting Felix G. Rohatyn, senior
partner in the investment banking firm of Lazard Freres, speaking to the
American Society of Newspaper Editors in 1984.

5 The *Economist*, 11 February 1989, p.81.

to impart economic vigour have led us back to some of the wilder, more primitive shores of capitalism.

'They threw in the towel,' Charlie said, 'the pollies and the bureaucrats. They spent all those years telling us they knew better than anyone else how to run the economy. Then, when they'd stuffed it up — when they didn't have a clue where to go from anywhere — they said "we're not going to be responsible any more — let everything run free — leave it to the market" — as though anyone knows what the market is or who runs it...'

'Wouldn't they say no one runs it — it's a power in its own right, detached and beneficent?'

'That's the good way of puttin' it, mate. But how can the market run free when the government spends thirty, forty per cent, maybe more of the GNP, when it takes as much in taxes, when it plays around with exchange rates and interest rates, when it raises more capital than you can poke a stick at on the money markets — or repays more loans? Not, mind you, that markets'd be more detached if governments didn't disrupt 'em so much. Markets are men. Markets are who's operating in them, who's manipulating them, who's controlling them.'

Capitalist buccaneers have reappeared, this time more exclusively in finance than in the 'real' economy.

In the 1960s, investors, both institutional and individual, looked for a long, unbroken series of reported quarterly earnings increases. In the 'eighties — when such increases might go on for years before being marginally reflected in stock price — they looked more often for the asset-rich, price-depressed company that might bring them a 30- or 50-percent profit overnight through a takeover offer.[6]

Gyrations in interest rates and volatility in financial markets have been a gift from the gods to those who can shuffle financial paper, especially on a grand scale. Of the Fed's yo-yo handling of finance in the early years of the Reagan Administration, William Greider wrote:

But what damaged American production was rewarding for

---

6 Brooks, op. cit., p.28.

American finance, especially for the major banks active in international markets. The rising dollar meant simply that the value of their overseas dollars was rising too. It also meant that market demand was growing for the commodity that American financial institutions traded — US financial assets. As long as the Fed held interest rates high — higher than competing returns in foreign countries — capital naturally flowed across boundaries, seeking the higher returns available in American financial instruments. And, as the demand for dollars increased, the dollar would naturally get harder and harder in foreign exchange. In other words, the stronger dollar was good for business - if your business was finance.[7]

The banks and the financial buccaneers seldom had it so good. The smart ones still do.

The Passing of the Caring Society

But the caring society of the 1960s has been largely superseded. The rich care less for the poor countries and the rich everywhere care less for their own poor than they did. That the tide of socialist economics has receded we can acknowledge without much regret; but we can be less complacent that the tide of caring, which was part of the social democratic morality, has ebbed along with it.

The uncaring past has, so far, been robustly but not unashamedly resurrected. Some residue of caring and consciousness of human rights and suffering still modifies the starkness of the new capitalism; and the pendulum which swung so abruptly to deregulated societies and a more *laisser-faire* world community could swing back. President Bush's campaign rhetoric about a kinder and gentler society might yet gather substance. But the essential elements of proud and rampant capitalism are likely to persist. That should mean, adapting Adam Smith's *Wealth of Nations* to the modern situation, that freedom for the buccaneers will be the invisible hand bringing us all a better material life in a better physical and social environment.

Although we have yet to see whether it will, what we are concerned with here is less the philosophy than the

---

7 Greider, op. cit., p.416.

practicalities of what it will mean for the individual — for you and me — in Western societies. Will we passively accept what goes on around us, applauding the active participants including the adventurers, the marauders and the buccaneers? Or will we — you and I — participate actively ourselves in the new, worldwide capitalist society?

The active participant stands the best chance of doing well. Two points can be made. First, people in developed Western societies are much richer than previous generations. (Even the poverty line, though regrettably many still live below it, is drawn at a higher real-income level than applied to earlier generations.) But, second, wealth is still unevenly distributed: in the United States at the start of the 1980s, '54 percent of total net financial assets were held by the 2 percent of families with the greatest amount of such assets and 86 percent by the top 10 percent; 55 percent of the families...had zero or negative net worth'.[8] Inequalities are probably even more marked now. In Britain, much the same trends have been evident, with financial assets being even more heavily concentrated in the hands of fewer people in the middle and later 1980s. In 'egalitarian' Australia, income and wealth show the same widening inequalities: household income, 8.2 times as much for the rich as for the poor in 1984, grew to 9.7 times in 1985-6. The World Bank calculated that 10 per cent of Australian families enjoyed about a third of all household income in the 1970s while the bottom 25 per cent received only 5 per cent, a more unequal income distribution than in any other Western country. Between 1972 and 1982, the proportion of people living in poverty increased from 8.2 per cent to 12.5 per cent, or, according to another survey, from 10.5 per cent in 1982 to 13 per cent in 1986. A study by the Australian National University found that the richest 1 per cent of the population owned one-third and the top 10 per cent at least 60 per cent of the country's wealth; while a Labor Member of Parliament estimated that the total wealth of the 200 richest Australians more than trebled from $A7.3 billion in 1984 to almost $A25 billion in 1987 — during the term of office of the Hawke *Labor* Government.

Although the statistics on which these findings are based

---

8 Report of the Federal Reserve Board, quoted by Greider, op. cit., p.39.

are imperfect and the various surveys are not always comparable, the assessments, all by responsible observers, agree that the marked and persistent trends of the last fifteen years or so have been in the direction of greater inequalities in income and wealth.[9] This uneven distribution, whether in Australia or elsewhere, can best be remedied not by expropriating the rich, but through effective acquisition of income-earning assets by a wider spread of the population.

The Quest for Economic Democracy

That is more possible than it was. Many people now can exercise a variety of options in utilising their financial and other economic resources; they are better educated and better informed; they have more leisure; they are free to utilise their time with some flexibility; and facilities are available to allow them, if they wish, to participate actively in their own economic system. They don't need to surrender that system, its operation and benefits to the professionals, including the adventurers, the marauders and the buccaneers. No one need any longer classify himself irretrievably as a 'worker' or 'employee', as distinct from those who command the economy from the heights. 'Workers' can be investors, traders, builders, even — if their ambitions drive — commanders of small or large parts of the economy. Nothing economic is really beyond anyone who, as the old saw goes, sets his mind to it. Nor is anyone restricted to an unrewarding lifetime niche from which his destiny denies him any escape.

Is it a good thing if we participate actively in this way? Can we confidently assert that what is good for us is good for the country — and for the economy and the international community? The answer to these questions must be 'yes'. The more of us who participate actively and with understanding in the new capitalism, the more successful it should be, the more equally the rewards should be shared and the sooner our society should be able to resume its responsibility of care for the less fortunate.

People in Western societies already devote more time and

---

9 This data is drawn from the *Bulletin*, Sydney, 25 April 1989, pp.54–5.

energy than they did to matters of personal investment, as a derivative of their higher income and wealth and a concomitant of the society in which they live. They can opt out, as some chose to do in the 1960s. But the majority do not — and do not *want* to. The not-unreasonable prospect — or hope — might be that more and more of them will see the new capitalism and their own more numerous options as providing an opportunity and a challenge, rather than as something to fear and therefore as something to walk away from by abdicating responsibility to the large financial institutions.

In an ideal situation, this will intensify as the years pass. People's welfare will depend more and more not on how well they work — important though that might be — as on how well they invest. People who are richer and have more options can choose to save more — or less — according to their wishes and the demands made by their particular time of life. They can choose to invest in one thing or another. They can invest throughout their working lives, during part of it or when they have retired, have more resources and see themselves as having more free time.

'The working man's not going to achieve his breakthrough by chasing the traditional trade union goals,' Charlie said.

'What else is there? Participation by labour in ownership and management?'

'Through the union movement? No, that's got whiskers on it. The workers don't believe in it themselves.'

'Management buy-outs?'

'Management's not labour but it's a step along the right lines. It could turn out to be a fad. Looking back from 1995, we might wonder what it was all about. A sort of eccentricity arising from the financial turbulence of the eighties.'

'But it could offer something.'

'If it gets across the idea that ownership — real investment — is the right of everyone, yes. What I want to see is a million — a hundred million — managers and workers being owners in the sense that some of them at least will join the adventurers, the marauders and the buccaneers, not leave the whole thing to an arrogant few...'

'Arrogant?'

'No, that's the wrong word. It's not that they're arrogant.

Not all of them anyway. It's just that they've realised how easy it is. They wake up one morning and say to themselves, "Hey, I've got the hang of this. It's dead simple. I can make a million without hardly moving a muscle. How is it everyone's not doing it?" Now what I want is for everyone to latch on to that notion. It's the breakthrough for the working man and it can give us a genuine economic democracy — a democracy of opportunity, if not of achievement.'

'Haven't we had that in Australia for a long time?'

'In theory, yes. In practice, the democracy of opportunity has concentrated on the fields of education and professional qualification — and it hasn't done even that too bloody well. What we want now is democracy of opportunity in investment and enterprise — something that will give us a better spread of income and wealth — the only thing in the end that'll do it.'

The development of a property-owning society has been actively encouraged by some governments. As a matter of policy, the Thatcher Government in Britain has sought to extend property ownership so that more become capitalists, big or small; using such devices as mortgage concessions for house purchase and, fortuitously more than by preconceived design, through 'privatisation'. The Chancellor of the Exchequer, in his 1989 Budget, gave the process further support through reinforcing such devices as Personal Equity Plans, though direct equity investment seemed to be encouraged less than unit and like investment through large financial institutions. In practice, the latter would reinforce the already formidable power of those institutions and their managers, rather than bring the little investor directly on to the investment and enterprise market in greater numbers.

If the process has been given particular form in Britain, something of the substance is emerging elsewhere, though hesitantly and without any clear definition as to where it is going or should be going. Actually or potentially, the process could involve all age groups: the young with their need to get started, not only in careers but also in accumulating financial and economic assets; the middle-aged looking for family financial security and, on the horizon, a secure retirement; the elderly with their often considerable accumulation of retirement resources looking for investment. This process makes it all the more necessary that knowledge of effective investment be spread throughout the community.

This is the more so since, despite the rise in real incomes and the massive accumulation of economic assets, the great majority still remain asset-poor. Though richer, most people fail to make the most of their greater income to enlarge their asset holdings; they fail to take that step which will change their almost total dependence on personal exertion to greater reliance on and support from ownership of financial assets.

Even in the United States, where stock market and other more sophisticated forms of investment are spread most widely, only a small proportion of people have substantial investments and many have no real assets at all.

American families, on average, had $24,000 in financial assets, according to a survey of consumer finances conducted by the Federal Reserve Board. But this was an instance where the average of all Americans was grossly misleading, distorted by the concentrated wealth in the upper half. The median was only $2,300, which meant that precisely half of American families owned financial assets, including checking deposits, savings accounts or any others, that totaled less than $2,300. More than a fourth of all families had less than $1,000 and another 12 percent had none...37 percent of American families had no savings account at all. Another 29 percent had savings balances below $2,000...Half of the elderly households, sixty-five years old or older, had no savings account at all. Another 11 percent had less than $1,000...Only 29 percent of the elderly had more than $5,000 in savings...Half of the families in America...had checking balances of $500 or less... When equity in homes was added to the family balance sheet, alongside financial assets, the median family's net worth was $24,500 — $22,000 of it in the family home. [10]

In Australia, tight money, high interest rates, deregulation and the raft of economic measures which, for the most part unintentionally, have redistributed income and wealth from the poor to the rich, have reduced the

---

10 Greider, op. cit., pp.38, 43, 166.

extent of popular investment even in their own housing. A recent survey [11] suggests that 5 per cent of Australians are now living in shared accommodation and that this percentage will almost double to 9 per cent or 1.5 million Australians by the year 2000.

So even the United States has a long way to go before any significant investment is spread over a majority of the population. In other countries, the achievement of anything approaching 'popular' or 'democratic' participation in even the simpler investment forms is likely to take much longer. Having said that, I must also acknowledge that the situation is changing. Apart from government encouragement, competition for investment funds from an increasingly dense jungle of institutions is focusing the attention of individuals more and more on investment possibilities. The general press as well as specialist publications have helped the process. 'Personal investment' has become a regular feature in the popular as well as the quality newspapers — and on radio and, in more limited measure, on television, so that people of widely differing social and economic backgrounds are now being educated and drawn into active and direct participation in investment. I still need to register some reservations. For example, most investment is indirect, through various funds, insurance and pension schemes. Although some statistics, such as those for individual shareholders in British, (including privatised) companies, suggest a rapid evolution in direct investment, these figures are probably misleading and perhaps politically motivated. Nevertheless, the trend they disclose may be broadly accurate.

At the same time, there are dangers even in such of these trends as may be superficially valid. What small investors should *not* want is to collect a few share certificates of British Petroleum or British Coal or a water-distribution company which might gather dust in some drawer like a postcard celebrating Queen Elizabeth's coronation. There might be some 'prestige' in being a shareholder; it might feel good to fly in 'your own' airline, in which you own a minimum parcel of shares, but will that be enough if the

---

11 By BIS Shrapnel Pty Ltd, as reported in the *Australian*, 27 April 1989.

dividends are poor and the value of the shares steadily declines? But much more than that: it changes nothing in the reality of the economy or its power centres.

The Economic 'Uncle Toms': Free the Slaves!

To change that reality, investment must be a continuing experience — and should be hard-headed, quite different from the open-eyed innocence and gullibility of the more vulnerable among the economic Uncle Toms. Investment in some formerly nationalised industry might set you off along the road to equity investment — but that's all it should be: a beginning, a first try about which you will reflect and on which you will build in ways most beneficial *to you*. If it's not, the holding of a few shares by a crowd of small investors might create the illusion of democratic capitalism, concealing the reality that a mass of small shareholders do little more than inflate share values for the benefit of the major owners and controllers of financial assets, whether individuals or institutions. What we don't want is another three-card trick which seems to be democratising investment while it really redistributes income even more inequitably to the few per cent who already hold or control most of the financial assets.

At the outset, you should beware of several things:

(1) Don't let others take your money from you to make profitable investments themselves. Those who will try will not necessarily be scoundrels or confidence men. Most will be reputable institutions inviting you to lend your money to them at low rates of interest or to take up pension or superannuation arrangements which, though beguiling, offer you poor returns. Examine with very great care *any* proposal to use your money for investment by others. It may profit you more to invest your own money directly yourself.

(2) Don't fall for the slick share deal. Some fashionable shares *may* be worthwhile. But the shooting stars are the ones to avoid, unless, early in their fashionable career, you take a calculated risk to get in before they reach for the heavens and then get out quickly while the going is good. But whether they're shooting stars or long-established blue chips, examine their present status and performance

carefully and buy, hold or sell accordingly. And don't forget that a share's value is what the market puts on it. If the market is bullish about a share, you should consider buying even though you know the fundamentals are poor. But then you must be prepared to get out quickly before the market wakes up to how poor those fundamentals are.

(3) Don't delude yourself that all property investment is good; and don't be fooled by loose talk about the 'long run'. The long run might be too long for your limited destiny. Just as there will be people who will try to get you to buy poor shares, so there will be many who will try to sell you poor property. Never buy property sight unseen or be taken in by a glossy prospectus. Resist buying a ranch in faraway Texas or in Sturt's Stony Desert. Practise being a sceptic and a cynic; and buy only when you've set your own doubts comfortably at rest.

Self-confidence

Along with the practice of scepticism should go the practice of self-confidence. Remember that there is nothing very difficult about making profitable investments. Don't be frightened by marble-clad institutions, by esoteric jargon or by the 'geniuses' of the financial world. If you're careful about your first investment and exercise good judgement, that will help build self-confidence. If you can do it once, you can do it again — and again.

Remember too that even the richest, the most expert, the financial 'geniuses', make mistakes. Millions were caught in the stock market crash of October 1987, many of them until then regarded as brilliant big-time investors and entrepreneurs. So do your best to avoid mistakes but don't be too depressed if occasionally you make one. Don't hitch your star too closely to *any* expert; and never so closely that you'll suffer from the mistakes he'll inevitably make. Become your own expert. Your judgement can be as good as anyone else's; and no one will be as attentive to your best interests as you should be yourself. So never entrust your fortune to the imagined god-like judgement of any financial guru.

Within this general safeguard, you should avoid too great reliance on unit/investment trusts of various kinds. The chances are the rewards they will offer will be small and, in any event, might not be as 'safe' and assured as they appear. After all, those managing the trusts must get their cut — and, when you read the small print, it could be hefty. But, quite apart from that, to rely too heavily on investments made by other people is to abandon your future to them. None of us should do it. Especially, to the extent that we do rely on investments made by others, we should gather all the information we can about the managers of the trusts and the investments they're making. Never fly blind. We should always know where we're going and who is taking us there. And if we know these things, why not make our own investments ourselves? Why not get the managers' cut as well as the rest? Why not maximise our own gains — in a way no one else, intent on his own fortunes, will ever do?

That doesn't mean you should not take advice. You should. Grab it from wherever you can get it. But assess it yourself. Be confident, as I've said, that your own judgement can be as good as anyone else's. As your experience grows, it will be better than most others'. So receive advice, pass it through the computer of your own mind and experience and set out on your next investment project with a good assessment of prospects and risks.

Increasingly, too, you might be able to rely not only on the computer of your own mind but also on using expert systems to run through your personal home computer — what has been called 'smart advice from dumb machines'. These expert systems can be used to interpret data from stock, currency and commodity markets or any other in which you might be interested. In the end, you will still have to make the decisive judgement, but you will be making that judgement at the end of the line when the data has gone through several phases of analysis.

Unlike the jobs computers have done in the past — like totting up payroll figures — there are no right or wrong answers in most expert-system applications. There is only better or worse. This means that humans must be prepared to argue a bit with the machines in order to get the most out of them. Expert-system builders at Britain's PA Consultants describe three stages in the acceptance of a system they built to advise stockmarket arbitragers. At first, the arbs paid no attention to the machine. Then the computer identified a big money-making opportunity, which, because the arbs weren't paying attention, they missed. So for the next few weeks the arbs did everything the machine advised, until, inevitably, it goofed and they lost money. Finally, the arbs recognised that the machine has strengths and weaknesses, and learned how to treat it accordingly. [12]

These systems aren't yet in widespread use. But they will be. Part-time investors working from home will be able to be as effective as stock market arbitragers and other full-time professionals. They will still have to form their final judgement as to when, how and how much to invest. That judgement — the 'yes' or 'no' that will mean profit or loss — will, in a sense, be as hard or easy as ever. But the basis on which part-time investors make their judgement will be so much better that a sea-change could take place in 'democratic' or 'populist' investing. The barriers could come down, enabling anyone to invest sensibly in any market anywhere in the world. All you need is to acquire a user-friendly computer and a relevant expert system.

An Organised Life

As that indicates, much more important than taking advice from others — indeed, much the most important element in anything you do — is to have your life well organised. You don't need to plan every last minute of every day; but try to manage your time well, so that you have time for work, time for play — and time for making a little extra on the side. That makes for a productive life and helps greatly towards a happy one. Organisation and management. And a reasonable degree of discipline. That doesn't mean standing to attention twenty-four hours a day. Don't discipline yourself into a strait-jacket. But don't fritter away that part of your time that could be painlessly applied to making money. Follow the rules that have been outlined in this book or, if you have better rules, follow those. But don't let yourself slip into sloppy ways, at least where making money is concerned.

---

12 The *Economist*, London, 18 January 1989.

If you're disciplined in making money, you'll be able to let your hair down in other things — in enjoying life the way you want. In things other than making money — sailing to romantic Pacific islands, having a ball in season and out, buying ocean-going yachts for the sheer pleasure of it without thought of a 10 per cent return, inviting charming and attractive guests to your elegant pad on the shores of the Mediterranean — in these things, you can let your discipline slip. That, after all, is what you became rich for. If you use a fair measure of discipline in making money, you can afford some indiscipline in spending it.

So organisation and management. A seasoning of discipline. And steady homework. Know what you're investing in. Make well-directed enquiries. Assess the managers of any enterprise to which you're thinking of entrusting your money. You don't need to work so hard in becoming a millionaire that you'll ever have to raise a sweat. But you'll need to flex your mental muscles regularly and feed them enough data to keep them supple and healthy for their daily workout. This flexing of your mental muscles can be less tiring than jogging and less time-consuming than keeping up with the daily racing and sporting pages. Of course, you can work harder if you want to. That's up to you. But all you really need is so to organise your life that you allot enough 'jogging time' each day to enable you to keep a finger on the pulse of business affairs. Do that and you'll be on your way to making your millions with the easy assurance of the legendary 'financial genius'.

A Real-world 'Monopoly'

So you'll need organisation and management, a dash of discipline and a 'jogging' allotment of homework. The regime isn't painful; and, with the right approach, can be almost no sweat at all. That right approach is to be serious about your investments but make a game of them too. A twentieth-century Dutch philosopher, Johan Huizinga, worried about 'a far-reaching contamination of play and serious activity'. Because 'the two spheres are getting mixed', 'the indispensable qualities of detachment, artlessness, and gladness are...lost'. He was right that the 'gladness' of sport should not be overwhelmed by an obsession with financial rewards; nor should economic activity be 'contaminated' by irresponsibility. But within those limits, your investment activities can bring you rewards and at the same time be good fun: a game of Monopoly that is for keeps; a game that is a part-time occupation, entertaining and rewarding. You can take an interest in the personalities of the investment world; and an interest in your fellow shareholders in a company. They won't all be pop-stars but some will shine. Go along to a company meeting or two. Most will be pretty dull, unless the company's in crisis or there's a get-up-and-go shareholder who wants to spark some life into a fuddy-duddy set of directors and managers. But even company meetings get less dull when you own a part of the company, you know what the mine looks like and you can follow the company balance-sheet.

Take a look at the stock exchange in action. See the operators on the floor. You might be interested in the new technology evolving so rapidly to handle worldwide trading. You might be interested in the psychology of trading: why some stocks go up and some, though sound and well run, stumble along in the doldrums. Why does no one get excited about the enormously profitable, well-run Unilever — with a turnover of about $A35 billion and an operating profit of about $A2 billion a year — but become frantic about all sorts of shooting stars and penny dreadfuls? Is it true that some stocks can, like an actor or a politician, be charismatic while others, despite their quality, lack the capacity to appeal to the investor? Is charisma important? Should you buy stocks that, on the basis of their quality, *should* go up or stocks that, whatever their quality, *will* go up? What happens when a company decides to change its image? 'Mike Angus promised more openness when he took over as chairman of the UK half of Unilever in 1986 and the investor relations roadshow has been on the move since,' the *Financial Times* reported on 13 January 1989. 'The result in recent months has been an almost universal shift from "hold" to "buy" in brokers' ratings...'

That shift in ratings did not immediately inspire action by investors but Unilever managers were confident it would 'be translated into institutional buying, especially in the US market, once the bout of buy-out, bust-up and bid speculation in the consumer sector starts to wane'. So this could be an interesting situation for you as an investor. Is this the moment, with the 'brokers' ratings' going up, to buy Unilever? Will the company's changed image make a big difference to the company's market price? What about that 'buy-out, bust-up and bid speculation in the consumer market'? How long will that last and, therefore, how long might it be before the change in Unilever's image can make any impact? Should you wait a while before you buy Unilever shares? If you wait too long, will the price go beyond your reach so that you'll never be able to afford a small slice of ownership in one of the world's greatest multinational companies?

These are fascinating questions in the real-life Monopoly game. But they're not the only ones. If you're more mathematically inclined, you might like to indulge yourself by probing the intricacies of chartist projections or other systems for forecasting trends. There's an annual 'Chart Seminar' you might like to take in on your next excursion to London, Paris, Copenhagen or Zurich. That could be amusing as well as enriching.

But don't let yourself be mesmerised by the more arcane systems. Treat them as part of the data to enhance your interest and enable you to play a better game. But the most important thing is to know the market well and how people there behave. Get to know how real economies work; find out all you can about the world. Don't be overwhelmed by mathematical or graphic abstractions. But don't forget either that charts and other systems influence or determine the decisions of many investors. That's an element you must take into account in making your own decisions about when to buy or sell.

It is for you to determine what aspects interest you most and how far you want to pursue them. Your interest in investment shouldn't mean reducing your interest in music or football or television but rather adding a new form of relaxation — which will, incidentally, finance much of what else you want to do.

In indulging that 'relaxation', don't press yourself too hard — unless, of course, you want to. You might develop such a passion for making millions that it becomes your dominant preoccupation. If so, well and good. But, if that happens, you will have passed outside the more modest investing circle I've been talking to here. For the more modest, less obsessed people, the normal practice will be to start along the investment road in a small way. A first humble stake. A small loan. An inexpensive purchase and a short wait. A first coup. Then repeat — and repeat. Enquire into new forms of investment. Keep your appetite sharp. Don't invest in something just because it's novel; but don't ignore the new. You might find new inspiration — and profit. But, if you do invest, make sure beforehand that the novel has real potential for profit, superior to the old and tried.

Never forget timing. Buy the right share or the right house at the wrong time and you could spend months or years regretting it. Buy the right house or the right share — or the right stamp or painting — at the right moment and your ships could keep coming in. Buy in a slump — or as near to it as you can get. Never buy in a runaway boom. That's the time to sell. To buy, wait patiently until the cycle comes round again and, in the meantime, invest in something else — if you can find it — that is in a slump right now. If you can't find it, then don't invest in anything. 'The windows of opportunity are small,' someone said, 'and move past very quickly'. That's true; but don't deceive yourself into imagining windows that aren't really there. Wait patiently until a 'window' really does appear. Then act quickly.

Buy in a slump but never invest in anything just because it's in a slump. Some things have slumped for good. Some will never boom — never have a lively market again. Don't invest in an ostrich farm when the fashion for ostrich feathers has passed. If the fashion looks like coming back and there's a shortage of ostriches, it could be worth thinking about — provided it comes back this year and not the end of next century. But, as a general rule, buy low into something whose market, though secure, is, like most things, subject to fluctuations in supply and demand. If prices are very volatile, you might be taking a risk unless your footwork is very good. You might need to hop in through that 'window' quickly and jump out again, into the fireman's catcher, like a streak of light. Don't overestimate your capacity to escape. Don't imagine you're a Houdini. Limit your risks. Take none you don't have to.

That brings us back to a very important point: this is not a manual for gamblers. It advocates that you minimise risks and maximise gains. It doesn't put the risk *into* but seeks to take as much as possible of the risk *out of* everyday investing. It is designed to set you on a safe, secure, sober road to becoming a millionaire. The rest is up to you. Don't work too hard on it. Have fun on the way. Meet interesting people. And make enough to get yourself a fine house, perhaps a little villa in the South of France, maybe a boat to take out on the harbour and, in your old age, friends to console you with their love and affection. We can hope that, very soon, you'll be well on your way along that happy road, you'll have your bank manager in the palm of your hand and you'll be looking round for the most convenient marina to park your ocean-going yacht.

Charlie's Recipe for Riches

'What's *your* recipe for getting rich?' I asked Charlie.
'Start poor.'
'Most people do.'
'Be uncomfortable in your poverty.'
'Most people are.'
'Grab someone else's money...'
'Legally?'
'No future in crime, mate. I don't say that 'cause I'm moral, just 'cause I'm sensible. But, when you're lookin' for money, don't hang back. Get in there and ask — and ask and ask. Like it is with the sheilas, ninety-nine might knock you back but it's that last one who says "Yes" that brings you joy. Look at the big boys. What's their real talent? Mobilising capital, they'll call it in their high-falutin' jargon. More down to earth, it's just being able to ask for money in a way that'll mean you get it.'
'What else?'
'Be impatient. Never, never reconcile yourself to poverty.'
'What if you've been handed the wrong genes?'
'Aw, come on, mate. That's just a cop-out. You're a sucker if you let family or fate or any of that crap hold you back.'
'Be self-confident?'
'Absolutely. Take a good look at the "GREAT MEN" around you. How "great" are they? Every damned one of them, mate, turns out to be a piker, sooner or later...'

'Feet of clay?'

'Not only feet, mate. All the way up. But don't forget, if they're not solid metal, you're not either. They're no better than you but you're no better than them, get me?'

'So be self-confident but not conceited?'

'Never get a big head. Never think things can't go wrong. They can. And if they can, they will. So keep your eye on the ball.'

'But things can still go wrong. What then?'

'My Dad used to say, "You can tell a great fighter not by how hard he hits, but *how well he comes back after he's been hit*".'

'What if he's lucky and never *gets* hit?'

'Don't you believe it, mate. In investment, as in everything else, there'll be times when you'll take a whacking. You should have organised things so you'll live through it. But you'll cop it, no doubt about that — no matter what precautions you take. If you fold, then you're the boy for the pension scheme. But if you keep your head, dance away from the punches and then come back swinging in the next round, chances are you'll die rich.'

'So apart from being poor and uncomfortable, the other big ingredient is guts?'

'It helps. Everyday good sense you'll need a lot of. Keep informed. Remember Ivan Boesky.'

'The insider trading man?'

'He made billions by knowing just a little bit more than anyone else. Story [13] is he employed one man to do nothing but check on the movement of corporate jets. If he knew where the jets were going, he knew where things were happening. Some of those things would be takeovers. Some of them would fuel Boesky's risk arbitrage.'

'But you don't want us to ape Boesky?'

'Not in all he did. None of that illegal insider stuff. But keep yourself informed — be a little bit ahead of the rest of the market — legally — yes, that's what you should aim at. And not just today and give up tomorrow. Keep at it. The biggest thing is persistence. Don't give up — don't let up.'

'"If you can force your brain and nerve and sinew to serve your turn long after they are gone, and so hold on

---

13 See Metz, op. cit., p.13.

when there is nothing in you except the will which says to you, 'Hold on'..."'

'Aw, now, mate, that's going a bit far. You don't have to be a hero to make yourself a few quid.'

'Just ordinarily persistent - as most of us aren't?'

'Look, mate, you know how it is, as well as I do. Till we're twenty, twenty-five, we're full of zip, zing, fire. Driven by competitive urges. We work hard. Play hard. We want to change the world. We're full of ideas — moral, political, you name it, we've got a better way of doing it. Then suddenly, it's all over. We start giving things up — football, surfing — especially thinking. By the time we're forty, we're not going anywhere any more — except where the tide we caught in our twenties carries us. Now what I'm saying is this: if you can be one of the exceptions, if you can continue right on doing new things, having new ideas — and there's no reason you shouldn't — in your thirties and forties and fifties and right on up, then you'll be a winner. Most of the competition'll have been burnt off early. You'll be pretty much on your own. You don't need to do anything you couldn't do when you were twenty. Just keep right on as if you were. Persistence. Stamina. That's what you need. And in the end it doesn't cost you any more. You've got to run the course anyway, you might as well do it with vigour and flair...'

'But we don't all have vigour, Charlie — fewer still flair.'

'Only think you don't, mate. I knew a bloke once. Never said, "G'day". Always "Happy New Year". Didn't matter what season it was - Christmas, Easter, Melbourne Cup Day, the lot. "Happy New Year". Surprised you at first. But gave you a lift. Made you think you were starting all over — fresh. So...'

'Forget about the past when you thought you didn't have vigour and flair?'

'Smack on, mate. Just believe you've got 'em — because really you have. And, if you believe it and act on it, that's what it'll be. A Happy New Year. This year and next — and the one after. A lot happier anyway than they would have been...'

Bibliography

(This list includes the publications quoted in the text as well as others of interest. The reader should not or need not tackle them all at once but rather dip into them over time, as required.)

Books

Aitken, M.J., Burrowes, A.W., Mulholland, R.D. *Investing on the Australian Sharemarket*. South Melbourne: Macmillan, 1983.

Asia and Pacific Review 1989, World of Information, Saffron Walden, England, 1989.

Australian Finance Conference. *How to Manage Money and Credit*. Sydney: Australian Finance Conference Limited, 1988.

Bond, Bruce. *Money Thoughts. The ABC of Money Management*. Melbourne: Lothian, 1986.

Brooks, John. *The Takeover Game*. New York: E.P. Dutton, 1988.

Bruck, Connie. *The Predators' Ball*. New York: The American Lawyer/Simon and Schuster, 1988.

Casey, Douglas. *Strategic Investing*. New York: Simon and Schuster, 1982.

The CCH Tax Editors. *1989 Australian Master Tax Guide*. Sydney: CCH Australia, 1989.

Cumes, J.W.C. *The Indigent Rich: A Theory of General Equilibrium in a Keynesian System*. Sydney: Pergamon, 1971.

___, *The Reconstruction of the World Economy*. Melbourne: Longman Cheshire, 1984.

Cummings, Gordon. *FT Investors Guide to the Stock Market — 5th Edition*. London: Financial Times, 1989.

Davis, William. *The Rich, A Study of the Species*. London: Arrow, 1985.

Economist Publications. *Directory of World Stock Exchanges*. London: The Economist Publications, 1989.

Galbraith, J.K. *The Great Crash 1929*. Boston: Houghton Mifflin, 1955.

___, *Money: Whence It Came, Where It Went*. London: Andre Deutsch, 1975.

Greider, William. *Secrets of the Temple: How the Federal Reserve Runs the Country*. New York: Simon and Schuster, 1987.

Harrod, R.F. *The Life of John Maynard Keynes*. London: Macmillan, 1951.

Keynes, J.M. *The General Theory of Employment, Interest and Money*. London: Macmillan, 1936.

___, *The End of Laisser-Faire*. London: Hogarth Press, 1926.

Leacock, Stephen. *The Penguin Stephen Leacock* (ed. Robertson Davies). Harmondsworth, England: Penguin Books, 1981.

Macmillan Guide to International Asset Managers. London: Macmillan, 1989.

Metz, Tim. *Black Monday*. New York: William Morrow, 1988.

Mitchell, Neil. *The Generous Corporation: A Political Analysis of Economic Power*. Yale University Press, 1989.

New York Stock Exchange. *Marketplace: A Brief History of the New York Stock Exchange*. New York, 1982.

O'Shea, Daniel. *FT Investing for Beginners — 4th Edition*. London: Financial Times, 1989.

Plummer, Tony. *Forecasting Financial Markets*. London: Kogan Page, 1989.

Purcell, Hugh Dominic. *Private Investment: Microeconomics at the Personal Level*. Vienna: Technische Hochschülershaft Wirtschaftsununiversität, 1984.

Richards, Robert. *The 1989 Good Tax Guide*. Melbourne: Market Street Press, 1989.

Shulman, Martin. *Anyone Can Make a Million*. Toronto: Fitzhenry and Whiteside, 1962.

Securities Industry Association. *Security Industry Yearbook*. New York, published annually.

Smith, Adam. *The Wealth of Nations*. London: 1770.

Smith, Adam. *The Roaring '80s*. Sydney/Auckland: Bantam/Schwartz, 1989.

Stammer, Don. *Unlimited Success in Personal Investments.* Melbourne: Wrightbooks, 1989.

Trading in Futures — 5th Edition. Hemel Hempstead (England): Woodhead-Faulkner, 1989.

Trading in Gold — 2nd Edition. Hemel Hempstead (England): Woodhead-Faulkner, 1989.

Warner, Bill. *Australia's Financial Markets.* Sydney: Allen & Unwin, 1989.

Whittaker, Noel. *Making Money Made Simple.* Brisbane: Boolarong Publications, 3rd ed., 1988.

Newspapers

The *Australian*, Sydney.
The *Australian Financial Review*, Sydney.
Le Figaro, Paris.
The *Financial Times*, London.
Investors' Chronicle, London.
The *Wall Street Journal*, New York.

Magazines

Australian Business, Sydney.
The *Bulletin*, Sydney.
Business Review Weekly, Melbourne.
The *Economist*, London.

Australian Stock Exchange and Options Market Publications

Stock Exchange

Australian Stock Exchange Journal
Daily Diary
Weekly Diary
Weekly Dividends, Issues and Offers
Comparative Analysis
Stock Exchange Research Handbook
Financial And Profitability Study
Company Profit Announcements
Stock Exchange Statex Service

Options Market
Options: The Versatile Investment
Understanding Options
An Introduction to Put Options
Dealing in Options

Other

Australian Business Profitability, P.A. Consulting Services
    Pty Ltd, Sydney.
Business International, London and New York.
Economist Intelligence Unit, London.
The International, Financial Advice for Global Investors
    (published monthly by the *Financial Times*), London.
Jobson Year Book, Melbourne.

Index

103-4, 107-8
capitalism/capitalists 6-7,
230, 236-7, 239-42;
adventurers, marauders,
buccaneers 239-43
caring society 240-1, 242
cash flow 139-41, 155, 209
cash management trusts 179
Chapman, Arthur 209
Charlie, identified 49;
advises on Repco 78;
Happy Bounty coup 49-58;
insurance share loan
81-2, 190; building share
portfolio 81-91; building
property portfolio 96,
103-4, 109-19; buys
London/French property
114-19; redistribute from
poor to rich 129-31;
money loses value 122-3;
on films 181-2; on racing
182-4; stamps 196, 197,
200-1; buys jewellery 211-
12; on pensions, insurance,
superannuation 188-96;
on macroeconomic policy
227-33, 236-7, 239;
workingmen's goals 243-4;
recipe for riches 255-7
chartism/chartists 147, 253
Chicago Mercantile
Exchange 149, 157
China 79, 169-70, 231, 236-7
coins 202-4, 220
cold fusion 42, 167-8
collectables 119, 197-222;
first editions 208, 210;
vintage cars 208
collecting, male addiction
197-8; rules for 198-202
Colossus of Rhodes 134

commemoratives 218-22
commodities 156-70;
agreements 156-7; daily
reports 58, 161, 164;
markets 88, 90, 91, 156-7,
161-2, 164; jargon 165-6;
exchanges (LME,
Chicago, etc.) 157, 160-1,
164
communist countries,
changes in 79, 236-7; gold
168
computers 29; a tool of
trade 34; expert-analysis
systems 34, 249-50
computer-assisted trading
53, 89
consumer credit 17, 23, 236
copper 58-9
Crash, the Great 47, 137
credit 236; creating 16;
function of 18; rating 19-20;
squeeze 115, 226, 228-9,
232
credit cards 23, 30, 115, 236
currencies 91, 149-56;
stable/volatile 127, 149-50,
152-3; speculating in 118-19,
150-1; trading in 99-100;
borrowing in foreign 28,
114-19, 153-4; highly-
leveraged 155; currency
advisers/money-brokers
155-6

debt, for consumption 23;
investment 23
deflation 126, 189-90; Great
156, 190
delegated investment 170-81,
184, 195-6
democracy, economic 242,

Netherlands 92, 102
nickel, share boom 84-5
Nixon, Richard, stores
    money 23-4; stagflation
    228

oil, price hikes 86, 233; Bass
    Strait finds 86
'Old Masters' 48, 208, 213-16
Onassis, Aristotle 134
options 144-8; executive
    stock 144; warrants with
    shares 144; traded
    options 144-5; markets
    145-6; London Traded
    Options Market 145-6,
    148; Sydney Futures
    Exchange 146

Pacific Rim 237
Packer, Kerry 130
paintings 213-18
palladium, market for 167-8
Parbo, Sir Arvi 4
patron 26
pawnbroker 143, 213
Pitt Street farmer 111
plan, buying off 104-6, 107
poor, the working 1, 12, 49,
    112, 241-4; help rich 129-
    31; 'sacrificial victims'
    228-30; cared for less
    240-2
'populist' investment, see
    democracy, economic
Portugal, sharemarket 79
power, shifts in national
    231-7
privatisation 44, 235, 246-7
profit, and risk 27-8
property, as investment 92-4,
    248; building property

portfolio 109-19; market
    for 101-4, 142; location
    94-9; zoning 95; land
    value 97-8; home
    purchase 92-3; borrowing
    for 93, 100, 110, 112,
    138-9; fluctuations in
    market 101-6, 142-3;
    timing 92, 97, 99-108;
    demographic factors
    ('baby boom') 95, 101-2;
    buying off the plan 104-6,
    107; rural 107, 108-9,
    111, 119; commercial 74,
    83-4, 107; buying sight
    unseen 113, 248; negative
    gearing 103, 104, 131; tax
    breaks on mortgages 101,
    103; in Britain 24, 91, 94,
    100-2, 116, 141; in
    United States, 94, 102; in
    Japan 94; buying overseas
    114-19; assets 245-6
Pyramids 134

racing 182-4; many
    components 183; betting
    183; owning horses 48,
    183; breeding 182-4;
    syndicates 183
Rebozo, Charles G. 123-4
Reserve Bank Australia 115,
    130, 131
Rich, the, defined 2; helped
    by improvident poor 129-
    31; gain from interest-
    rate hikes 229
risk 27-8, 51-2, 80, 93, 99,
    127, 139-40, 142, 145,
    146, 153, 159, 161-3, 169,
    181, 254-5
risk arbitrage 165-6, 239,